JAPAN
made easy

Books by Boye Lafayette De Mente

Japanese Etiquette & Ethics in Business
How to Do Business with the Japanese
Japan Encyclopedia
Japanese in Plain English
NTC's Dictionary of Japan's Cultural Code Words
Discovering Cultural Japan
Japanese Influence on America
Japanese Secrets of Graceful Living
Korean Etiquette & Ethics in Business
Korean in Plain English
Chinese Etiquette & Ethics in Business
Behind the Japanese Bow
Survival Japanese

JAPAN
made easy

Second Edition

Boye Lafayette De Mente

Printed on recyclable paper

PASSPORT BOOKS
a division of *NTC Publishing Group*
Lincolnwood, Illinois USA

Cover photo courtesy of Japan National Tourist Organization. Tofukuji/Temple, Kyoto.

1997 Printing

Published by Passport Books, a division of NTC Publishing Group,
4255 West Touhy Avenue, Lincolnwood (Chicago), Illinois 60646-1975 U.S.A.
Manufactured in the United States of America.
Library of Congress Catalog Card Number: 95-67030

6 7 8 9 0 VP 9 8 7 6 5 4 3

 CONTENTS

PART III Useful Information   261

Japan is generally said to be made up of five islands—*Okinawa* (Oh-kee-nah-wah), *Kyushu* (Que-shuu), *Shikoku* (She-koe-kuu), *Honshu* (Hone-shuu), and *Hokkaido* (Hoke-kie-doe) from south to north—but there are actually some thirty-six hundred islands in the group, including dozens that are inhabited. The boomerang-shaped island chain lies just off the coast of East Asia, stretching for thirty-three hundred kilometers (about two thousand miles) from near the cold regions of Siberia's Kamchatka Peninsula to the subtropics of the western Pacific. Because of the large number of islands and the irregularity of their shapes, Japan has twenty-nine thousand kilometers of coastline. Total land area is 377,000 square kilometers or 142,000 square miles, making Japan approximately one twenty-fifth the size of the United States—or about the size of the state of Montana.

Some one billion years ago the Japanese islands were a part of the Asian mainland. Movement of the earth's plates resulted in a section of the Asian coastline breaking off and "floating" eastward. About 100 million years ago a huge lake appeared in the area that is now the Sea of Japan. The lake gradually expanded and within ninety-nine million years had linked up with the Pacific Ocean in the north and south, leaving the highest regions as a series of islands that were to become Japan. The remains of elephants and other animals found in Asia and on the North American continent also have been discovered in Japan, proving that the islands were once connected to these continents.

Over 70 percent of Japan's land area is made up of high mountains and hills, including over two hundred volcanoes and hundreds of geothermally active areas. The main island of Honshu has a high backbone of mountain chains running down its center. There are eleven peaks in the country that are over three thousand meters high, and thirteen that are over twenty-five hundred meters high. Mount Fuji, the highest, is 3,776 meters. This profusion of mountains helps make Japan one of the most scenic groups of islands in the world, with land- and seascapes that are the epitome of natural beauty.

Japan is divided into forty-seven prefectures and the metropolis of Tokyo. There is a further subdivision into eight geographic regions that are economically as well as politically important. These areas are the northernmost island of Hokkaido; the two southwestern islands of Shikoku and Kyushu, and five regions on the main island of Honshu: *Tohoku* (Toe-hoe-kuu), *Kanto* (Kahn-toe), *Chubu* (Chuu-buu), *Kinki* (Keen-kee), and *Chugoku* (Chuu-go-kuu).

With a population approaching 125 million concentrated in coastal lands along the eastern seaboard of Honshu, Japan is second only to the United States in the number of its large cities—ten with populations of more than one million each and nineteen with populations of over half a million each. Some twenty-seven million people live in the Tokyo-Yokohama area. The other major concentration of population is in the Kyoto-Osaka-Kobe area some 350 miles southwest of Tokyo.

Despite its small size in terms of overall landmass, Japan "feels" big because it is long and has such a rugged, varied landscape. Driving from the northern tip of Hokkaido to the southern end of Kyushu requires several days, and takes one from a subarctic type of climate to the subtropics.

Understanding the Essence of Culture

I believe that Japan is the best travel destination in the world for all of the important reasons: the character and personality of the people, the exotic nature of the culture, the ample availability and extraordinary efficiency of the transportation and accommodation industries, the manmade and natural scenic beauty, the quality and variety of food, the feelings of personal security, and more.

But ultimately whether or not a visit to Japan is worth *your* time, money, and effort depends primarily on your tastes, expectations, and mood; your knowledge of Japan; and your reaction to new and often unexpected situations. In other words, how would you react to Japanese culture—to what is *Japanese* about Japan? Your answer to this question depends on your own cultural upbringing, knowledge, and experiences.

One of the most important preparations for a successful trip to Japan is getting into the proper mood, which requires substantial knowledge of the essence of culture and how to experience it. But the nature or character of culture is not well or widely understood. First of all, it is intangible. It cannot be bought in restaurants or shops or packaged and shipped home. Westerners and Japanese alike have traditionally confused food, art, handicrafts, and architecture with culture. These things are all manifestations of culture but not culture itself.

You can use chopsticks and eat Japanese noodles, rice, raw fish, and miso soup all your life, and it will not add one whit to your understanding and appreciation of the Japanese. Seeing a Shinto shrine does not imbue you with any understanding or appreciation of Shintoism. You can collect woodblock prints, hanging scrolls, and *noh* masks or watch *kabuki* a thousand times and still have little more than an inkling of Japanese culture.

To achieve any significant insight into Japan, you must learn something about the philosophy and psychology of the Japanese: what motivates them; what guides them; what they regard as right or wrong; how they view themselves; how they see others; and how they live and communicate with each other.

Of course, you can learn a lot about a people by reading insightful books and by observing them, but the final step must be to experience their life; to absorb physically, emotionally, and intellectually the things that give the people their identity. This is especially true with the Japanese, because what you see in the facade of Japan does not reveal the essence of the country.

Unfortunately, the organized travel industry is not able to take the personal approach that would allow huge numbers of people to get behind Japan's facade systematically and not only learn a great deal about the people but enjoy themselves at the same time.

There are, however, many things you can do as an individual to go beyond the usual limitations of group travel without forgoing its advantages; still avoid the pitfalls one invariably encounters when traveling in Japan; and gain maximum pleasure and fulfillment from things Japanese by experiencing their feel, their taste, and their spirit.

Traveling for recreation is a wonderful privilege that by its very definition should be pleasurable as well as educational. But the old saying, "It's the little things that count," is especially true regarding a visit to Japan. This book covers hundreds of the little things that often make the difference between a wonderful experience and a terrible one. It is filled with practical information designed to smooth your way through routine as well as unexpected events. It is also a practical guide to key life customs in Japan and includes useful insights into the "whys" of typical Japanese behavior.

Finally, *Japan made easy* pinpoints a wide range of the special pleasures of Japan—literally hundreds of things, large and small, that make living and traveling in today's Japan fascinating and satisfying for those who can cross the cultural bridge.

Boye Lafayette De Mente

Tokyo

PART ONE

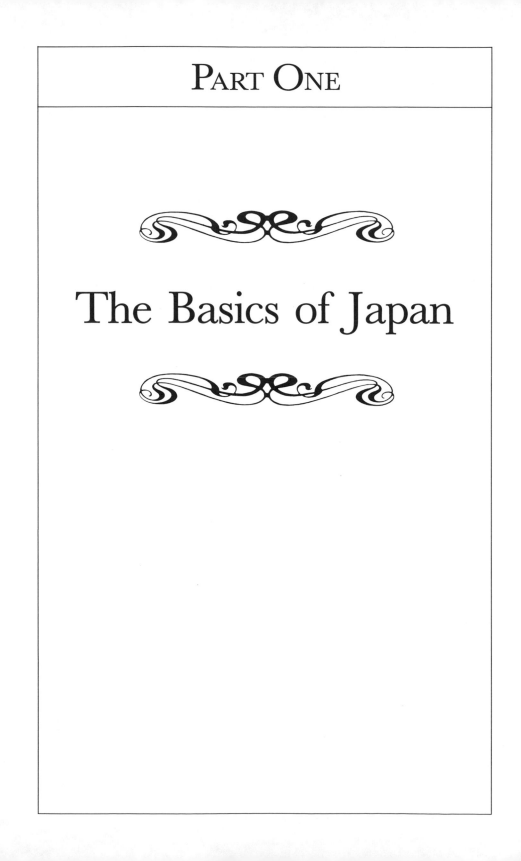

The Basics of Japan

CHAPTER 1

Smelling the Chrysanthemums

Legacy of the Past

Japan's transformation from a subsistence-level economy to one of the richest nations in the world in just two decades—the fifties and sixties—created a peculiar anomaly that has dogged the travel industry ever since. In image as well as reality, Japan went from being a travel bargain to being a travel luxury not only because of economic forces but also because of recent events in history.

During the last half of the forties and most of the fifties, the only hotel accommodations and dining facilities in Japan that were even halfway acceptable to foreign visitors were the very best the country had to offer: the most prestigious hotels, the top-name restaurants, and the first-class train coaches, all of which were available at that time at very low prices.

The travel industry naturally booked both businessmen and tourists into such well-known places as the Imperial Hotel and later the Hotel Okura, and recommended the best restaurants available. But starting in 1958, several things began happening simultaneously: the cash flow from Japan's successful export industries increased as if by magic; hotels, restaurants, and other travel-related businesses upgraded their facilities; and income spiraled upward. Of course, the yen price of goods and services in Japan also went up, but only in small increments, giving the Japanese unprecedented buying power.

By the early seventies, Japan's leading hotels and restaurants had become world-class luxury facilities, ranking far above what is normally rated as "first class." In the meantime, the foreign travel industry continued to look at its old favorites as the only viable choices it had. This approach devastated the budgets of its more economy-minded clients because of the superior value of the yen in relation to foreign currencies, especially the dollar.

As the value of the yen continued to increase in relation to the dollar, prices visitors had to pay in Japan also spiraled upward. When the dollar was abruptly devalued in the mid-eighties, things became even worse for the visiting travelers and businessmen: The cost of using taxis tripled, and the cost of hotel accommodations and meals more than doubled.

The overall result of these circumstances was that Western businessmen and tourists who normally would not stay at the most luxurious hotels in New York, London or Paris, or eat at restaurants catering to the very rich, were paying rich-man prices to stay in Japan's best hotels and eat in its better-known restaurants simply because the yen was three times more expensive than it had been before.

An obvious partial solution to the problem of the high cost of yen is to distinguish between luxury class and first class. Admittedly, there is a difference between some first-class hotels in Japan and first-class hotels in the United States, for example. Space is one of the most valuable commodities in Japan. A room in a Japanese hotel that qualifies as first class as far as other amenities are concerned is generally much smaller than a room in a Western hotel that is rated as first class. Further, this category of Japanese hotel will often not have a large, elaborate lobby. If this difference is acceptable, you have a choice of hundreds of hotels in Japan where the rates are moderate by world standards.

The way the Japanese classify hotels is often part of the problem. Luxury-class hotels are often not distinguished from "first-class" hotels. Also, hotels in Japan that would be accepted as first class in most countries are often called "businessmen's hotels," a category that is viewed in the popular mind to be well below the level of "real" first-class places.

Unless you are going to Japan on business and need to impress the people you are going to meet, there is no overwhelming reason you should stay in an unduly expensive hotel. Of course, if you can afford it and *want* the special experience of staying in a luxury hotel in Japan—and it is a very impressive experience indeed—that is another matter.

If you do want to economize on your travel expenses, the next challenge is to avoid high restaurant bills. This is easy enough to do if you will apply a little energy and time to the task. The first move is not to eat your meals in the dining rooms of luxury- or first-class hotels. Hotel dining room prices are anywhere from 50 percent to three or four times more than what ordinary outside restaurants charge for the same things. Hotel coffee shops are generally exceptions to this rule, however, with prices in the same range as outside restaurants on the same level. The second move is to stay away from exclusive restaurants that cater to people who are extraordinarily affluent—or spending company money.

Japan's major cities have more restaurants than other comparable cities in the world. In Tokyo, for example, there are some 100,000 restaurants, many located in office buildings, where there often are dozens; department stores, where they frequently occupy an entire floor; and many bakeries. Even in most residential neighborhoods you generally cannot travel more than a block in any direction without passing one or more restaurants.

The challenge is to know something about the different kinds of restaurants that are available in Japan, and take advantage of their variety and reasonable prices. If your itinerary is being arranged by a travel agency, you should work very closely with your agent. Become aware of both the class and cost of the hotels where you will be lodging as well as the wide variety of restaurants readily available. (See Chapters 9 and 14.)

Making a Rational Choice

You do not *have* to be trapped on a tourist treadmill that restricts you to premium-priced hotels, shops, and restaurants that offer few options for keeping your expenses below astronomical figures or experiencing Japan in three dimensions rather than one. The choice is yours. It is also up to you to make sure you have the freedom to sample the pleasures of Japan that are not on the typical itinerary.

To give the travel industry its due, it does, in fact, do a commendable job in trying to make sure that travelers experience more than one side of Japan while keeping them comfortable enough so that they will not complain. But since travel agents can only go so far and do so much, it is up to you to make sure your schedule provides you with ample opportunities to do things on your own.

There are two aspects of Japan that should guide you in planning your itinerary and schedule: modern or Westernized Japan, and traditional Japan. Both deserve some of your time. Modern Japan is of course epitomized by its great cities. Prime urban examples of East meeting West include Tokyo, Kyoto and Osaka, which boast huge shopping, restaurant and entertainment districts that are unmatched anywhere in the world; vast cultural opportunities; and masses of affluent, sophisticated people. Examples of traditional Japan, while abundant, are much more elusive and generally must be sought out deliberately by visitors.

In addition to offering lower lodging and restaurant prices, Japan's outlying cities, towns, and villages—particularly those not professionally developed as tourist attractions—invite the visitor to discover the country's unspoiled, stunning natural beauty, exotic customs, and traditional everyday lifestyles that have given Japan such a fascinating image in the first place.

The transportation and accommodations infrastructure in Japan is outstanding. Trains and buses go everywhere, and even the remotest towns have hotels and inns that are a legacy of the political policies of the Tokugawa Shogunate (1603–1868) and the extraordinary penchant the Japanese have had for traveling in their own country since the early years of the Tokugawa era.

My recommendation is to divide your time among the gold-plated amenities of Tokyo, Kyoto and Osaka and the special attractions of some of the other hundreds of cities, towns and villages that are substantially less expensive and much more "Japanese." Even Yokohama, Japan's second-largest city located only thirty minutes away from downtown Tokyo, is much less expensive than Tokyo, and much more "visitor-friendly" than the huge, sprawling capital. In addition to local hotels, Yokohama is served by a large and attractive Holiday Inn that sits on the edge of Chinatown and is within a five-minute walk of the famous Motomachi shopping area, the Silk Center, and the harbor.

Tokyo residents themselves like nothing more than to get out of the city as often as possible. Several days in Hokkaido, the northernmost island with its plains, horse ranches, lakes, forests, volcanoes, and hot springs, is regarded as a special treat—especially since prices there are from 20 to 50 percent below those in Tokyo. The same goes for Shikoku, smallest of the four main islands of Japan. A trip there is like taking a long step back into time, not only in the quality and style of life, but also in prices.

Throughout the island chain there are literally thousands of areas and towns of special historical interest, virtually all of them having nearby scenic wonders that have been nationally famous for centuries, as well as noted hot-spring resorts, inns, and hotels—all bustling with their own shopping and entertainment districts, and all conveniently accessible from Japan's numerous ports of entry.

Doing versus Seeing

The old reference to "smelling the roses" during your journey through life is perhaps the most appropriate saying to remember when you are traveling and experiencing new sights, sounds, smells, tastes, and textures. In fact, following this dictum is the secret of getting everything you should out of travel. Sadly though, too many people limit themselves to just sightseeing and cautiously sampling a few foods.

Beyond "room and board" considerations, the most important facet of a recreational trip to Japan is deciding what you want to do on the trip—what you really want to get out of it. Again, the primary criterion that determines the value of vacation or recreational travel is *doing* versus *seeing*. The more things you are able to "do" as opposed to just "see," the more you will get out of the trip.

Japanese culture lends itself to doing as well as seeing because it is very sensual, and deliberately so. Long ago the Japanese developed many foods, products, and customs that cater specifically to one or more of the five senses—with some designed to engage and delight a sixth and seventh sense. To understand and enjoy Japan fully, you must use all of your usual senses *plus* these two extra ones, which I identify as aesthetic and spiritual.

The Japanese appear to be the only society who made aesthetics a major aspect of their culture and a significant part of the traditional education of every individual. They were also the first people to synthesize the great religions of Asia and develop a spiritual culture that was compatible with change and technology and imbued them with an extraordinary energy and will to succeed.

In fact, present-day Japanese may be living in the best of all times because they have created a new, modern world without destroying their traditional one, and are able to move easily back and forth between the two as if time travel was possible simply by stepping through a door.

Obviously, you cannot experience traditional Japan by staying only in Western hotels, limiting your culinary excursions to a few Japanese restaurants, and spending a lot of time on trains and tourist buses. You must shuck your fears and inhibitions, shift into an adventure mode and set out deliberately to go not in harm's way but in the way of new and pleasurable experiences.

Before this book is done, I will suggest a hundred things that you can do in Japan which will guarantee that your trip will be as rewarding physically, emotionally, and spiritually as anything you may have experienced in the past.

Some Useful Phrases in Japanese

Good morning (until about 10:00 A.M.)
Ohaiyo gazaimasu   Oh-hie-yoe go-zie-mahss

Good day / Good afternoon (from about 10:00 A.M. to around 5:00 P.M.)
Konnichi wa   Kone-nee-chee wah

Good evening (from about 6:00 P.M. until midnight)
Komban wa   Kome-bahn wah

How are you?
O'genki desu ka?   Oh-gane-kee dess kah?

I'm fine, thank you
O'kage sama de, genki desu
Oh-kah-gay sah-mah day, gane-kee dess

This is the first time I have been to Japan
Kondo Nihon e hajimete kimashita
Kone-doe Nee-hone eh hah-jee-may-tay kee-mah-sshtah

I understand only a little Japanese
Nihongo ga sukoshi dake wakarimasu
Nee-hone-go gah suu-koe-she dah-kay wah-kah-ree-mahss

Please speak more slowly
Motto yukkuri hanashite kudasai
Moat-toe yuke-kuu-ree hah-nah-ssh-tay kuu-dah-sie

Please say it again
Mo ichido yutte kudasai   Moe ee-chee-doe yute-tay kuu-dah-sie

What is your name?
O'namae wa nan desu ka?   Oh-nah-my wah nahn dess kah?

My name is ———
Watakushi no namae wa ———
Wah-tock-she no nah-my wah ———

CHAPTER 2

Advance Planning

Backgrounding

One of my writing colleagues, Rowland Gould, veteran Asian editor/ correspondent and author of *The Matsushita Phenomenon,* was a master at assimilating cultural, social, and economic facts into stories that clarified contemporary events and situations. He called this process "backgrounding," which is also a very appropriate process in which people should engage before visiting Japan.

Backgrounding for the traveler primarily means reading a variety of books on Japan that cover the cultural, social, political, and economic history of the country—especially those written from a lively human perspective as opposed to the dry recitations of scholarly works.

Major publishers of English-language books on Japan include the Charles E. Tuttle Company of Tokyo and Rutland, Vermont; Kodansha International of Tokyo and New York; the Japan Times of Tokyo; and Passport Books (NTC Publishing Group) of Lincolnwood, Illinois. All of these companies distribute their books nationally as well as internationally, but it is often more practical to order from them directly by mail.

For mail-order catalogs of book titles, contact the publishers at the following addresses:

Charles E. Tuttle Company, Post Office Drawer F, Rutland, Vermont USA 05701. Tel: 802-773-8930. Tuttle is also the distributor for several other publishers of books on Japan, including John Weatherhill Inc. In other countries, see local listings under book distributors.

Kodansha International, Mail-Order Department, P.O. Box 1531, Hagerstown, Maryland, USA 21741. Tel: 1-800-638-3030. In other countries, see local listings under book distributors.

The Japan Times Ltd., 4-5-4 Shibaura, Minato-ku, Tokyo, Japan 108.

Passport Books (NTC Publishing Group), 4255 West Touhy Avenue, Lincolnwood, Illinois, USA 60646-1975. Toll-free tel: 1-800-323-4900. In other countries, see local listings under book distributors.

A leading retailer of books on Japan in the United States is the Japanese Kinokuniya bookstore chain, which has branches in San Francisco, Los Angeles, Torrance (CA) and New York. Other retail sources include Nippan Books of Los Angeles, Zen Oriental Books of New York and the Japan-American Society in New York.

Here is a brief list of "backgrounding" books on Japan that I recommend. There are, of course, dozens of others available from the publishers named above. I suggest that you read at least five or six books altogether, more if possible.

Different People—Pictures of Some Japanese, by Donald Richie
    (Kodansha International)
    Richie, one of the best contemporary foreign writers in Japan, provides us with perceptive portraits of some 50 Japanese from all walks of life.

Encounter with Japan, by Herb Passin (Kodansha International)
    This classic account of the author's life in Japan following World War II, mixed with historical fact, brings out the essence of the Japanese way in a warm and evocative style.

Japan—A Short Cultural History, by George Sansom (Charles E. Tuttle Company)
    A sweeping chronicle of the rise and development of the Japanese civilization, the book describes its extraordinary pageantry and color as well as the patterns and nuances of the everyday life of the people.

Japanese Inn, by Oliver Statler (Charles E. Tuttle Company)

Statler gives a masterful telling of the human side of Japanese history from the vantage point of an inn on the great walking road that connected the Imperial capital of Kyoto with the Shogun's capital in Edo (Tokyo).

Japanese Pilgrimage, by Oliver Statler (Charles E. Tuttle Company)

Here is another slice of Japanese history told in conjunction with travels around the kingdom of the Shogun during the Tokugawa Era (1603–1868), when the main threads of Japanese culture were refined and institutionalized.

Shimoda Story, by Oliver Statler (Charles E. Tuttle Company)

The story of Townsend Harris, the first American diplomat to be stationed in Japan, is a fascinating and revealing portrait of the Japanese and their ongoing fight to protect and preserve their unique way.

Japan: Images and Realities, by Richard Halloran (Charles E. Tuttle Company)

Noted correspondent Richard Halloran presents a clear and provocative image of the real Japan as a fragile but formidable world power.

Memories of Silk & Straw, by Dr. Junichi Saga (Kodansha International)

The book contains a delightful selection of short stories about life in a small town, collected by a country doctor from his aged patients, who ranged from a blacksmith and tofu maker to a local gangster.

Discovering Cultural Japan, by Boye De Mente (Passport Books)

This concise guide to the cultural attitudes and behavior of the Japanese cites the things that make Japan unique and fascinating to the visitor.

Japanese Secrets of Graceful Living, by Boye De Mente (Phoenix Books)

Here, in a highly readable form, is the essence of the universally appealing Japanese culture, which offers the promise of a balanced life through recognition of man's true nature and his physical, intellectual, and spiritual needs.

Everything Japanese (The Japan Almanac)—An Encyclopedic Reader of Things Japanese, by Boye De Mente (Passport Books)

This book offers a treasure trove of information about Japan, answering virtually any question anyone might have. Over eight hundred topics are covered, including art, cities, cuisine, government, history, literature, religions, sports, famous people, and more.

Shadows of the Rising Sun, by Jared Taylor (Charles E. Tuttle Company)

A penetrating analysis of contemporary Japan is given by Taylor, who was born and raised in the country.

The Book of Tea, by Kakuzo Okakura (Charles E. Tuttle Company)

This delightful book, written in English by the author, delves into the Japanese view of beauty, art, and man's relationship with nature.

The Code of the Samurai, by A. L. Sadler (Charles E. Tuttle Company)

The Samurai, Japan's elite sword-carrying warrior class, ruled the country from 1192 until 1868, imposing their manners and ethics on all Japanese to a considerable degree. Knowledge of the beliefs and behavior of the Samurai is essential to an understanding of Japanese culture.

The best source in Tokyo for books and other publications in English on Japan is the main shop of Maruzen (established in 1869), 2-3-10 Nihonbashi, Chuo-ku, opposite Takashimaya Department Store. The second floor of the large Maruzen building is devoted entirely to foreign language books. A shipping service is available if you buy more than you want to carry. The store opens at 10:00 A.M.

Getting into the Right Mood

There are several typical reasons for reading a number of books on historical as well as contemporary Japan, which include gaining general knowledge, specific information and an overall perspective of the country. One of the more esoteric and yet very important reasons is to get yourself "in the mood" to experience and enjoy Japan first-hand. Merely reading travel industry promotional brochures is certainly not sufficient and can be misleading.

It is often the mood with which one approaches Japan (or any other country) that determines how well the trip goes. As much as 90 percent or more of the mood factor is predetermined by our cultural bonds—expectations and prejudices based on our own experiences and outlook. Many people, no matter how sincerely they might want to or how diligently they might try, cannot break these cultural bonds without considerable help. They are the ones who can view foreign things from a safe distance but generally cannot force themselves to experience them fully. That is like admiring an apple but never eating one. There is no comparison.

One of the goals of this book is to encourage you to decide in advance that you are not going to let your own cultural conditioning prevent you from physically and emotionally experiencing Japan. It also will help you incorporate a long list of the things you intend to do into your itinerary.

At the very top of your list of things to do should be one very important thing you will *not* do—and that is complain about things that are different from the way they are at home—whether it is the way your morning toast looks or the fact that most signs are in a foreign language.

Another characteristic of successful travelers is an intense curiosity and the courage to follow up on incidental things that pique their interest. But as a result of package tours being minutely scheduled to the point that most activities are practically robotized, giving curiosity free reign has become virtually a lost art. The only way around this problem while still taking advantage of the conveniences of group tours is to insist that more than the usual amount of "free time" be built into the trip schedule.

One of the biggest complaints of people who have visited Japan in group tours *is* the tight schedule, which generally keeps them on the road from morning to night. You can prevent this from happening to you by working with your travel agent in advance.

Power of an Introduction

There is nothing quite like having a personal contact in a city or country you are visiting for the first time. This is especially true in a country as culturally different from ours as Japan, where the typical foreign visitor becomes virtually illiterate as soon as he or she steps off the plane or ship. For this reason, I recommend that you use any contacts you may already have there, or make one or more if you don't have any.

Interpersonal relations among the Japanese are based on relatively strict, well-defined customs. One of the most sensitive and important of these customs involves obtaining an introduction to someone you want to meet for either social or business purposes.

The difference an introduction makes in the reception one gets, regardless of the purpose, really can be remarkable because the *shokaijo* (show-kie-joe) introduction system is so deeply ingrained in the Japanese that they often do not react at all if it is not followed. There is a strong obligation for them to go out of their way when one does follow protocol, however.

If you are going to Japan strictly for pleasure, you still can use business or professional connections to help you come up with one or more personal introductions. Sources for such connections include the academic field (colleges or universities having affiliations in Japan); service clubs such as the Kiwanis and Rotarians, which are immensely popular in Japan; sister-city organizations; the Young Presidents' Association; professional organizations in science; women's organizations that have affiliations in Japan; and sports clubs with Japan associations.

One approach that has been used with wonderful results is contacting the English-speaking clubs of Japanese universities. Explain that you are going to be in Japan for pleasure from ——— to ———, and that you would like to meet one or more members of the club during your stay. This frequently results in club members volunteering to become interpreter/guides for you. The addresses of Japanese universities are available from Japanese embassies and consulates abroad, Japan Trade Center offices (overseas branches of the Japan External Trade Organization, generally known as JETRO), the libraries of local universities, some public libraries, and the U.S. embassy in Japan.

The Seasons

Japan is usually described as having a temperate climate. Don't be misled. In summer it gets very hot and humid throughout the southern and central portions of the country, except in the highlands. In winter it gets cold everywhere except for the southern extremes of Kyushu and Okinawa, which is some four hundred miles south of Kyushu. All of Japan's largest cities—Tokyo, Yokohama, Nagoya, Kyoto, Osaka and Kobe—which are more or less in central Honshu, the main island, are in regions that get hot in summer and cold in winter.

With the exception of the lowlands in the extreme southern portion of the country, Japan has four very pronounced seasons, which are beautifully reflected in its traditional culture. A great variety of traditional foods and activities are directly related to the various seasons, and are a significant part of the visible and tangible manifestations of Japanese culture. Over and above physical comfort, these are the kinds of things that could influence your decision on when to travel in Japan, and many of them are in my list of things you should do while in Japan (See Part II).

National Holidays

You also should consider Japan's national holidays in your advance planning. Being in Japan during national holidays can be good or bad, depending on what you want to do during those periods. While many retail outlets are closed and public transportation can be especially crowded, the festivals and other special events during holidays can be highlights of your trip (See Part II). The present national holidays are as follows:

January 1–3	New Year's **Ganjitsu** Ghan-jeet-sue
January 15	Coming-of-Age Day **Seijin no Hi** Say-e-jeen no He
February 11	National Foundation Day **Kenkoku Kinen Bi** Kane-koe-kuu Kee-nane Bee
March 21	Vernal Equinox Day **Shunbun no Hi** Shune-boon no He

April 29	Green Day
	Midori-no Hi Me-doe-ree-no Hee
May 3	Constitution Day
	Kenpo Kinen Bi Kane-poe Kee-nane Bee
May 5	Children's Day
	Kodomo no Hi Koe-doe-moe no He
September 15	Respect-for-the-Aged Day
	Keiro no Hi Kay-e-roe no He
September 23	Autumnal Equinox Day
	Shubun no Hi Shuu-boon no He
October 10	Health-Sports Day
	Taiiku no Hi Tie-ee-kuu no He
November 3	Culture Day
	Bunka no Hi Boon-kah no He
November 23	Labor Thanksgiving Day
	Kinro Kansha no Hi
	Keen-roe Kahn-sha no He

Some Useful Phrases in Japanese

Is today a national holiday?
Kyo wa saijitsu desu ka?   K'yoe wah sie-jee-t'sue dess kah?

Is today a holiday/vacation (regular day off)?
Kyo wa O'yasumi desu ka?
K'yoe wa Oh-yah-sue-me dess kah?

Is the post office open today?
Yubin kyoku wa kyo aite imasu ka?
Yuu-bean k'yoe-kuu wah k'yoe aye-tay ee-mahss kah?

The weather is fine today, isn't it!
Kyo wa ii o'tenki desu, ne!
K'yoe wah ee oh-tane-kee dess, nay!

CHAPTER 3

When To Go and What To Take

Picking the Right Season

Given Japan's four precise seasons, when you go will impact on almost everything you do: the clothing you take and wear, your physical comfort and convenience, the cultural events you can see or participate in, even some of the foods you eat. While there are some variations because of geographic location, spring generally begins in late March and lasts through June; the summer season is from July through mid-September; fall is from mid-September through November; and winter, the longest season, is from December to late March.

The Japanese islands lie mostly in the so-called North Temperate Zone, and stretch some twenty-six hundred kilometers (sixteen hundred miles) from north to south. As far as their north-south geographic location is concerned, they compare with the portion of the United States' East Coast from Bangor, Maine to Jacksonville, Florida.

But the nearby landmass of Siberia, Northern China and the Korea Peninsula, along with a ridge of spinelike high mountains running north to south through Japan, play a vital role in the climate. The result is lower temperatures and more snowfall in the northern and northwestern areas than is generally experienced along the Eastern Seaboard in the United States.

Mean winter temperature in Tokyo is 38.7°F, and humidity averages 60 percent. In spring the mean temperature is 55.6°F, with humidity averaging 68 percent. Snow seems to fall in Tokyo in thirty- to forty-year cycles. From the early 1950s until the mid-1980s, it snowed only a few times each year. Since 1985 it has snowed twenty to thirty times each winter. Summertime temperatures in Tokyo range from 75° to 85°F, with a mean humidity of 80 percent. It cools off in the fall to a mean of 62.1°F, with humidity averaging 77 percent. Temperatures in Kyoto are a little lower in winter and a little higher in summer than those in Tokyo because of its proximity to mountains and distance from the ocean.

There is little significant difference in the seasonal temperatures in Nagoya, Osaka, and Kobe and the dozens of towns and cities in between. Like Tokyo, they are hot and humid in summer and fairly cold to very cold in winter. The exceptions along this central Honshu belt are areas on the tips of peninsulas that jut out into the warming currents of the Pacific Ocean. They are warmer in winter and seldom have snow.

The further south of Osaka-Kobe you go, the warmer the winters tend to be, although it occasionally snows in Kagoshima on the southern tip of Kyushu. And the eastern side of the island chain is always warmer than the western side. The further north of Tokyo you go, the longer and the more severe the winters. By the time you reach the northern island of Hokkaido—or if you go into the mountains of central and northern Honshu—you are in genuine snow country, where the winters are long and cold. Summers in the central mountains and the northern portions of Honshu and in all of Hokkaido are short and cool. The isolated island prefecture of Okinawa, 685 kilometers (some four hundred miles) south of Kyushu, is semitropical, with mostly warm, sunny winters and hot, humid summers that are mitigated, however, by steady ocean breezes.

During winter months (December through March), clothing should be very warm but not heavy unless you are going into the central mountains or northern Japan, where snows are deep and temperatures are often near or below zero. In spring and fall, clothing should be light but warm, again unless you are going to venture into the high areas or the northern country, where temperatures can drop below freezing as late as the end of May and as early as the beginning of October.

Summer, which runs from June through September along the Pacific side of central and southern Honshu and the islands of Shikoku, Kyushu, and Okinawa, calls for very light clothing that is compatible with high temperatures and high humidity.

There are monsoon-type rainy seasons throughout Japan in spring and late fall, but it can rain, particularly in the mountains, anytime. The spring rains usually begin in early June and last for five or six weeks. A warm jacket often feels good during this period if you are at higher elevations. There is also a typhoon season in Japan, sometimes beginning as early as August, with September known as "typhoon month." At least one and sometimes two or three typhoons sweep across wide areas of Japan each season, with heavy rains and high winds. The southern portions of the islands are usually in the direct path of the typhoons, while Osaka, Kyoto, Nagoya, and Tokyo usually get only the fringe rains and winds, which, however, can be heavy and disruptive.

Raincoats and umbrellas are virtually daily essentials in June, and come in handy for short periods in fall and winter.

Generally speaking, the Japanese dress better and more formally than most people around the globe. Japan's businessmen and army of white-collar workers are sticklers for formal wear during office hours. Most people you see out on the town at night are also well-dressed: The men wear jackets and ties and the women wear fashionable attire. When vacationing and engaged in recreational pursuits, the Japanese dress to fit the occasion, with casual but very trendy sportswear being the norm.

Fashion is a major industry in Japan, and the Japanese are extremely brand-name conscious. In addition to domestic lines of clothing, virtually every top European designer is represented in Japan, with boutiques even in outlying provincial cities offering imported fashions. The visitor will want to keep this in mind when considering what to bring and what to wear.

Note: Japanese laundries and dry cleaners, particularly those associated with hotels, provide excellent and rapid service. In hotels shirts are automatically starched unless you clearly specify otherwise.

Seasonal Things

Japan has hundreds of festivals and other public events spread throughout the year, along with numerous regularly occurring cultural shows and exhibits that range from kabuki and noh to pottery and lacquerware. The challenge is to select a variety of things that correspond with the timing of your trip. (See Part II).

Again, unless you are into winter sports, the special attractions of Japan in winter are hardly sufficient to give winter precedence over other seasons for recreational travel. If you do opt for a warmer season, the biggest winter event you will miss is New Year's, with its shopping for year-end gifts; **Bo Nen Kai** (Boe Nane Kie), or "Parties to Forget the Old Year"; ringing in the new year at Buddhist temples across the country; and colorful processions of people making their **hatsu mairi** (hot-sue my-ree), or first visit to a shrine in the new year (for many, this is done at the stroke of midnight).

For most, the two best periods for visiting Japan are April and May, and from mid-September through mid-November. Third in the order of preference would be mid-July through mid-September. Each of these periods has its pluses and minuses. Spring, for example, is not the best time to go north of Tokyo or into the highlands if you don't like cold weather. These areas are best visited during mid-summer and in the fall—unless, of course, you are not bothered by cool or cold weather and want this incomparable experience of enjoying some of the hundreds of hot-spring resorts that dot Japan's northern country; they are at their best when the outside world is still white with snow.

Midsummer, with its hot days and high humidity, is naturally the ideal time to head north into the high country, or to the beaches. Fall in Japan is noted for warm days and cool, crisp nights, and for the canopy of golden colors that come with the turning of the leaves. All of the seasons are thus marked by their own characteristics, special dress, and attractions, giving you an opportunity to choose the one most suitable.

Japan's spring begins gradually, creeping up the islands and heralding its arrival in successive areas and cities by the appearance of the country's famed cherry blossoms. The season begins in Kagoshima on the tip of Kyushu, the southernmost main island, in early March, arriving in Tokyo in early April and in Sapporo, Hokkaido, on the northernmost main island, in May.

Observing the annual blossoming of the country's cherry trees has been an institutionalized celebration for more than a thousand years, and there is perhaps no more dramatic way that nature could mark the end of winter in Japan. The psychological release engendered by strolling among the trees, their blossoms continually wafting away on the slightest breeze, provides a sensual pleasure that one can savor for days afterward. For a person who has become attuned to the annual experience, just glimpsing a cloud of cherry blossoms from a moving train or car is enough to banish the cold hand of winter and rekindle the spirit of spring.

It has long been a tradition for Japan tours to begin in the early spring, often coordinated with **hana mi** (hah-nah me) or cherry-blossoming viewing, but this is your decision which should be based just as much on what else you want to do and your preference of weather. It can be cool this early in the spring, often requiring sweaters or light jackets. In the mountainous areas of central and northern Japan, where many tours regularly go, it is usually still quite cold in April and May, especially if there is a cloud cover and a wind.

Competing with the Japanese

One factor that should be taken into consideration if you are planning a winter, spring, or summer trip is competition from vacationing Japanese, not only for hotels, inns, and transportation, but for all the other facilities as well, from toilets to walking or standing space.

The Japanese are among the most well traveled people in the world. Very specific and highly distinguishable traveling groups include business travelers, employees on company-sponsored recreational trips, school-sponsored student outings, farmer co-op outings, packaged tours of all kinds, women's groups and religious pilgrims (a large and growing group).

With almost 125 million people squeezed onto a landmass that is only about 142,000 square miles in size, of which over 70 percent is uninhabited mountains, things have to work smoothly to prevent mass gridlock. For example, lining up to get near the great Buddha in Kamakura, much less inside it, is not the same as lining up for rides at Disneyland. You can help yourself and the rest of the traveling public by avoiding the main rush periods.

The main traveling/vacation periods in Japan are over New Year's, from the end of December until about 7 January; the first week in May (Golden Week); and in mid-August, when millions of people return to their ancestral homes as part of the traditional *O'bon* (Oh-bone) "paying respect to ancestors" festival.

Some Useful Phrases in Japanese

Will it get cold tonight?
Komban samuku narimasu ka?
Kome-bahn sah-muu-kuu nah-ree-mahss kah?

Shall I take a coat?
Koto wo motte ikimasho ka?
Koe-toe oh mote-tay ee-kee-mah-show kah?

I would like to buy an umbrella
Kasa wo kaitai desu   Kah-sah oh kie-tie dess

CHAPTER 4

Reservations and Other Details

Independent or Group Travel

There is obviously much to be said for both independent and group travel. A review of the primary factors involved should help you to decide which way you want to go.

Some of the advantages of group travel arranged by a travel agent include the following:

1. All you have to do is tell the agent where you want to go, when you want to go, how many days you want to be gone, and pay the cost.
2. Travel agents receive wholesale prices from airlines and hotels and are able to pass some of these savings on to you.
3. Most of the details of traveling abroad, from obtaining passports and visas to arranging for airport-to-hotel ground transportation and all local tours, are taken care of for you.
4. While overseas you are accompanied by a guide and/or interpreter who provides all kinds of other miscellaneous services as well, relieving you of most direct responsibility.

Probably the main disadvantage of group travel is simply that you are a member of a group and are treated as such, required to follow a detailed schedule that you cannot alter without causing problems.

If you choose to travel independently, you have to make all of your own travel arrangements, obtain your own travel documents, and take care of yourself. But none of this is as difficult as it might seem to someone who has not traveled abroad. The travel industry handles millions of independent travelers daily, and has it down pretty pat.

To get a passport, you need proof of your identity and citizenship, preferably a birth certificate. In the United States application forms (Form DSP-11) are available from the nearest federal building. Mail the filled-out form, along with the current fee and two passport-size photos measuring two by two inches, to the nearest designated passport office.

Arranging for air travel abroad is no different than making reservations for a domestic flight. There are a number of ways you can go about arranging for hotel accommodations in Japan. The easiest, of course, is to make your reservations with one of the international hotel chains, such as Holiday Inn, which you can call toll free from anywhere and book reservations anywhere in their system.

Booking through Holiday Inns International is especially convenient since they are the largest hotel chain in the world and operate their own in-house international reservation system called Holidex. There are Holiday Inns in Narita (adjoining the New Tokyo International Airport), Tokyo, Yokohama, Kyoto, Osaka, Nagasaki, and Toyohashi. In the United States, the toll-free Holiday Inn number to call for reservations worldwide is 1-800-465-4329.

Other hotel chains with international reservation systems include Hilton, Hyatt and Sheraton.

Who Needs Visas?

As of 1988, American citizens no longer need visas to visit Japan for either tourism or business for up to ninety days if they have transit or return-trip tickets. They still need valid passports, however. Citizens of the following countries do not need visas to visit Japan, provided they do not intend to stay for more than three months or engage in business: Argentina, Bahamas, Bangladesh, Barbados, Belgium, Canada, Chile, Colombia, Costa Rica, Cyprus, Denmark, Dominican Republic, El Salvador, Finland, Greece, Guatemala, Holland, Honduras, Iceland, Iran, Israel, Italy, Lesotho, Luxembourg, Malaysia, Malta, Mauritius, Norway, Pakistan, Peru, Portugal, San Marino, Singapore, Spain, Surinam, Sweden, Tunisia, Turkey, Uruguay and Yugoslavia.

Visitors from the following countries may stay in Japan without visas for six months as long as they do not work or engage in business: Austria, West Germany, Ireland, Liechtenstein, Mexico, Switzerland, and the United Kingdom. New Zealanders may visit Japan for 30 days without visas.

Other nationalities must have visas to stay in Japan for more than seventy-two hours. If they have confirmed, ongoing reservations, they may stop over in Japan without visas for up to seventy-two hours. Tourist visas to Japan are issued without charge by Japanese embassies and consulates abroad.

Health Requirements

Smallpox and cholera shots are required for entering Japan only if you are coming from an infected area.

Customs Regulations

Travelers visiting Japan may bring in personal belongings, plus up to four hundred cigarettes, one hundred cigars, or five hundred grams of pipe tobacco; three bottles of liquor; two ounces of perfume; and gifts or souvenirs valued up to ¥100,000, duty free. Prohibited items include firearms, narcotics, any type of ammunition, and pornographic materials. A written declaration is required for any unaccompanied baggage.

Japanese Customs inspectors sometimes check the baggage of returning Japanese very closely, particularly if they are coming from Southeast Asia. The baggage of young men from Middle Eastern and Near Eastern countries is usually checked thoroughly. Generally, Americans and Europeans are waved on through, sometimes with a cursory check of the hand-luggage.

The Traveler's Friend

Japan's National Tourist Organization (JNTO), which operates travel information centers abroad as well as in Japan, is an excellent source of both general and specific information on economical accommodations and tours in Japan. JNTO publishes a number of booklets and directories of its own and acts as a distribution center for numerous brochures, newspapers, and other travel publications produced by private companies.

JNTO's overseas information centers include the following:

United States
Rockefeller Plaza, 630 Fifth Avenue, Suite 2101, New York, New
    York 10020
401 North Michigan Avenue, Suite 770, Chicago, Illinois 60601
2121 San Jacinto Street, Suite 980, Dallas, Texas 75201
360 Post Street, Suite 601, San Francisco, California 94108
624 South Grand Avenue, Suite 1611, Los Angeles, California 90017

Canada
165 University Avenue, Toronto, Ontario M5H 3B8

England
167 Regent Street, London W.l.

France
4-8 Rue Sainte-Anne, 75001, Paris

Switzerland
13 Rue de Berne, Geneve

Germany
Kaiserstrasse 11, 60311 Frankfurt/M

Mexico
122 Reforma, Fifth Floor, B-2, Mexico City 6, D.F.

Brazil
509-S/405 Avenue Paulista, Sao Paulo 01311

Australia
Level 33, The Chifley Tower, 2 Chifley Square, Sidney

Korea
10 Da-Dong, Chung-Ku, Seoul

Hong Kong
Peter Building, 58 Queen's Road, Central

Thailand
Wall Street Tower Building, 33/61 Suriwong Road, Bangkok

JNTO has three Tourist Information Centers (TIC) in Japan: a main branch in Tokyo, plus sub-branches at Tokyo International Airport in Narita, and in the Kyoto Tower Building in Kyoto.

The main center in downtown Tokyo is staffed by English- and French-speaking personnel. It is open from 9:00 A.M. to 5:00 P.M. daily, except Sundays and national holidays. The center maintains extensive files on tourism facilities, and it undertakes to answer inquiries on the spot as well as by phone and mail—which means that travelers planning on visiting Japan may write for information in advance.

Among the services provided by the TIC are arranging for home visits and licensed guides. It is especially helpful to people who are traveling independently and wanting to take in out-of-the-way places. Here is the address of the main TIC office in Tokyo:

> Tourist Information Center
> Kotani Building, First Floor
> 1-Yurakucho, Chiyoda-Ku, Tokyo
> Tel: 3502-1461
> Teletourist Service Number (events in Tokyo): 3503-2911

This location is on Hibiya Avenue, one block east of the southeast corner of the Imperial Palace grounds, and two blocks north of the back of the Imperial Hotel. The building is on the south side of the avenue, next to the elevated train tracks that separate the Hibiya-Yurakucho area from the Tsukiyabashi-Ginza area, and about one hundred yards south of Yurakucho Train Station.

The Hibiya, Ginza, and Yurakucho Subway Stations, where five lines (the Hibiya, the Chiyoda, the Yurakucho, the Mita, and the Marunouchi Line) intersect, are beneath the area in front of the TIC. A sixth subway line, the Ginza, is three blocks away, and is also accessible from Hibiya Station via an underground passageway. The Hibiya Station subway exit that comes out within a dozen or so yards west of the TIC (on the same side of the street) is Exit A4. Exit A2 brings you up directly across the street from the TIC. If you come out of A4, walk straight ahead for about fifty feet. If you are on the Marunouchi Subway Line, get off at the Ginza Station, walk to the south end of the platform (toward Kasumigaseki, Akasaka Mitsuke and Shinjuku), take the exit on the right side after passing through the turnstiles, go up and out, and walk straight ahead under the elevated train tracks. The TIC building adjoins the narrow street on the other side of the tracks, on your side of the street. The TIC door is rather inconspicuous, so don't walk past it.

If you are traveling by commuter train, get off at Yurakucho Station and take the Hibiya Exit. When you come out of the station, the Sogo Department Store will be on the right. Cross the street and go left, walking parallel to the elevated train tracks past the twin-towered Yurakucho Denki Building. If you look straight ahead, you should be able to see the TIC building on the other side of the first street you come to (about one hundred yards from where you exited Yurakucho Station). A Japan Air Lines (JAL) Gift Plaza will be on your right (on the first floor of the south tower of the Yurakucho Denki Building) before you cross the street to the TIC building.

The Kyoto Tower Building, where the Kyoto branch of the TIC is located, is just outside of Kyoto Station on the southwest side. From the station, take the *Minami Guchi* or South Exit. Tel: 075-371-5649.

Some Useful Phrases in Japanese

I would like to make a reservation
Yoyaku wo shitai desu   Yoe-yah-kuu oh she-tie dess

I would like to confirm my reservations
Yoyaku wo kakuritsu shitai desu
Yoe-yah-kuu oh kah-kuu-reet-sue she-tie dess

Is this the exit for the Ginza?
Kore wa Ginza no deguchi desu ka?
Koe-ray wah Geen-zah no day-guu-chee dess kah?

Which is the way to Ginza Street?
Ginza Dori wa dochira desu ka?
Geen-zah Doe-ree wah doe-chee-rah dess kah?

Is it far?
Toi desu ka?   Toy dess kah?

How many minutes will it take on foot?
Ashi de nanpun gurai kakarimásu ka?
Ah-shee day nahn-poon guu-rye kah-kah-ree-mahss kah?

Is it better to go by taxi?
Takushi de iku ho ga ii desu ka?
Tock-she day ee-kuu hoh gah ee dess kah?

CHAPTER 5

Playing It Safe

Japan's Security Blanket

Japan's laws and customs proscribing physical violence and public or street crime were very detailed and as a rule severely enforced during the country's long feudal age (1192–1868). Law enforcement officials carried swords which they were authorized to use to maintain peace. Because of this policy the people were conditioned for centuries to obey laws, and until recent decades one could spend years in the country and never witness a public brawl. Such crimes as mugging were virtually unheard of. Still today, the Japanese are among the most law-abiding people in the world. One does not have to fear the onset of darkness or avoid walking in the streets at night. Generally speaking, there are no parts of any city that are more dangerous than any other.

Crime and the criminal element in Japan, like everything else, is highly structured, identifiable and usually predictable. One of the oldest and strongest codes of professional Japanese criminals is that they do not prey directly on the public. Ordinary people who occasionally resort to crime will embezzle or burglarize a home or business, but robbing a person is rare.

Japan's ancient traditions and codes remain in sufficient force so that they provide a security blanket for the people at large, resulting in a feeling of safety that adds a special dimension to life in Japan. It is indeed a remarkable thing to go to Tokyo or other Japanese cities from New York, Los Angeles, Mexico City, or any other city where fear of public violence runs deep, and experience the personal security one takes for granted in Japan.

The Honesty Factor

Another characteristic of the Japanese that is a legacy of their traditional culture and also contributes to personal security is an extraordinarily high degree of honesty. During Japan's extended feudal age, which actually did not end until 1945, the Japanese were probably more conditioned in personal honesty than any other people in history. Honesty was taught as the only way of life. Dishonesty, when it occurred, was dealt with harshly.

While the culture trait of honesty is no longer taught with the same dedication and force, it remains strong enough to distinguish the Japanese and reinforce Japan's role as a preferred destination for foreign travelers.

It is common, for example, for Japanese in all walks of life to go out of their way to locate the owners of lost or forgotten property and return it to them. Stories of foreign visitors forgetting cameras or other personal articles in public places and eventually having the property returned to them by some private individual, after a search that would tax an experienced detective, often make the national news.

The Marvelous *Koban*

Tangible evidence of Japanese concern with law and order is provided by the *koban* (koe-bahn), or "police boxes," that dot Japanese cities. These police substations date from the early days of the Tokugawa Shogunate. Once Ieyasu Tokugawa had destroyed the other contenders for power and established his own military dictatorship in 1603, the country settled in for a long period of peace.

Suddenly several hundred thousand sword-carrying samurai warriors were without battles to fight. The less-refined warriors took to drinking and brawling in the streets, frequently using their sharp blades on passersby. The shogunate established the *koban* system to help stop these **tsuji giri** (t'sue-je ghee-ree), or "street corner cut-tings." In those days, "cutting" was a synonym for "killing."

Today, policemen stationed in Japan's *koban* spend most of their time just watching over things, giving directions to people trying to find addresses in their area (See Chapter 12 for why one has to go to the police to find an address in Japanese cities), and helping drunken revelers into taxis after an evening on the town.

Koban police in downtown areas of Japan's major cities have also become old hands at helping foreign visitors who have gotten lost, lost something, or are trying to find a shop or restaurant in the area.

Common Sense and Precautions

Despite the absence of street crime in Japan, and the overall safety of one's person or property, it is still wise to use common sense and to take normal precautions. This includes not leaving sums of money or other valuables in hotel rooms; not carrying large sums on your person (you might lose it); and not knowingly or deliberately inviting trouble with tough-looking young men in low-class drinking areas. Remember, too, that you are in a foreign country where the laws and customs are different; getting involved in any situation in which you might be subject to questioning or arrest can be inconvenient to say the least. (See Chapter 6).

Some Useful Phrases in Japanese

Where is the nearest police box?
Ichiban chikai no koban wa doko desu ka?
Ee-chee-bahn chee-kie no koe-bahn wah doe-koe dess kah?

Please keep this money for me
Kono okane wo azukatte kudasai
Koc-no oh-kah-nay oh ah-zuu-kot-tay kuu-dah-sie

Do you have a safety deposit box?
Kinko ga arimasu ka?   Keen-koe gah ah-ree-mahss kah?

Is this area safe?
Kono chitai wa anzen desu ka?
Koe-no chee-tie wah ahn-zen dess kah?

I am looking for this address
Kono jusho wo sagashite imasu
Koe-no juu-show oh sah-gah-ssh-tay ee-mahss

Is it far from here?
Koko kara toi desu ka?   Koe-koe kah-rah toy dess kah?

Please draw a map of the area
Sono chitai no chizu wo kaite kudasai
Soe-no chee-tie no chee-zuu oh kie-tay kuu-dah-sie

How many minutes will it take by taxi?
Takushi de nanpun gurai kakarimasu ka?
Tock-she day nahn-poon guu-rye kah-kah-ree-mahss kah?

How much will it cost to go by taxi?
Takushi de iku to ikura gurai shimasu ka?
Tock-she day ee-kuu toe ee-kuu-rah guu-rye she-mahss ka?

I lost my camera
Kamera wo nakushimashita
Kah-may-rah oh nah-kuu-she-mah-sshtah

I am staying at the Ginza Tokyu Hotel
Ginza Tokyu Hoteru ni tomatte imasu
Geen-zah Toe-que Hoe-tay-rue nee toe-mot-tay ee-mahss

My room number is 645
Watakushi no rumu namba wa roku-yon-go desu
Wah-tock-she no ruu-muu nahm-bah wah roe-kuu-yoan-goe dess

I am going to Kyoto tomorrow
Ashita Kyoto e ikimasu   Ah-ssh-tah K'yoe-toe eh ee-kee-mahss

CHAPTER 6

Dealing with Emergencies

Getting Rid of Fear

You do not have to be afraid of visiting Japan. The possibility of an emergency that cannot be dealt with quickly and effectively is probably more remote than it is in your own country. Given the highly structured and efficient systems in Japan, particularly the systems associated with the travel industry, there may indeed be less danger to you while you are in Japan than on other occasions. In addition, the Japanese are especially solicitous of foreign visitors and are usually more sensitive and helpful than people in other countries.

Ambulances, Doctors, Drugs, and Hospitals

If you should become ill while you are in Japan, you can get excellent medical care. If you are at your hotel, call the front desk and ask the clerk to contact a doctor. All hotels have a list of doctors to call in emergencies. Some of them have staff doctors on call twenty-four hours a day. If you are out touring, your Japanese guide will know what to do.

If ambulance service and hospital arrangements are necessary, your hotel will also take care of these matters for you. If you are only a short distance away from your hotel and fall ill, return to the hotel (by taxi, subway, etc.) if you can. If you cannot, ask someone—a passerby if necessary, but preferably a shop clerk, restaurant waiter or clerk, office worker, or policeman—to call the hotel for you and request whatever service you need. If you are quite ill and no one around you speaks English, say the following: **Byoki desu. Kyukyu-sha yonde kudasai.** (Bee-yoe-kee dess. Que-que-shah oh yone-day kuu-dah-sigh.), which means, "I am sick. Please call an ambulance."

If you are in the countryside or at a tourist attraction or out-of-the-way inn, take the same approach to getting help. As a rule, the Japanese go out of their way to aid foreign travelers in distress. The main thing is to make someone aware that you do need help. If you need an ambulance and you have to do the calling yourself, the universal number, good anywhere in Japan, is 119 (which is also the number to report a fire).

The names, phone numbers, addresses and specialties of several foreign doctors are normally listed in the leading English-language visitor publications found in your hotel, tourist information centers, airline offices, and travel agencies. There are a number of these in all of Japan's major cities. Some of the doctors are foreign, but all speak English. Clinics and hospitals that cater to foreign patients are also generally listed in local travel literature.

As for patent medicines, pharmacies are more common in Japan than in the United States and most European countries. Many leading hotels have pharmacies in their basement shopping arcades. Others are located in major shopping districts, near terminals, and on neighborhood shopping streets. If you are out on the town and need one, just say, "**Kusuri-ya wa doko desu ka?** (Kuu-sue-ree-yah wah doe-koe dess kah?)," or "Where is the medicine shop (drugstore)?"

Japanese drugstores carry the usual drugs and medicines as well as antibiotics that can be obtained in the United States or Europe only with a doctor's prescription. In Japan doctors who are in private practice or have their own clinics are authorized to sell prescription drugs directly (and the sale of drugs is a major part of their business).

Among the Tokyo hospitals that have English-speaking personnel, along with private rooms, Western food, and outpatient service, are the following:

St. Luke's International Hospital **Sei Roka Byoin** (Say-e Roe-kah B'yoe-een), 10-1 Akashi-cho, Chuo-Ku, Tokyo. Tel: 3541-5151.

Tokyo Medical and Surgical Clinic, No. 32 Mori Building, 3-4-30 Shiba Koen, Minato-ku, Tokyo. Tel: 3436-3028.

Tokyo Sanitarium Hospital **Toyko Eisei Byoin** (Tokyo A-e-say-e B'yoe-een), 3-17-3 Amanuma, Suginami-ku, Tokyo. Tel: 3392-6151. Operated by the Seventh-day Adventist Church.

International Catholic Hospital **Seibo Byoin** (Say-e-boe B'yoe-een), 2-5-1 Naka-Ochiai, Shinjuku-ku, Tokyo. Tel: 3951-1111.

Dental Care

If you require emergency dental care while in Japan, there are several dentists in Tokyo and other major cities who cater to foreign clientele. They are listed in local English-language phone books, and advertise in the classified ad sections of local English-language newspapers.

The Law and the Police

It is rare for travelers in Japan to have any kind of run-in with the law. When it happens it usually involves someone who attempted to smuggle in contraband (guns, ammunition, drugs, pornography), or who was involved in a traffic violation, traffic accident, or a dispute over prices in a rip-off bar or cabaret. You can easily avoid the first category. If you are involved in a traffic violation, stay very calm, very subdued, and apologize profusely, saying you are very sorry for endangering people, for inconveniencing the police department, for failing to obey the regulations, for not being familiar with the rules. If no one was injured or endangered, you are likely to get off with a warning.

If you are involved in a traffic accident, stay very calm, very sub-dued and apologize even more profusely. If it was another party's fault, apologize to everyone concerned, adding that you did your best to avoid the accident, but since it was the other party's fault it hap-pened anyway. If it was your fault, apologize to everybody who comes near you, repeatedly. In either event, be prepared to spend a lot of time answering questions and filling out documents. At the earliest opportunity, call the owner of the car, whether it's a rent-a-car company or a private owner. They will have insurance on the car and will know who to contact.

If substantial injury or damage has been inflicted, contact your embassy or the nearest consulate, give them all the details about yourself and the accident, and ask for their help and advice.

No matter who is at fault, stay cool and collected. If you get angry, lose your temper and sound off, it will go much worse for you. If you are guilty of some offense it is especially important for you to apolo-gize to everyone. To the Japanese, expressing genuine sorrow when you are at fault in any situation is regarded as greatly reducing the degree of guilt and the need for additional punishment.

In Case of Arrest

In Japan a person arrested for committing a crime or on suspicion of committing a crime can be detained by the police for seventy-two hours without formal charges while the case is investigated. If there is sufficient evidence to indicate guilt, the case is turned over to the Prosecutor's Office, which can hold a suspect for up to sixty days, in increments of ten days each time, for further investigation.

If it is decided to prosecute a case, a document detailing the charges and hearing is prepared. The detainee or defendant must sign and fingerprint the document, which will then be submitted as part of the prosecution's case.

As in the United States and elsewhere, a person arrested in Japan has the right to remain silent and consult a lawyer—**bengoshi** (bane-go-she). The American Embassy maintains a list of lawyers who speak English and handle international cases. Other nationalities may also contact the American Embassy and ask for this referral service.

Another option, and one that has some advantages, is to contact the Legal Aid Society **Horitsu Fujo Kyokai** (Hoe-reet-sue Fuu-joe K'yoe-kie), a nonprofit group operated by the Japanese Bar Association and financed by a fee schedule that is paid after the trial is over. (If you go to a regular lawyer, most of them require payment in advance.)

Since the LAS is a nonprofit organization, the fees charged for its services are generally well below those of independent lawyers. The society is operated within the Japan Federation of Bar Associates, 1-1-1 Kasumigaseki, Chiyoda-ku, Tokyo, Japan 100. Tel: 03-3580-2851.

Crimes involving juveniles (those under the age of 20) are generally sent to the Family Court. Investigations cover the family as well as the suspect, and parents are often called to testify.

In the Event of Fire

Fires were once an almost daily and nightly occurrence in Japan's paper-and-wood towns and cities, but with the substitution of modern gas and electric stoves for the traditional *hibachi* (he-bah-chee) fire pots, conflagrations are no longer common.

Western-style buildings, all with the latest fire-prevention facilities, are especially safe. In addition, most large buildings, including hotels, have inhouse security personnel who function as fire watchers as well as guards. In some luxury hotels, these security guards patrol the floors on a twenty-four-hour basis.

As always, you should inform yourself of the nearest fire escapes and exits in hotels, particularly in Japanese-style inns.

When the Earth Quakes

There are several thousand recorded earthquakes each year in Japan. Generally during the course of a year there will be three to a dozen that will be severe enough to rattle furnishings and otherwise attract attention. About once a year a quake is bad enough to cause damage somewhere near the epicenter.

The visitor to Japan is not likely to experience a bad earthquake because they are really not that frequent, and the epicenter is usually some distance away from main cities. Even in the event of a more serious quake, the Japanese have made great improvements in earthquake-proof construction techniques, so that large areas of many cities are relatively safe from medium to strong earthquakes.

Many of the earthquakes that occur in Japan that are strong enough for you to notice are often over before you have time to take any action. Others may last for several minutes, and include one or more aftershocks. If you are in a large modern building when a serious shock hits, the best thing to do is to get away from windows and get under something like a table, or stand in the doorway if the shock continues—do not immediately start running to get out of the building.

If the rocking and rolling continues but you can walk, turn off any gas that may be on, and turn on any water faucets to catch as much water as you can in the sink, bathtub or containers in case the water-pipes break. If you are in a small wooden building such as a restaurant or inn, and the quake is obviously a serious one, get to an outside doorway if you can, but do not run into the street, where you might be hit by falling debris. If you are in the street, run inside the doorway of the nearest large building and remain there until the quake is over.

If you prefer to be as safe as possible, you might want to pick up an earthquake survival kit, available in Japan in various stores. In addition to such things as a flashlight and a rope ladder for descending buildings on the outside, these kits contain emergency medical supplies and foods. The same kits are also very useful in the event of fires or other emergencies. The kits are known as **bosai pakku** (boe-sie pahk-kuu).

TELEPHONE HOT-LINE NUMBERS

AMBULANCE / FIRE   **119**

POLICE   **110**

LOST AND FOUND

Narita International Airport, Terminal 1, from Tokyo	0476-32-2802
Narita International Airport, Terminal 2, from Tokyo	0476-34-5000
Metropolitan Police Department, Tokyo	03-3581-4321 (English spoken)
JR East Infoline, Tokyo	03-3423-0111 (English spoken)
TRTA Subway Center, Tokyo	03-3837-7111 (English spoken)
Taxis, Tokyo	03-3648-0300
JR Nagoya Station	052-546-2241
JR Kyoto Station	075-351-6134
JR Osaka Station	06-341-8088
JR Shin Osaka Station	06-3302-7335
JR Kobe Station	078-341-0880
JR Hakata Station	092-471-8111

CREDIT CARD SERVICES

American Express (toll-free, 24 hours, English)	0120-376-100
Master Card	03-3254-6751
VISA Card (24 hours, English)	03-3459-4700
Diners Club of Japan	03-3499-1311

Some Useful Phrases in Japanese

Help!
Tasukete!   (Tahss-kay-tay!)

Policeman
Keikan   (Kay-e-khan);
also **O'mawari-san** (Oh-mah-wah-ree-sahn),
the colloquial term.

Police station
Kei satsu   (Kay-e sot-sue)

Police headquarters
Kei satsusho   (Kay-e sot-sue-show)

Earthquake
Jishin   (Jee-sheen)

Health insurance
Kenko hoken   (Kane-koe hoe-kane)

Medical examination hours
Shinsatsu jikan   (Sheen-sot-sue jee-kahn)

Hospital visiting hours
Menkai jikan   (Mane-kie jee-kahn)

Nurse
Kangofu   (Kahn-goe-fuu)

I have diarrhea
Geri wo shite imasu   Gay-ree oh ssh-tay ee-mahss

I have a fever
Netsu ga arimasu   Nate-sue gah ah-ree-mahss

I caught a cold
Kaze wo hikimashita   Kah-zay oh hee-kee-mahssh-tah

I have a headache
Zutsu ga shite imasu   Zoot-sue gah ssh-tay ee-mahss

I feel nauseated
Hakike ga shite imasu   Hah-kee-kay gah ssh-tay ee-mahss

Call the police, please
Keikan wo yonde kudasai   Kay-e-khan oh yone-day kuu-dah-sie

I will complain to the police
Keikan ni hanashimasu   Kay-e-khan nee hah-nah-she-mahss

My husband is sick. Please call a doctor
Shujin ga byoki desu. Oisha-san wo yonde kudasai
Shuu-jeen gah b'yoe-kee dess. Oh-ee-shah-sahn oh yone-day
kuu-dah-sie

CHAPTER 7

Money Matters

Avoiding Exchange Rip-Offs

It is very convenient to have fifteen thousand or twenty thousand yen with you when you arrive in Japan to avoid exchanging money at the airport to pay for transportation into the city. Also, Japanese yen is expensive enough without paying the high commission rates incurred when you buy it from a commercial foreign exchange trader located in international airport gateways to Japan. In many cases, the commissions charged by these traders are well above 10 percent.

It is better to buy your yen from a bank. Contact your local bank first. If it doesn't have yen for sale, it should be able to tell you which bank does have it. If you are unable to buy yen conveniently before leaving for Japan, there are exchange bank facilities located in the customs area of the New Tokyo International Airport at Narita as well as at Japan's other international airports. If you are arriving by passenger ship you can buy yen on the ship.

The customs area banks at Narita are located against the wall after you pass through the customs checkpoints. If there is a long line at the bank windows or you miss them, the same banks have small windows on the opposite side of the wall, accessible from the large reception/waiting area. After you exit from customs, make a sharp left or right (depending on which door you come out of). The inconspicuous bank windows are more or less behind the exit doors.

In Japan all first-class and luxury hotels are authorized to sell yen. These hotels have foreign exchange windows, usually next to the cashier at the front counter. Many duty-free shops are also licensed to sell yen, as are most banks. In banks look for the **Gaikoku Kawase** (Guy-koe-kuu Kah-wah-say), or "Foreign Exchange" window.

If the clerk does not speak English, say "**Doru wo en ni shitai desu** (Doe-rue oh inn nee she-tie dess)"—"I would like to change dollars into yen." The clerk will give you a small form to fill out.

Minding Your Money Matters

Prior to 1868 the great mass of employed Japanese did not work for wages. Their needs were more or less taken care of by their employers, and the concept of putting an hourly, weekly or monthly monetary value on their time and labor, as is done now, was alien.

The privileged *Samurai,* an elite warrior class which made up a sizable proportion of the population, felt strongly that talking about money or dealing in money matters was degrading and beneath them. It was considered arrogant and uncultured to flaunt one's wealth, and there was a law prohibiting such behavior.

In today's Japan spending freely and living ostentatiously is commonplace, but there are some holdovers from the old attitudes about money. It still is considered impolite to flaunt money openly or to hand anyone except a tradesman or clerk money that is not wrapped in paper or an envelope. Gifts of money are customarily presented in **noshi bukuro** (no-she buu-kuu-roe), special envelopes made for that purpose. *Noshi* refers to cords that are used to tie the envelopes.

Noshi bukuro are most commonly used for weddings and funerals, important social events in the lives of the Japanese, especially businessmen. People attending weddings and funerals put an appropriate amount of money (ranging from ten thousand to fifty thousand yen or more, depending on their relationship with the family concerned) in the envelope and leave it on a special table provided for that purpose. For a wedding, the money envelope cords are white and red, and the envelope is imprinted with the **kanji** (kahn-jee) character **Kotobuki** (Koe-toe-buu-kee), meaning "Congratulations." Gold and silver cords are used on money envelopes on other happy occasions. For funerals, the envelope cords are black and white, and the envelopes bear the characters **Go Rei Zen** (Go Ray Zen), meaning "Before the Spirit of the Departed."

The Japanese virtually never contest a bill or argue about the cost of an item—except in a recognized bargaining situation—and are very embarrassed when someone else does. It is a good idea to check bills and figures, however, because younger clerks and sales staff in particular do make mistakes. You can be sure your bill is correct if the clerk uses a **soroban** (so-roe-bahn), or abacus, to add it up. Otherwise, check it. If you find an error, apologize and point it out.

Japanese who are experienced in dealing with foreigners, particularly the younger generation, can be just as casual about money as any Westerner, but the visitor should be safe rather than sorry by handling money modestly and observing the old protocol in money-giving situations.

The Japanese are noted for their hospitality and are much quicker than most people to pick up tabs in restaurants and bars. Of course, there are times when it is proper to accept such hospitality graciously, and times when it is not—even though your Japanese friend has made the gesture. On these latter occasions, you often have to get physical to get to the bill before he does or retrieve it from him if he gets it first.

Traveler's Checks

Traveler's checks from recognized companies and banks are widely accepted in Japan. It is not a good idea, however, to try to use them in neighborhood businesses or in small, out-of-the-way towns and villages. Such places also are not accustomed to accepting regular bank checks.

Another point: Avoid using large-denomination traveler's checks to make small purchases in small shops. It is better to exchange these checks for cash at your hotel or at a bank.

Credit Cards

Credit cards are as commonly used in Japan as in the United States or Europe. Virtually all of the American and European cards as well as several Japanese cards are accepted by many restaurants and shops catering to an international trade. Nontourist, Japanese-style shops, restaurants, and inns are often the exception to this rule, requiring cash payment. Cards accepted are often displayed in a front window or on a wall just inside.

Banking on It

For those who are going to spend any substantial amount of time in Japan, some knowledge of how Japanese banks work would be helpful. Once you get beyond the language barrier, there are only a few differences between a Japanese bank and most foreign banks.

In Japan very few payments are made by check. Most payments are done by bank transfer, called *furi komi* (fuu-ree koe-me). In fact, companies that pay by check may be considered old-fashioned or even a little bit devious, since the money remains in their account longer if payment is by check, and there may be occasions when a check is no good—something that cannot happen with a bank transfer.

Another difference is that Japanese banks do not complete a customer's transactions while he waits at the counter. After the customer turns in the deposit or withdrawal slip or initiates whatever action is desired, he is given a numbered chit and asked to sit in the lobby, which has a selection of magazines to read while waiting. When the internal transaction is finished, he is called by number or name to return to the counter to complete the business.

The Japanese view this system as providing the customer with special service, since he gets to sit down and relax. Some banks even have private rooms where mothers can nurse their babies and change diapers, and other areas where young children can play. Many also have public bulletin boards, called *Den Go Ban* (Dane Go Bahn), where customers may post private messages.

Japanese banks also usually have one or more employees stationed in their lobbies to provide both security and assistance to customers. These staff members usually wear uniforms and/or arm bands, but they are not armed. They help newcomers operate the automatic tellers, advise them about which forms to fill out, and indicate the windows to go to for the service they want.

As usual, the functions in Japanese banks are strictly divided by category, with separate tellers for each. The name of the function is on a sign next to the appropriate teller, usually in Japanese ideograms (*kanji*/kahn-jee) and Roman letters, and the window is usually numbered as well.

The Tip Trap

The old Japanese attitude toward money is probably one of the reasons they are sensitive about tipping. Giving a Western-style tip (to cab drivers, waiters, bellhops, etc.) is considered impolite as well as disruptive of both the ideal relationship between employees and guests, and interpersonal relations among employees.

This does not mean the visitor gets by without paying a surcharge—which is what a tip is—on all meals and hotel services, however. Hotels and first-class restaurants in Japan add from 10 to 15 percent to the guest's bill as a service charge. This, says management, is later shared among all of the employees in the form of general benefits, thereby eliminating personal competition for tips and giving all employees the same incentive to do their best for guests.

About the only tips given directly are to airport and train station redcaps, tour guides, and drivers of rented cars. Many restaurants, hotels, taxis, and the like have signs posted requesting that patrons refrain from tipping. Also, the personnel of Japanese Railways are under strict orders to return any tip that is given to them.

If you get very special service from a maid or bellboy in a hotel or inn and want to show your appreciation despite the ban on tipping, you may have to resort to a gift of some kind rather than money.

There are a few exceptions to the no-tipping rule. In Japanese-style inns it is fairly common for guests to leave cash tips under their pillows for room maids (a custom some Japanese follow when they are abroad). When a Japanese throws a party for important guests at an inn or restaurant, he may have a cash tip delivered to the location *before the party takes place* to ensure that he gets special service.

Surprising to some, perhaps, is the fact that the no-direct-tipping practice in Japan does not result in any loss of service. In fact, the extraordinary service one gets in hotels, inns, and Japanese-style restaurants is one of the reasons the country is so popular as a travel destination.

There are many advantages to the Japanese system, and after a long stay there a return to the United States or Europe, where tipping in all kinds of situations is expected, can be a very disagreeable change.

Yen coins come in units of 1, 5, 10, 50, 100 and 500. (Before the imposition of a retail sales tax in 1989, about the only places that used one-yen coins were supermarkets. In other places, prices were always rounded off to 10.) Paper currency comes in one thousand, five thousand, and 10,000 yen notes.

Money Vocabulary

Bank
Ginko   (Gheen-koe)

Bank account
Koza bango   (Koe-zah bahn-goe)

Bill (charge)
Okanjo   (Oh-kahn-joe)

Bill (paper money)
Satsu   (Sot-sue)

Cash
Genkin   (Gane-keen)

Change
Otsuri   (Oh-t'sue-ree)

Check
Kogitte   (Koe-geet-tay)

Checking account
Toza yokin   (Toe-zah yoe-keen)

Counter number
Ban-no madoguchi   (Bahn-no mah-doe-guu-chee)

Deposits
O-azukeire   (Oh-ah-zoo-kay-ee-ray)

Dollar
Doru   (Doe-rue)

Foreign Exchange
Gaikoku kawase   (Guy-koe-kuu kah-wah-say)

General savings account
Sogo koza   (Soe-go koe-zah)

Handling charge
Tesu ryo   (Tay-sue rio)

Money
Okane   (Oh-kah-nay)

One hundred yen
Hyaku en   (H'yah-kuu inn)

Five hundred yen
Gohyaku en   (Go-h'yah-kuu inn)

One thousand yen
I-sen en   (E-sin inn)

Two thousand yen
Ni-sen en   (Nee-sin inn)

Three thousand yen
San-zen en   (Sahn-zen inn)

Four thousand yen
Yon-sen en   (Yoan-sin inn)

Five thousand yen
Go-sen en   (Go-sin inn)

Ten thousand yen
Ichi-man en   (E-chee-mahn inn)

Ordinary savings
Futsu yokin   (Fute-sue yoe-keen)

Receipt
Ryoshusho   (Rio-shuu-show)

Remittances
Gosokin   (Go-soh-keen)

Traveler's checks
Toraberazu chekku   (Toe-rah-bay-rah-zoo check-koo)

Withdrawals
Hikidashi   (He-kee-dah-shee)

Yen
En   (Inn)

CHAPTER 8

Japan's International Airports

The New Tokyo International Airport

The New Tokyo International Airport (commonly referred to as Narita International Airport) is located on the outskirts of the city of Narita in Chiba Prefecture some sixty kilometers east of Tokyo. It consists of two terminals, Terminal 1 and Terminal 2, that are about one kilometer apart. Both terminals have the same facilities in virtually the same design layout, and are user friendly, with English signs posted everywhere. There are full-fledged railway stations beneath each terminal.

Which terminal you arrive at is of little significance, but it is, of course, vital that you know which terminal you are to depart from when leaving Japan so you can go to the right terminal. [All public transportation going *to* the airport stops at Terminal 2 first, and then proceeds on to Terminal 1.]

If you have to go from one terminal to the other there is free shuttle-bus service that departs from the "arrival floor/levels" every 10 to 15 minutes. The trip takes from five to eight minutes. Boarding areas for the terminal shuttle buses are designated by numbered bus stop signs. At Terminal 1, the airport shuttle bus stop is Stop No. 5. At Terminal 2 the shuttle bus stops are No. 8 and No. 18.

Free baggage carts are available in the Customs area, and may be taken outside the terminal—to the limousine bus stops in front of the terminals, to the taxi stands, and to the adjoining parking lots.

Once through Customs you exit into a large Arrival Lobby where you will find limousine bus ticket counters, other airport service counters, information desks, and escalators and stairs leading to the underground railway stations that serve the terminals. If you need to exchange foreign currency for yen, you may do so while you are still inside the Customs area, or after you exit into the Arrival Lobby. The banks serving the facilities have service windows on both the Customs side as well as the Arrival Lobby side.

Getting Into Tokyo/Yokohama

Modes of transportation from New Tokyo International Airport to a variety of destinations include limousine buses, trains, a train/subway, taxis and private cars for hire. Taxis are convenient but very expensive [several hundred dollars]. They also may get caught up in freeway and city traffic, extending the one-hour trip to two hours or more and running the cost up significantly. The taxi stands and private-car areas are on the second lane over from the front of the two terminals. [The first lane is reserved for buses.]

Limousine buses provide scheduled service from both terminals to a number of destinations, including Tokyo hotels, the Tokyo City Air Terminal (TCAT), Haneda Airport (Tokyo's domestic airport), and Yokohama. The buses depart from numbered stops just outside the Arrival Lobbies. Your bus ticket, available at limousine bus ticket counters in the Arrival Lobby, will be imprinted with your destination, departure time and the bus stop number. The bus stop numbers are on very conspicuous vertical street-side signs, and are easy to spot. Terminal 1 also has overhead digital readout signs for each bus stop that continuously give the destinations and departure times for each bus.

Porters stationed at each limousine bus stop take charge of your check-in baggage, giving you claim tickets and placing your luggage in the baggage compartment of the appropriate bus. It takes anywhere from seventy minutes to two and sometimes three hours to reach central Tokyo destinations by bus, depending on traffic conditions.

Two train lines, the Keisei Line and Japanese Railways (JR), each operate two services between Narita and the central Tokyo area. Keisei operates the Keisei Skyliner and Keisei Limited Express trains, connecting the airport with the Keisei-Ueno Station and Nippori Station in north central Tokyo. JR operates the high-speed luxurious

Narita Express (N'EX) between the airport, Tokyo Central Station, Shinjuku Station on the west side of Tokyo, Ikebukuro Station on the northwest side of the city, with periodic service on to the Yokohama N'EX Station.

A fifth choice is a combination train and subway line, the Toei Asakusa-Keisei Line, which also serves the airport and central Tokyo. This is the least expensive, and slowest, of the train services to and from the airport. The Toei-Keisei begins at the airport as an above-ground train and becomes a subway on the outskirts of Tokyo.

If you are going to central Tokyo and choose the Toei/Keisei Line you may want to get off at Higashi Ginza Station, which adjoins the famous Ginza area on the east side, and connects with the Hibiya Subway Line (from which you can transfer to other subway lines that will take you almost anywhere in central Tokyo). Other major stations on the subway portion of the line include Asakusa, Nihonbashi, Mita and Gotanda.

The Narita Airport train stations are located directly beneath the two terminals, one level down. [Terminal 1's station is the end of the line for all of the train/subway lines.] Both stations are accessible from the respective terminals via escalators and stairs located in the central areas of the Arrival Lobbies, and clearly marked by large floor as well as ceiling signs.

In the railway terminals, information booths, ticket windows, ticket counters, ticket vending machines and entry-ways to the train platforms are all clearly marked in English. In both stations there is a *Vju* Travel Plaza ticket office, called *Biu* (Beu) in Japanese, where you may buy tickets for either the Keisei trains or the Narita Express. If you have ticket vouchers it is the only place in the stations where you can exchange them for tickets.

At each of the ticket windows and ticket vending machine locations the various stops and ticket charges are posted on the walls. If you do not know your stop or cannot figure out the correct fare, you may want to go the glass-enclosed Travel Plaza ticket office to buy train tickets. Keep in mind that if is generally necessary to buy tickets on the luxury-class Narita Express 30 minutes prior to its scheduled departure time. N'EX trains are easily identifiable because of their stream-lined shape, cream-grey color trimmed in red, and attractive N'EX logo.

Via N'EX it is 53 minutes from Narita to Tokyo Station, 74 minutes to Shinjuku Station and 87 minutes to Ikebukuro Station. It is 31 minutes from Tokyo Station to the N'EX station in Yokohama. At Tokyo Central Station, N'EX trains arrive on tracks 3 and 4, five levels below ground (B-5 floor), on the West side of the huge station. Access to and from the N'EX platforms is via the SOBU LINE Exit and Entrance.

In Tokyo's equally large Shinjuku Station, the Narita Express also arrives and departs from Tracks 3 and 4, which are on the west side where several major international hotels are located [the hotels are three to eight blocks from the West Entrance of Shinjuku Station].

Limousine Bus Routes

With over 15 million passengers going to and from Narita annually, demands on the various transportation systems are enormous. Most foreign visitors choose to utilize the limousine buses that serve the airport rather than the subway line and trains because it is easier to buy tickets for the buses—fares are the same for most destinations and there are clerks handling ticket sales instead of vending machines, so passengers don't have the hassle of trying to read the destination boards to find out what ticket to buy and how much to pay. More important, however, is the fact that most of the buses take passengers who are staying in first class hotels right to the front door of their hotels—and pick them up there when they leave—so they don't have the serious language and other problems involved in getting from one place to another in Tokyo, especially with heavy luggage.

There are 19 limousine bus routes between Narita and key points in Tokyo and Yokohama. Two of these routes are between Narita and the *Tokyo City Air Terminal* (TCAT), and the *Yokohama City Air Terminal* (YCAT). During busy periods, buses leave and arrive at TCAT every five to ten minutes. Buses going directly to Tokyo hotels leave every five to 30 or so minutes, depending on the time of day and the route. Here are the routes and the hotels they serve:

AKASAKA ROUTE
New Otani Hotel   Akasaka Tokyu Hotel
Akasaka Prince Hotel   ANA Hotel Tokyo

ASAKUSA STATION ROUTE (VIA SHINKIBA STATION)
Asakusa View Hotel   Hotel East 21 Tokyo

CHIBA (JAPAN RAILWAYS) STATION ROUTE
Hotel Pacific Chiba

GINZA ROUTE
Palace Hotel

Imperial Hotel

Dai-ichi Hotel Tokyo

Ginza Tokyu Hotel

Ginza Tobu Hotel

Renaissance Hotel

Ginza Dai-ichi Hotel

HANEDA AIRPORT ROUTE
Haneda Tokyu Hotel

IKEBUKURO ROUTE
Holiday Inn Metropolitan Crown Plaza

Sunshine City Prince Hotel   Four Seasons Hotel

KAIHIN MAKUHARI STATION, KEMIGAWAHAMA STATION AND JR CHIBA STATION ROUTE
Makuhari Prince Hotel

Hotel Green Tower

The Manhattan

Hotel Francs

Hotel Springs Makuhari

Hotel New Otani Makuhari

Kemigawahama Station

JR Chiba Station

Hotel Pacific Chiba

KUDAN ROUTE
Koraku Garden Hotel

Hotel Edmont

Fairmont Hotel

Hotel Kayu Kaikan

Diamond Hotel

Hotel Grand Palace

SHIBA ROUTE
Tokyo Prince Hotel   Hotel Okura

SHINAGAWA/EBISU ROUTE
Hotel Meridien Pacific Hotel

Takanawa Prince Hotel

New Takanawa Prince Hotel

Radisson Miyako Hotel Tokyo

Hotel Laforet Tokyo

Westin Hotel Tokyo

SHINJUKU STATION ROUTE
Keio Plaza Hotel

Century Hyatt Tokyo

Tokyo Hilton

Shinjuku Washington Hotel

Park Hyatt Tokyo

TACHIKAWA STATION ROUTE
Tachikawa Grand Hotel   Palace Hotel Tachikawa

TAKESHIBA/RINKAI/FUKUTOSHIN ROUTE
Hotel Intercontinental Tokyo Bay

Hotel Nikko Tokyo   Tokyo Big Sight

TOKYO CITY AIR TERMINAL ROUTE
Royal Park Hotel (Connected to TCAT by an underground passageway)

TOKYO DISNEYLAND ROUTE
Sheraton Grand Tokyo Bay Hotel & Towers

Tokyo Bay Hilton

Dai-ichi Hotel Tokyo Bay

Tokyo Bay Hotel Tokyu

Sunroute Plaza Tokyo

YOKOHAMA CITY AIR TERMINAL ROUTE
Yokohama Royal Park Hotel Nikko

Inter Continental Hotel

Yokohama Prince Hotel

When Leaving for the Airport

Getting to Narita International Airport from Tokyo can be more complicated than getting into the city, depending on which mode of transportation you choose. There is no problem if you chose a taxi or limousine bus and depart from the front of your hotel. If you choose the subway or a train, however, you have the problem of getting yourself and your baggage to the appropriate train station and getting on the right train.

If you choose to go to Narita via the Narita Express you may board at the N'EX station in Yokohama, or at Ikebukuro, Shinjuku or Tokyo Stations in Tokyo. Generally the best way to get to any of these stations is by taxi, unless you have very little luggage and are staying at one of the few hotels that is within a short walk of one of the above stations or a subway station.

If your choice is the Keisei Skyliner or Keisei Limited Express you must first get to Keisei-Ueno Station or Nippori Station. If you go by subway or commuter train to Ueno, keep in mind that the Keisei train station where you board the train for Narita is about a ten-minute walk from the main Ueno Station where both commuter trains and subways stop.

If you opt for the Toei Asakusa Subway/Keisei Line, you can board at a number of Toei Asakusa line stations (including Mita, Higashi Ginza, Nihonbashi, and Asakusa in the central area)—keeping in mind that not all of the trains on the line go all the way to the two airport terminals in Narita.

Subway trains that *do* go to the airport have blue neon Kanji (Japanese ideogram) signs over the cab of the front car saying Narita Kuko (Narita Airport), as well as blue signs on the sides of some cars saying Kyuko (Limited Express). NARITA KUKO is also posted in Roman letters on the front train and on some of the coaches. These special Narita Airport subways run every fifteen to twenty minutes.

If you go to Narita by subway or any of the train lines, make sure you get off at the right terminal. When going *to* the airport, Terminal 2 comes up first, If your flight departs from Terminal 1, which is about two minutes further on, be sure to stay on the subway or train until it reaches that terminal—which is the end of the line. [Signs in both of the terminals say NARITA STATION, which can be confusing.]

Checking in at TCAT

When departing from Japan you may prefer to check in at the Tokyo City Air Terminal (TCAT), located in the Hakozaki-cho area of east-central Tokyo. If your airline has a check-in counter at TCAT you can check your baggage all the way through to your destination, get your seat assignment and boarding pass, go through Immigration, and then board a limousine bus for Narita—where you have nothing to do except pay the airport tax [you buy tax vouchers from vending machines prior to entering the Immigration area), turn in a plastic pass given to you by Immigration, and get to the boarding area on time.

After checking in on the ground-floor level of TCAT you proceed to the second floor where you buy a limousine bus ticket, then go on to the third floor to pass through Immigration and board your designated bus. Buses leave TCAT for Narita every 5 to 10 minutes in a very efficient system that takes most of the pain out of getting to the airport.

Most passengers going to Narita via TCAT go to the terminal by taxi, or by shuttle bus from the *Yaesu Guchi* (Yie-sue guu-chee) side of Tokyo Station. You may also go to the terminal by the Hibiya Subway Line, getting off at *Suitengumae* (Sue-ee-tane-guu-my) Station, and following the signs to the terminal (via an underground passageway). Exits 1A and 1B.

Note that not all airlines have check-in counters at TCAT. If your airline does not provide check-in service at TCAT (and you can inquire when you confirm your reservations), you can still utilize the terminal's limousine bus service to the airport. It means, however, that you must personally take your luggage all the way to the bus boarding area in the terminal, have it checked onto the bus, then retrieve it at Narita and go through the usual inspection and check-in procedures.

Also keep in mind that flights departing from Gates C81 through C88 and D91 through D99 in Terminal 2 leave from an adjoining building; not from the main terminal. These gates are served by shuttle buses, which leave from the second floor of the main terminal. Gate E70 is also served by a shuttle bus, which departs from the first floor boarding lounge.

At this writing, some 30 airlines have complete check-in service at the central Tokyo facility. They are:

Aeroflot Russian International Airlines
Air China
All Nippon Airways
American Airlines
AOM French Airlines
Asiana Airlines
Austrian Airlines
Canadian Airlines International
China Eastern Airlines
Delta Airlines
Finnair
Garuda Indonesian Airways
Iberia Airlines of Spain
Iran Air
Japan Air Lines
Japan Asia Airways
KLM Royal Dutch Airlines
Korean Air
Northwest Airlines
Olympic Airlines
Pakistan International Airlines
Philippine Airlines
Quantas Airways
Sabena Belgium World Airlines
Singapore Airlines
Swiss Air
Thai Airways International
United Airlines
Virgin Atlantic Airways

About half of these airlines do not have their *own* counters at TCAT. They are served by Japan Airlines, United Airlines and Northwest Airlines, so it is necessary to look for their smaller, less conspicuous signs. Japan Airlines presently provides check-in service for around half of the listed airlines.

Going to the Right Terminal

Passengers arriving at Narita from abroad do not have to be concerned about which terminal their airline uses, since both terminals have duplicate service and transportation facilities. But departing passengers should make a note of which terminal they are to leave from in order to avoid a last minute mistake that can be costly in terms of time. Also it is helpful to keep in mind that arriving airport limousine buses stop twice at huge Terminal 2, at the Nort and South Entrances, in that order. They stop on the 4th (departure) floor of Terminal 1.

Airlines whose check-in counters are in the *North* end of Terminal 2 (in the order listed) include:

All Nippon Airways (ANA)	Biman Bangladesh Airlines (BBC)
Asiana Airlines (AAR)	China Eastern Airlines (CES)
Austrian Airlines (AUA)	Continental Micronesia Inc. (CMI)
Delta Air Lines (DAL)	Egyptair (MSR)
Sabena Belgian World Airlines (SAB)	Garuda Indonesian Airways (GIA)
Scandinavian Airlines System (SAS)	Iberia Airlines of Spain (IBE)
THY Turkish Airlines (THY)	Iran Air (IRA)
Japan Air System (JAS)	Iraqi Airways (IAW)
Aeroflot Russian International Airlines (AFL)	Japan Asia Airways (JAA)
	Malaysia Airlines System (MAS)
Air China (CCA)	Olympic Airlines (OAL)
Air India (AIC)	Pakistan International Airlines (PIA)
Air Lanka (ALK)	Philippine Airlines (PAL)
Air New Zealand (ANZ)	Quantas Airways (QFA)
Air Pacific (FJI)	Swiss Air (SWR)
AOM French Airlines (AOM)	Thai Airways International (THA)

Terminal 2, South Entrance

Japan Airlines (JAL)—which takes up virtually all of the South end of the terminal.

Terminal 2, a virtual city within itself, attracts large numbers of people who go there not to leave the country but to enjoy the ambiance of the place, to dine in its dozens of restaurants and to shop in its arcades.

Terminal 1, South Wing (Entrance)

Air France (AFR)	Korean Air (KAL)
Alitaria (AZA)	Lufthansa German Airlines (DLH)
American Airlines (AAL)	Northwest Airlines (NWA)
British Airways (BAW)	Singapore Airlines (SIA)
Canadian Airlines International (CDN)	United Airlines (UAL)
Cathay Pacific Airways (CPA)	Varig Brazilian Airlines (VRG)
Finnair (FIN)	Virgin Atlantic Airways (VIR)
KLM Royal Dutch Airlines (KLM)	

Connections for Domestic Flights

The domestic terminal at Narita adjoins Terminal 2, and is accessible from the terminal via a causeway from the Departure Lobby, which is on the third floor level. If you arrive at Terminal 1 with connecting reservations on a flight departing from the domestic terminal you will be directed to a shuttle bus boarding area for the short trip. For passengers connecting with domestic flights originating at Haneda Airport, Tokyo's main domestic airport, there is door-to-door limousine bus service from Narita to Haneda—a trip that takes from 90 minutes to two or more hours.

Kansai International Airport

Kansai International Airport (KIA) is located on "Airport Island," a man-made islet in Osaka Bay, five kilometers offshore. It is Japan's first hub-airport, serving both domestic and international flights, as well as Japan's only airport that operates 24-hours a day.

In addition to its unusual location, KIA boasts the world's largest passenger terminal, a flamboyantly avant-garde building designed by the famous Italian architect Renzo Piano.

The main Passenger Terminal Building (PTB) is distinguished by a huge "canyon atrium" that has 12 see-through elevators. The PTB consists of a main terminal and north and south wings connected by a "Wing Shuttle" train. Travel time from the main terminal to the end of either wing is one and a half minutes. Shuttle trains run every 1–2 minutes.

The International Arrival Lobby is located on the first floor of the main terminal. Customs is on the second floor. The International Departure (check-in) Lobby is on the fourth floor. Departure gates are on the third floor. The domestic lobby for both arrivals and departures is on the second floor.

Altogether, there are 26 restaurants and 44 shops and retail stands on the second and third floors of the terminal, plus a 24-hour convenience market in the basement.

Airport Island is connected to the shore, at Rinku Machi (Rinku Town) by a spectacular 3.75 kilometer Airport Access Bridge that includes a six-lane expressway over train tracks and hugh pipelines carrying water, gas, and electricity. Public transportation to the airport includes two high-speed train systems, water-jet shuttles, and buses.

The Kansai Airport Express "Haruka" train, operated by Japan Railways (JR), runs between the airport and Kyoto Station via Tennoji Station and Shin (New) Osaka Station. It is 29 minutes from KIA to Tennoji Station, 45 minutes to Shin Osaka Station, and 75 minutes to Kyoto Station. All seats on the 200-passenger Haruka trains are reserved.

Nankai Railways operates a "Rapito" ("rapid") express train between KIA and Nanba Station in central Osaka. It is 29 minutes from Namba Station to the airport. All 252 seats, both "super" and "ordinary," on this six-coach train are also reserved.

K-Jet hydrofoil ferry service is provided between the airport and Port Island in Kobe (29 minutes), Tenpozan Port in Osaka (30 minutes), Awaji Island (35 minutes), and Tokushima on Shikoku Island (80 minutes).

Check-in can be completed by passengers at "City Air Terminals" (CATs) in Kyoto, Osaka, and Kobe. Immigration procedures can be completed at the Kobe City Air Terminal (Kobe-CAT).

Travelers using Kansai International Airport might take advantage of passing through Osaka's Nambu district (the Osaka gateway to KIA) to visit **Namba Walk**, one of the country's largest and most impressive underground shopping malls.

Namba Walk, with 280 stores, runs east and west from North Namba to Nippon Bashi (Japan Bridge). In addition to its shops, the mall is noted for its beautiful plaza areas (and state-of-the-art restrooms).

Some Useful Phrases in Japanese

Is this the boarding place for Tokyo?
Kore wa Tokyo no noriba desu ka?
Koe-ray wah Tokyo no no-ree-bah dess kah?

What number is the boarding place for the Hyatt Hotel?
Haiyato Hoteru no noriba wa nan ban desu ka?
Hie-yah-toe Hoe-tay-rue no no-ree-bah wah nahn bahn dess kah?

Where do the Narita shuttle buses leave from?
Narita no shataru basu ga doko kara demasu ka?
Nah-ree-tah no shah-tah-rue bah-sue gah doe-koe kah-rah day-mahss kah?

Does this bus go to Tokyo Station?
Kono basu wa Tokyo Eki ni ikimasu ka?
Koe-no bah-suu wah Tokyo Aa-kee nee ee-kee-mahss kah?

CHAPTER 9

Hotel Matters

Classes of Hotels

Japan was the first country in the world to have a nationwide network of roadside inns and luxury hotels. This extraordinary phenomenon came about as the result of a political decision made in 1635 by the grandson of Ieyasu Tokugawa, who founded Japan's last great shogunate dynasty in 1603. In 1635, shortly after becoming shogun, Iemitsu Tokugawa mandated that some 250 of the country's 270 fief lords, called **daimyo** (dime-yoe)—literally, "great names," or "lords"—would maintain residences in Edo (Tokyo), keep their families there at all times, and spend every other year in the capital in attendance at the shogunate court.

This policy, known as **Sankin Kotai** (Sahn-keen Koe-tie), or "Alternate Attendance," specified when the *daimyo* would travel to and from their fief capitals to Edo, what routes they would take, and how many samurai warriors and servants they were required to bring with them, based on the size and wealth of the individual fiefs. Lords of the larger fiefs had to bring entourages of several thousand people, causing a procession of marchers that stretched for a mile or more. These caravans came to be known as *Daimyo Gyoretsu* (Dime-yoe G'yoe-rate-sue), or "Processions of the Lords."

Each of the *daimyo gyoretsu* marched at a pace of about thirty miles a day, which meant that those from the more distant fiefs were on the road for three to five weeks each way. It also meant that they needed food and lodging along the way. Hundreds of post stations, spaced at specific intervals, sprang up to service the fief lords and their retainers on their journey to and from Edo.

There were three categories of accommodations at each of these stopovers. First were luxurious *honjin* (hone-jeen), or "headquarter hotels", where the fief lord and his personal attendants stayed; next were the *waki-honjin* (wah-kee-hone-jeen), or "annex headquarters," where the chief retainers stayed; and third were the **hatago** (hah-tah-go), where the warriors and lower retainers were lodged.

With the appearance of this vast network of inn-hotels along all of Japan's main roadways and the continuation of peace for decades, other people, ranging from peddlers, gamblers, itinerant priests, and religious pilgrims to messengers and officials of the shogunate government in Edo and the Imperial Court in Kyoto, became frequent travelers, filling the chain of inns with colorful crowds.

This system was to continue for almost 250 years, until the fall of the Tokugawa Shogunate in 1868. The volume of travelers is indicated by the number of inns along just one of Japan's main highways. The famous **Tokaido** (Toe-kie-doe), or "Eastern Sea Road," which connected Edo (Tokyo) and Kyoto, boasted 111 *honjin,* sixty-eight *waki-honjin* and 2,905 *hatago* inns. Over a dozen of these former "post stations" stage annual reenactments of the *Daimyo Gyoretsu,* attracting visitors from around the world.

It was this feudal control system that resulted in Japan's travel and hospitality industries achieving a size and levels of quality and service that were not to appear anywhere else in the world until well into the nineteenth century. When one speaks of inns, hotels, and traveling in Japan, one talks about a part of Japanese life that has long and sanctified traditions, and has been far more intimately intertwined with the daily lives of more people over a longer period of time than in any other country.

In today's Japan these traditions of quality and service continue. There are still some seventy thousand inns in the country and several thousand hotels. While no longer classified as *honjin, waki-honjin* or *hatago,* the inns still come in several grade levels, ranging from very luxurious and expensive to very basic and inexpensive.

The traditions of the *honjin,* which were designed to provide the quality of service that would meet or exceed the expectations and whims of kings, queens, princes, and princesses, have been transferred to Japan's luxury-class, Western-style hotels. The *waki-honjin* are represented by first-class hotels and the *hatago* by the so-called businessmen's hotels.

Hotel Facilities and Services

Luxury and first-class hotels in Japan are world-renowned for the variety of their facilities and services. They are certainly not just places to stay overnight. They combine the functions of convention centers, wedding halls, meeting places for business and other social affairs, dining centers, shopping centers, and cultural milieus. Some of them are so large and elaborate that they are like cities within themselves, and are themselves tourist attractions. It is all of these extras that you are paying for when you stay at these name hotels.

The main point in choosing your hotel is to distinguish among the various classes and grades within classes, and pick one that is suitable for your purposes and budget. Whether making your own hotel arrangements or going through a travel agent, you can exercise considerable control over the cost by designating which class of hotel you prefer. Keep in mind, also, that luxury and first-class hotels in Japan add up to thirty percent taxes to the basic room cost, so the room rates you are quoted are only part of the story. Some businessmen's hotels also add taxes to their base rates. Those that do not will generally have "service charges and taxes included" printed on their tariff sheets.

Stretching Your Hotel Money

The Japan National Tourist Organization (JNTO) can provide you with long lists of hotels and inns that offer moderately priced facilities. One such list is entitled "Reasonable Accommodations in Japan." It contains the particulars on some 250 hotels and inns throughout the country that are experienced at accommodating foreign guests. The places are classified on the basis of *Inexpensive* (under four thousand yen) and *Moderate* (four thousand to seven thousand yen). Twenty-eight of the listings are in Tokyo. The listing is free from JNTO.

Public Youth Hostels

Japan's large network of public youth hostels, operated by prefectural governments, offers some of the best bargain accommodations in the country and are ideal for young people traveling alone or in pairs. Several dozen of the hostels belong to the Japan Hospitality Public Youth Hostel Group specifically formed to offer their facilities to foreign visitors, youth hostel members or not.

Some of the public hostels are located in cities; others in scenic spots around the country. Major cities that have hostels include Tokyo, Nagoya, Kyoto, Osaka, Hiroshima, and Nagasaki. There is also a hostel at famed Nikko, in the mountains north of Tokyo.

The Tokyo International Youth Hostel, for example, is located on the eighteenth floor of a spectacular high-rise building next to Iidabashi Station in central Tokyo.

For a list of hostels in the cities named above, contact the JNTO and request the Japan Hospitality Public Youth Hostel Group brochure.

Breakdown of Selected Tokyo Hotels

Here is a partial list of the different classes of hotels in Tokyo.

LUXURY HOTELS (twenty thousand yen and up)
Akasaka Prince Hotel (Akasaka area)
ANA Hotel Tokyo (Akasaka area)
Capital Tokyu Hotel (Akasaka area)
Century Hyatt Hotel (Shinjuku)
Hotel Okura (Toranomon area)
Imperial Hotel (Hibiya-Ginza area)
New Otani Hotel (Akasaka area)
Tokyo Hilton International (Shinjuku)

FIRST-CLASS HOTELS (twelve thousand yen and up)
Akasaka Tokyu Hotel (Akasaka)

Ginza Daiichi Hotel (Ginza)
Ginza Tobu Hotel (Ginza)
Ginza Tokyu Hotel (Ginza)
Holiday Inn Tokyo (Hachobori-TCAT area)
Hotel Grand Palace (Kudanshita-Iidabashi area)
Hotel Pacific Meridien (Shinagawa area)
Keio Plaza Hotel (Shinjuku)
Miyako Hotel (Shirogane-dai-Shinagawa area)
New Takanawa Prince Hotel (Shinagawa area)
Pacific Hotel (Shinagawa area)
Palace Hotel (Marunouchi-Otemachi area)
Shiba Park Hotel (Shiba Park-Shimbashi area)
Shimbashi Daiichi Hotel (Shimbashi)
Shinjuku Prince Hotel (Shinjuku)
Shinjuku Station Hotel (Shinjuku)
Shinjuku Washington Hotel (Shinjuku)
Sunshine City Prince Hotel (Ikebukuro)
Takanawa Prince Hotel (Shinagawa-Takanawa area)
Tokyo Prince (Tamuracho-Shiba Park area)

BUSINESSMEN'S HOTELS (six thousand yen and up)
Asakusa Plaza Hotel (Asakusa)
Diamond Hotel (Ichiban-cho)
Fairmont Hotel (Kudan Minami area)
Hotel Ginza Daiei (Ginza area)
Hotel Ibis (Roppongi)
Hotel Juraku (Kanda-Ochanomizu area)
Hotel Listel Shinjuku (northeast Shinjuku area)
Hotel Sunroute Tokyo (Shinjuku)
Marunouchi Hotel (Marunouchi-Otemachi area)
Mitsui Urban Hotel (Ginza-Shimbashi area)
New City Hotel (Shinjuku)
President Hotel (Aoyama)
Roppongi Prince Hotel (Roppongi)
Shibuya Tobu Hotel (Udagawa-cho)
Tokyo City Hotel (Nihonbashi)
Yaesu Fujiya Hotel (Tokyo Station area)
Yaesu Terminal Hotel (Tokyo Station)

Some Useful Phrases in Japanese

Do you have any vacancies?
Aite iru heya ga arimasu ka?
Aye-tay ee-rue hay-yah gah ah-ree-mahss kah?

I want a room with a bath
O'furo tsuki no heya ga hoshii desu
Oh-fuu-roe t'sue-kee no hay-yah gah hoe-she-e dess

This room is too small
Kono heya wa chiisai sugimasu
Koe-no hay-yah wah chee-sie sue-ghee-mahss

How much is the room rate?
Heya dai wa ikura desu ka?
Hay-yah die wah ee-kuu-rah dess kah?

May I see the room?
Heya wo mite mo ii desu ka?
Hay-yah oh me-tay mo ee dess kah?

Is there a TV in the room?
Heya ni terebi ga arimasu ka?
Hay-yah nee tay-ray-bee gah ah-ree-mahss kah?

Does it also have a refrigerator?
Reizoko mo arimasu ka?
Ray-e-zoe-koe moh ah-ree-mahss kah?

CHAPTER 10

Inn Matters

Going Back in Time

Japan's great collection of **ryokan** (rio-khan), or inns, some of which date back centuries and played leading roles in many exciting events in history, are like doorways to the past. Designed, decorated, furnished, and operated in a manner set hundreds of years ago, the inns offer present-day Japanese unprecedented opportunities to indulge themselves in a lifestyle perfected by their ancestors and perpetuated down to the present time.

Many of these same timeless inns also offer their accommodations and services to foreign visitors, as both history lessons and real-life adventures in Japan's traditional culture.

For those who are not familiar with *ryokan,* they are usually small, one or two stories, have six to about fifty rooms, and are surrounded by a landscaped garden or natural scenery. Hundreds of the more famous inns around the country are located in areas especially selected for their beauty: mountain precipices, stream-laced valleys and gorges, choice seascapes, and lakesides.

Public floor areas in inns are made of polished wood. Room floors consist of **tatami** (tah-tah-me), thick mats made of an aromatic reed woven to a fine mesh, bordered with fabric ribbons, and placed on wooden frames. Inner doors are made of sliding paper panels. One style, called **shoji** (show-jee), is made of white rice paper that is very thin and virtually translucent. The other style, called **fusuma** (fuu-suu-mah), is made of multiple layers of thick paper decorated with paintings of traditional scenes.

The entry foyer of an inn is called the **genkan** (gane-khan). Take off your street shoes in the *genkan,* step up on a polished wooden floor, and don a type of house slipper. These soft slippers are worn only on areas where there is wood, stone, or tile. They are not worn into rooms that have *tatami* reed-mat floors, but are left in the hallway outside your room, or in the *genkan* vestibule of your room if it is elaborate enough to have its own private foyer. There are other slippers for wearing in toilets.

Interiors of inns are designed to function as and give the feeling of large summer or resort-type homes in which all the patrons are honored guests. Each room functions as a combination "front" room, sitting room, dining room, and bedroom. Each has its own **tokonoma** (toe-koe-no-mah), or "beauty alcove," and often a lanai that overlooks natural scenery outdoors.

Inns are not designed to provide tight hotel-like privacy, but to encourage the guest to relax, expand, and communicate with his surroundings. This relaxation process begins in the *genkan* entrance foyer of the inn, when you remove your street shoes and put on hallway and public-room slippers. In addition, the sliding, thick-paper room doors (*fusuma*) are not lockable. Maids frequently come and go without knocking before they enter, just as they may do in a private home among family members.

Your room will be furnished with a low table and probably a low dresser/mirror for dressing and makeup purposes. Floor cushions and bedding will be stored in wall closets. A suite will have an adjoining sitting room, usually with Western-style lounge chairs and a table for drinks and card-playing. If there is a large lanai, it may be furnished with lawn-type chairs. Your maids, assigned to you as soon as you check in, will set up your table in the center of the room if it hadn't been set up in advance, and then take **zabuton** (zah-buu-tone) sitting cushions from the wall closets and put them around the table for you. Most inns have *zaisu* (zah-e-sue), or legless tatami chairs that are available on request.

The maids then lay out **yukata** (you-kah-tah) robes for everyone, at which time you may take off all of your outer street clothing and don it (men sometimes just take off their jackets).

Almost immediately after you sit down you are normally served *O'shibori* (Oh-she-boe-ree)—small dampened towels that are hot in the winter and chilled in the summer—to wipe your face and hands. Next comes tea and usually tiny cakes of sweetened bean paste or fruit.

After a brief period of resting and refreshing yourself, the traditional procedure after checking into an inn was to take a bath to remove the dust and fatigue of travel. Nowadays, if you arrive early in the day, this ritual may be postponed until evening.

Bathing is done in small private baths that will accommodate a couple, or in larger baths, which may accommodate several dozen people at the same time. **Yukata** (you-kah-tah), thin cotton robes, are provided as casual loungewear and bathrobe. You undress in your room, don a *yukata,* slip into your slippers left just outside your door, and shuffle to the bathroom, guided by a maid if you wish. Your *yukata* is left in an outer room of the bath, usually in a wicker basket provided for that purpose. As you must have heard or read elsewhere, you scrub and rinse off before getting into the bathtub, which is intended for soaking, not washing.

At night your maid comes in, folds the table up and puts it away, and then spreads *futon* (fuu-tone) sleeping mats on the floor for you. The bottom portion of the *futon* which serves as a mattress is quite thick. But just as any new bed sometimes takes two or three nights to get used to, it may take you that long to become accustomed to *futon*-style sleeping. Once you do, the practicality of this style of bedding and sleeping becomes obvious.

The traditional inn has no common dining room or bar. Guests are served in their own rooms by maids. Any drinks or snacks are also brought in by maids, who may be summoned any time by using an intercom phone or a call button. Larger inns that cater to big parties, especially company outings and tourist groups, generally have a large Japanese-style banquet hall where the groups take their meals and drinks. Some of these halls are big enough to seat up to five hundred or more people.

Modern Inns

Rooms of some of the more modernized *ryokan* have refrigerators that are kept well-stocked with beer and various snack items. Guests take whatever they want from the fridges, keeping record of what they eat and drink on a form provided for that purpose. Inn rates for individuals usually include breakfast and sometimes dinner as well.

Checkout time in *ryokan* is normally 10:00 A.M.. Many inns in out-lying areas, especially the smaller ones, close and lock their front doors at set times in the evening; some as early as 11:00 P.M. This closing time is called **mon gen** (moan gane). If you are staying at a small, family-run inn, be sure you find out whether the front door is locked at night and at what time; you may want to make arrange-ments to be let in at a later hour.

Ryokan catering to upscale Japanese guests and foreign visitors now usually have air conditioning, and some have central heating as well. When requesting reservations at inns you should specify if you want one or both, especially in midsummer or midwinter.

Generally speaking, the inn style of accommodations is more in keeping with life in resort and rural areas. But many choose to expe-rience their special ambience in cities as well.

Budget Inn Guide

Several dozen of Japan's lower-priced inns, located from one end of the island chain to the other, are members of a group called the Ja-pan Economy Accommodation Federation (JEAF), whose stated aim is to offer foreign visitors an opportunity to experience life in a tradi-tional Japanese inn at a very reasonable cost. The primary qualifica-tion for membership in JEAF is that the nightly rate for a single room is under five thousand yen. (The average is around four thou-sand yen.)

A directory of the JEAF inns is available from Japan National Tourist Organization (JNTO) offices around the world. See JNTO listings in this book for the office nearest you. Reservations at JEAF inns must be made in writing (phone reservations are usually not ac-cepted if the inn does not know you), with a one thousand yen de-posit per person. Travel agents can, of course, make guaranteed reservations at inns.

Japanese Inn Group

Another group of inns that caters specifically to foreign guests call themselves the "Japanese Inn Group." For an English-language directory of the sixty-six members of the group, write to Japanese Inn Group, c/o Hiraiwa Ryokan, 314 Hayao-cho, Kaminoguchi-agaru, Ninomiyacho-dori, Shimogyo-ku, Kyoto 600, Japan. The directory contains maps.

You and Your *Yukata*

Most visitors who treat themselves to the special pleasures of the Japanese inn are quick to recognize the extraordinary contribution the *yukata* makes to the attractions of living Japanese style. The *yukata* began as an undergarment for the kimono. As the centuries passed, people also began using it as a nightgown and bathrobe. Eventually, *yukata* makers began adding colorful motifs to the cotton fabric of the robe, and it gradually developed into casual wear for the home, resorts, and festivals. Long before the beginning of the modern era, *yukata* had become the national leisure costume of Japan.

The *yukata* owes much of its ongoing appeal to its popularity as a combination bedroom, bathroom, and outdoor leisure garment, and to the intimacy of the *ryokan* and resorts where its use is most common, especially during the summer months, when it is frequently worn without undergarments.

Further, the nature of the *yukata,* hugging the body from neck to ankle, makes it necessary for the wearer to move in a relatively slow, controlled manner, thereby adding to the qualities of gracefulness and physical discipline that are pleasing to the eye and the spirit.

The patterns and cuts of the *yukata* differ for men and women, but it takes a bit of exposure before the unfamiliar eye automatically discerns the difference. *Yukata* that are designed primarily as sleeping gowns have sleeves that are extra long.

There are a number of considerations to keep in mind regarding *yukata.* Probably the most common mistake made by foreign visitors when they are first introduced to the multi-purpose robe is "lapping" the front right-over-left instead of left-over-right. In the past, the former lapping method was done when the wearer was dead. There is also a right way and a wrong way for the *yukata* sash to be tied. Men wrap the sash low around their hips, with the knot on the right side. Women wrap the sash (or *obi*) high around their waist and tie it in back.

During the winter months, a padded version of the *yukata* called **tanzen** (tahn-zen) is provided by many inns. Summer, of course, is the best season for *yukata,* when you will find that the clean, crisply starched, colorful garment will add another dimension to your stay in Japan.

Hot-Bath Behavior

To some, the main attraction of Japanese inns is their **O-furo** (Oh-fuu-roe), or "hot baths." The most distinctive feature of the famous *O'furo* is that you bathe before getting into the tub or pool. The bathrooms, both public and private, are designed for bathers to soap, scrub down, and rinse off *outside* the bath on tiled or slat-board floors that are slanted and have runoff drains. After one has experienced this kind of bathing a few times, the idea of scrubbing off *inside* the tub, and then lying there in all that soap and grime, is enough to make one shudder at that style of unsanitary bathing.

Most inns that cater to foreign guests have two types of baths: a smaller one for singles, couples, and families that often is referred to as the **kazoku buro** (kah-zoe-kuu buu-row), or "family bath"; and a larger one, usually coed, for general group bathing. Very large inns may have several baths of different sizes.

The routine at a Japanese hot bath is very simple. You may undress in your own room and wear a *yukata* to the bath, or wear your clothing to the bath anteroom and undress there. Whatever you wear to the anteroom is left there on a shelf or in a wicker basket. Soap and towels are provided except at public baths; in an inn you take your own from your room. The traditional Japanese towel, called a **tenugui** (tay-nuu-goo-ee), is small and made of thin cotton. It is used as both a washcloth and drying towel. You take the smaller towel into the bathroom with you, using it to cover your private parts when you are walking around, then as a washcloth, and finally as a preliminary drying cloth before you step out of the bathroom into the anteroom.

After undressing in the anteroom you go through a sliding door into the main area of the bath. Depending on the size of the bath, there will be anywhere from one to dozens of hot-and-cold water spigot combinations along one or more sides.

Select one of the water outlets, squat in front of it or sit on a low wooden or plastic stool, and then proceed to douse yourself with water, soap yourself down, and scrub. After washing and rinsing yourself thoroughly, enter the bath and soak for as long as you wish. One of the special pleasures of bathing with a friend is having them scrub your back—and then doing the same for them, of course.

Temperatures in the typical Japanese hot bath vary from 95°F to as high as 140°F. Unless you are in a private bath it is not cricket to add cold water to the bath just to suit yourself. It will soon become obvious to you that the cooler water is at the bottom of the tub or pool, and that any movement increases the burning effects of the water.

After a period in the tub or pool, the usual procedure, especially for those who soak for a long time, is to douse oneself with several buckets of cool or cold water. Then wipe or sponge off most of the water with your wet *tenugui,* return to the anteroom, finish drying, and put on your *yukata* for the trip back to your room.

In most private-home baths and baths in some smaller inns, there are no wall spigots for hot water. The hot water to be used for the initial dousing and scrubbing is drawn from the tub by means of a small wooden bucket, a large dipper, or a washpan.

Although the routine described above is the proper one, in the winter time when it is cold it is common for men, especially in public bath houses, to breach etiquette. Instead of scrubbing first, they enter the tub first to warm up. Then they get out and wash, and later get back into the pool a second time to soak.

Of course, this results in the water getting dirtier than usual, but even after several dozen unwashed persons have soaked in a large tub or pool for a few minutes, the water still looks cleaner than if just one person soaps up and scrubs down in a small Western-style tub. Also, in most hot-spring spa baths the water is constantly being renewed with fresh water.

As has been widely publicized, the Japanese do not regard unisex bathing as scandalous, extraordinary or even exciting; they have been doing it since the beginning of their civilization. I'm happy to report that more and more Westerners are discovering that mixed bathing has very real therapeutic effects contributing to a more stable personality.

If you have the opportunity and inclination to group-bathe while in Japan—and I highly recommend the custom—the only additional etiquette involved is to very nonchalantly cover yourself (just the bottom, ladies!) with your *tenugui* towel when you enter and leave the bath, and when walking around inside the bathroom. Not everyone bothers to do this, but it is considered polite.

Of course, it *is* scandalous for anyone to make any kind of fuss over being "caught" nude in a bath or upon seeing others nude in a bath.

For those who do not for one reason or another sample the special delights of the Japanese inn, there are some Western hotels that have Japanese-style hot-bath facilities that go along with some suites, or they have separate "massage" baths where guests may get a touch of one of the more sensuous facets of Japanese culture. (See Chapter 15).

Some Useful Phrases in Japanese

I would like to bathe before eating dinner
Yuhan wo taberu mae ni O'furo ni hairitai desu
Yuu-han oh tah-bay-rue my nee Oh-fuu-roe nee hie-ree-tie dess

Is it a private bath?
Shiritsu no O'furo desu ka?
She-ree-t'sue no Oh-fuu-roe dess kah?

Will it accommodate two people?
Futari demo hairemasu ka?
Fuu-tah-ree day-moe hie-ray-mahss kah?

Please bring me two clean towels
Kirei na taoru wo ni mai motte kite kudasai
Ke-ray-e nah tah-oh-rue oh nee my moat-tay kee-tay kuu-dah-sie

This O'futon is too short. Do you have a longer one?
Kono O'futon wa mijikai sugimasu. Motto nagai no wa arimasu ka?
Koe-no Oh-fuu-tone wah me-jee-kie sue-ghee-mahss.
Mote-toe nah-guy no wah ah-ree-mahss kah?

CHAPTER 11

Communicating with the Japanese

Crossing the Language Barrier

Difficulty in communicating is the main source of the more serious problems experienced by travelers in Japan. These problems most often arise when the rushed visitor speaks hurriedly—usually in English and frequently with a strong accent—and mistakenly assumes that he has gotten his point across.

Japanese tend to be reluctant to admit it when they do not clearly understand what is said to them (whether the speaker is a foreigner or another Japanese), because this would "inconvenience" and possibly antagonize the speaker—not to mention the "face" the Japanese might lose.

When there is any doubt about whether you have been understood, you can often solve the problem by printing what you want to say, since most Japanese can read English with far more fluency than they can speak or understand it when spoken. Simply asking a person if he understands—when there is doubt—is usually not enough. The tendency, again, is for him to say "yes" whether he does or not.

Few if any of the problems that arise from language differences are insurmountable handicaps, unless the visitor deliberately chooses to be unsympathetic and contrary. But the problems, particularly those pertaining to transportation arrangements, are time consuming, frustrating if the traveler is not prepared for them, and costly if he ignores them.

Of course, the traveler who stays on the well-marked "tourist trail" is least apt to encounter serious communication problems, while those who like to pioneer their own paths would be wise to brush up on their patience and pantomime.

Another approach that is both more fun and fruitful is to obtain a simplified, phoneticized Japanese-language guide prior to leaving for Japan and learn a number of key questions and answers in advance. Japanese is easy to pronounce (it's almost exactly like Spanish), and a vocabulary of a few dozen words can work wonders.

A completely phoneticized guide to Japanese that I can wholeheartedly recommend is *Japanese in Plain English* (Passport Books). It gives you more than one thousand high-frequency words along with sample sentences that you can use in practical situations. You can appreciate how many linguistic doors you can open with a one-thousand-word vocabulary when you consider that most of us use less than one thousand words of our native language in our day-to-day existence.

Addressing People

Westerners, particularly Americans, are often on a first-name basis within moments after they meet someone for the first time. This has *not* been the custom in Japan and is still rare—but changing. As a general rule the visitor may call children and teenagers by their first names without disturbing protocol, but for older people, it is better to use their last names preceded by Mr., Mrs., or Miss—which is expressed in Japanese by the word **san** (sahn).

The Japanese are still considerably more formal in the use of names than their Western counterparts, and the distinction between first and last names is still rigidly maintained by the older generations. It would be unthinkable, for example, for a fifty- or sixty-year-old businessman to address one of his Japanese colleagues of the same age or older by his first name during office hours, even if he has worked with him for thirty to forty years.

Still today there are four main categories of name use, and one or two subcategories. The only group of people who always use first names (and without the usual *san* suffix) are parents referring to or addressing their own children. Older relatives referring to or addressing nieces and nephews use first names but customarily add the suffix *san*.

A group who commonly uses first names are close school chums who are in the same grade and are approximately the same age. They often have nicknames for each other and use them freely. But once they are out of school and enter the adult world, particularly when at work and in formal situations, they follow the formal etiquette of addressing each other by the last name plus *san*. They may revert to first names or nicknames when engaged in sports and at drinking parties, when it is permissible to forget formality.

Among adults, women generally address each other by their first names only if they grew up together and were close schoolmates, or if they are still young (in their teens or twenties), work together in an "informal" place such as a restaurant or club, and are good friends.

Women who have lived next door to each other for a lifetime, been good neighbors, and shared many intimate experiences still address each other by their last names, adding the title *san* (Honda-san, Sato-san, Suzuki-san, etc.).

Among adult men, only the closest of friends whose ties go back to their school days call each other by their first names, and only then in very informal situations. In a business office, it is customary to use last names or titles, regardless of the age or relationship. About the only exceptions to this rule are older managers who will address younger women who are longtime employees by their first names—and even this is an exceptional case.

Westernization of the Japanese is proceeding at a fairly steady pace, however, and more and more people now call new-found foreign friends by their first names automatically, a phenomenon that was launched after widespread reports that former President Ronald Reagan and former Prime Minister Yasuhiro Nakasone called each other Ron and Yasu immediately after their first meeting in the early eighties. By the same token, these people expect foreigners to call them by their own first names or a derivative.

The Japanese tend to be exceptionally tolerant of occidental residents and visitors, and they do not expect them to conform to all the meticulous rules of traditional Japanese behavior. With just a little foreknowledge and effort, however, the visitor can demonstrate that he has enough respect and goodwill for the Japanese to know as well as follow one of their more important customs.

All you have to do to be safe is call everyone by his or her last name, adding the *san* on all occasions except when addressing young children; in personal or informal situations with young, unmarried boys and girls whom you have come to know well; and with English-speaking adults who have adopted Western first names.

The Japanese are great on titles, and often use them in place of names. A teacher (of anything) or doctor is generally referred to as **sensei** (sin-say-e). The president of a company is invariably addressed as **shacho** (shah-choe) by employees and by outsiders who are younger or below him in rank; a manager is called **ka-cho** (kah-choe) or **bu-cho** (boo-choe), depending on his rank, instead of his name. A pilot is called **ki-cho** (kee-choe), and so on.

Addressing a Japanese by his or her title in informal situations smacks of flattery, but it is appreciated and wins points.

How to Greet People

Westerners in Japan, whether residents or visitors, are continuously faced with an awkward and sometimes embarrassing problem of how to greet Japanese acquaintances and respond to introductions. The problem is caused by the fact that for many Japanese, shaking hands is still an unnatural means of greeting someone, while most Westerners feel just as self-conscious and awkward about bowing.

The problem is not terribly serious, but it does act as a barrier between Japanese and Westerners, emphasizing to both parties how different their traditional lifestyles are, and making it more difficult for them to establish a fast and comfortable rapport with each other.

Of course, many Japanese who have worked or studied abroad or otherwise associated with Westerners for years have fully assimilated the handshake into their behavior, and many of the people the visitor meets will be in this growing group. For various other occasions, however, a few pointers can add to the confidence and ease of the traveler. After years in Japan, it seems to me that the best approach is to use a combination of Western and Japanese manners, depending on the circumstances.

If you are introduced to someone whose hand you cannot easily reach, or to a group of people, I suggest that you bow slightly from the waist and at the same time duck your head a bit. In this case, the bow is not only a lot more practical and simple, it is also the "right" thing to do. Older women, particularly, can be expected to bow rather than shake hands, unless they are very Westernized, which will be almost immediately obvious from their manner.

Then there are many cosmopolitan Japanese and experienced foreigners who combine the handshake and the bow, a practice that I recommend highly because it allows both parties to retain the flavor and feel of their own etiquette while meeting the other person halfway.

The important thing is to be alert and not force a handshake on anyone who does not respond naturally to it; be ready to bow when the occasion calls for it. As most Westerners are only too aware, the physical problems involved in shaking hands, especially with several people, often result in embarrassing situations.

The Japanese bow has a special advantage in that it is never wrong when used in a Japanese context, and more often than not it allows you to maintain your dignity. If you are formally introduced to someone and want to exchange name cards, the proper procedure is to face the person, ceremoniously hand over your name card, take the other person's card, look at it, and then bow. If you are standing quite close to the person, as often happens in groups, bow slightly to one side to avoid bumping heads.

How to Call People

Visitors to Japan who do not speak the language and are not familiar with the nonverbal communication signals of the Japanese are often at a loss when it comes to getting help in a store or office.

Unlike most Western places of business, the Japanese generally do not immediately descend upon visitors or prospective customers to see what they want, especially in department stores, shops, or offices that are not regularly patronized by foreigners. In the traditional Japanese value system, it is regarded as impolite to approach a visitor or customer aggressively without any sign from him.

Clerks and others may not respond to a questioning look or any other facial expression that in the West would get the desired reaction, often because they automatically assume they will not be able to communicate with you and are reluctant to get involved.

There are several accepted ways to get someone's attention nonverbally and call them to you. The first one is by waving your hand at them. Hold your hand up in front of you, palm down, and wave it up and down, very much like one waves goodbye in the West. Remember, however, that this signal *is not* to be used with an older person in a nonservice position or with anyone of rank or authority. It should be used *only* with friends, young clerks, maids, waiters, workmen, children, and so on.

The second method is to catch someone's eye and perform a relatively quick shallow bow, without breaking eye contact. This kind of bow can be used in any kind of shop, restaurant, or office. By bowing, which is a signal "in Japanese," you are asking that your presence be acknowledged; you're also clearly saying that you want something. This invariably triggers the desired behavior in the person you bowed to.

This bowing technique is especially useful when you are visiting a business office. Most Japanese offices do not have receptionists to greet and take care of visitors. By unspoken custom, responding to visitors is left up to whomever works nearest the door—usually the youngest and newest staff member. When you step into the office you are often right in among the working desks, or at most facing a counter that more than likely has no attendant.

When a foreigner suddenly materializes in a Japanese office where foreign visitors are uncommon, the tendency is for the occupants to hold back and in some cases avert their eyes to avoid having to get involved with someone whom they automatically presume does not speak Japanese. You often must take the initiative in catching the eye of someone you can bow to. Of course, in offices that regularly have foreign visitors there is always someone who speaks some English, is familiar with Western etiquette, and will normally approach you and/or speak up.

A third method requires that you speak a little Japanese. If so, you can use one of the phrases the Japanese themselves commonly call out to announce their presence in such situations. The easiest one of the phrases to memorize and use is **Gomen kudasai** (Go-mane kuu-dah-sie), which translates more or less as "Excuse me, please." If you do use this phrase, it will be presumed that you "speak" Japanese, so be prepared for the consequences.

In days past, it was common for men at drinking parties and traditionally styled restaurants to beckon waitresses and maids by clapping their hands loudly. While still in use, particularly by older men in traditional settings, this custom is no longer considered good manners and is not recommended.

If you try the bow approach to a young person in a place of business and get no reaction, follow it with a short hand wave. Quite frequently, people in places where foreigners are uncommon hold back because of embarrassment and lack of experience. Since the above signals are "in Japanese," using them helps, at least initially, to break the cultural and language barriers and put the person more at ease. If you think you might get into a situation in which the Japanese you approach do not speak English, prepare for this eventuality by having the purpose of your visit written out, or be ready to use some other ploy.

Another hand signal that is very useful is one that means "no." To say "no," just raise your right hand up to chin or nose level, with the palm facing left and the "bottom edge" out, and wave it back and forth three or four times. This signal is used informally and casually to friends, clerks, and other tradespeople, and especially to street peddlers or touts who offer you services or products you don't want.

Seating as Nonverbal Communication

There are two distinct categories of seating etiquette in Japan: one that involves open public seating on trains, subways, and buses, and the other pertaining to virtually all other situations. On public transportation, young children are typically given precedence over adults, with the infrequent exception of very old people. Even elderly grandmothers will often give up their seats for children, including rowdy youngsters. A common practice is to remove the shoes of the children and let them stand up on the seats to look out the windows and otherwise play around.

This custom is a manifestation of the Japanese tradition of indulging young children, a holdover from the past when childhood was the only carefree time in a person's brief life. Western visitors to Japan often express irritation at the practice, particularly when the children are loud and disruptive.

The "ladies first" custom is still rare in Japan, although it is seen now and then when young men give up their seats to older women or wives with infants in their arms. There is also a growing number of people who will give up their seats to the very elderly on public transportation, but the practice is still rare enough to be conspicuous when it happens.

Most of Japan's subway lines have special seats that are designated as reserved for the elderly. They are called "Silver Seats" (Shi-rue-bah She-toe) in reference to the gray or silver hair of the elderly. But people in general ignore the reserved signs, and in years of riding the subways I have seen only a few occasions when a younger person gave up a "silver seat" for a gray-haired person.

Just as in the West, one can "save" a seat in Japan (in a theater, on a train, etc.) by putting something in it: a jacket, bag, or some other possession. In the case of trains with open seating *and* open windows, I have seen people toss their possessions into seats through open windows before they board the train. This is not considered mannerly, but the Japanese who observe it and are displeased are normally too reserved and polite to complain about it.

For seating in homes, offices, meeting rooms, and so on, there is a certain formality based on sex, age, and rank that becomes more specific and strict as the situations become more formal. Every room, regardless of its location, has a "head" or a "power position" that is normally assigned to the person of highest rank; in a private home it is given to a guest, who is traditionally given "honorary rank" above that of the head of the household.

The best seat in the house, so to speak, is called the *kami-za,* or "godseat," which is probably best translated as the "seat of honor." In a private home this area is at the "head" of a room nearest the *tokonoma,* or "beauty alcove," where flower arrangements or hanging scrolls are displayed. In an office or meeting room the *kami-za* is at the head of the room, and is usually farthest from the door.

The Japanese are extremely sensitive to seating arrangements in even casual, informal situations, such as in a restaurant, and will normally insist that the ranking individual or guest sit in the seat that is perceived as being the "power seat." Most American visitors generally do not even think about this sort of thing in informal situations, and sometimes ignore it in formal circumstances as well. As a result, the Japanese typically take it upon themselves to show both social and business visitors where to sit when they enter any kind of room.

It is not only polite to abide by the seating etiquette when you are in a foreign country, it also demonstrates appreciation for the customs and feelings of the people, which is good politics. If you should be in a situation involving Japanese and are not sure where it would be proper for you to sit, the best idea is to hold back until someone advises you.

No One Will Laugh

The Japanese are not offended when foreigners cannot speak their language, and are not critical of people who speak it poorly. On the contrary, they are surprised and pleased when foreigners speak even broken Japanese, and are supportive when someone tries. You do not have to be concerned at all about making a fool of yourself or encountering arrogant or insulting behavior. The more you try to use Japanese during your visit, the more you will learn and the more you will enjoy the experience.

As I'm sure you appreciate, being able to communicate directly with people is one of the special pleasures of traveling abroad.

Some Useful Phrases in Japanese

My name is De Mente
Watakushi no namae wa De Mente desu
Wah-tock-she no nah-my wah De Mente dess

What is your name?
Anata no namae wa nan desu ka?
Ah-nah-tah no nah-my wah nahn dess kah?

This is my wife, Margaret
Kono kata wa kanai no Margaret desu
Koe-no kah-tah wah kah-nie no Mah-gah-ray-toe dess

We (I) live in the American state of Arizona

Amerika no Arizona shu ni sunde imasu
Ah-may-ree-kah no Ah-ree-zoe-nah shuu nee sune-day ee-mahss

Where do you live?
Anata wa doko de sunde imasu ka?
Ah-nah-tah wah doe-koe day sune-day ee-mahss kah?

Have you ever been to America?
Amerika e itta koto ga arimasu ka?
Ah-may-ree-kah eh eat-tah koe-toe gah ah-ree-mahss kah?

How many days were you there?
Nan nichi gurai imashita ka?
Nahn nee-chee guu-rye ee-mah-ssh-tah kah?

We will be in Japan for just two weeks
Nishukan dake Nihon ni orimasu
Nee-shuu-kahn dah-kay Nee-hone nee oh-ree-mahss

CHAPTER 12

Mastering Japan's Maze

Honing Your Homing Pigeon Instincts

For first-time visitors to Japan, one of the most frustrating problems that must be faced is how to get around in Tokyo and the other major cities without assistance. Not being able to speak Japanese means they can communicate verbally only with the very small percentage of Japanese who speak their language. Not being able to read Japanese-language signs means they are suddenly cut off from most visual communication as well. For most practical purposes it is as if they were suddenly struck both speechless and blind.

No matter how brilliant or accomplished the foreign visitor might be in his own culture, he becomes virtually helpless in Japan, unable to do many of the smallest things for himself. Suddenly finding oneself in this situation and unable to communicate with most people can be a major shock, particularly if experienced over a prolonged period of time.

This situation is further compounded in Japan by a totally different addressing system. Finding an address in Japan is very much like finding the proverbial needle in a haystack. In the first place, most streets in Japanese cities do not have names (and when a street has no name, there is often no way you can tell a newcomer where it is and make any sense). The only streets that are named—and this is a recent phenomenon—are the very few major thoroughfares running through and connecting large districts within the cities. Tokyo, for example, has thousands upon thousands of streets, but fewer than one hundred of them have names.

In the second place, the addressing system in Japan has nothing whatsoever to do with any street the house or building might be on or near. Addresses are based on areas rather than streets. In metropolitan areas these "address areas" start out with the city. Next comes the **ku** (kuu), or ward, then a smaller district called **cho** (choe), and finally a still smaller section called **banchi** (bahn-chee).

The original meaning of *cho* is "town," and *banchi* means "land or lot number." Most of Japan's larger cities began as collections of communities (towns) that grew together. The original name of many of these little "towns" has been maintained as present-day *cho,* sometimes read as *machi* (mah-chee).

A city ward can be quite large in area (several square miles) and have a population ranging from several hundred thousand to two million or more. A *cho* is usually several square blocks in area, but no *cho* is actually square in shape. They come in all shapes but square, and there are dozens of *cho* in the larger wards. The smallest units, the *banchi*, or "lots," also vary in size and shape, and usually have three or four and sometimes many more houses or buildings on them. Prior to a reformation of the addressing system in Tokyo in the sixties, there was one notorious *banchi* that had over one hundred buildings on it, all with exactly the same address.

In the third place, only three of Japan's large cities—Sapporo, Nagoya and Kyoto—have streets laid out in grid fashion. For the most part, Japan's city streets originated as lanes in small clusters of villages and towns that eventually grew together without the benefit of planning. Tokyo is therefore the world's largest urban maze.

In the sixties, Japan's addressing system was greatly improved by extending the *banchi* numbers so that each building would have its own exclusive number, and redrawing borders of some of the odder-shaped *banchi* and *cho.* An effort was also made to make end numbers go up in sequence from one building to the next. Still, the problem of finding individual addresses remains serious because both streets and the dimensions of the various large and small areas are irregular in size and shape, and no obvious way exists to tell where one area ends and another begins.

Very small metal or plastic address plates are sometimes affixed to the fronts of buildings or gates (for private homes that have gates). The *cho* names and numbers and the main lot numbers—also very small in size—are also sometimes affixed to telephone poles, streetlight poles or the corners of major buildings. But there is not enough uniformity or consistency in these latter address plates to make it easy to find an address. If you read Japanese, finding the address is usually possible, but not easy.

A typical Tokyo address, written in the proper order in Japanese, goes like this: Tokyo, Shibuya Ward, Nishi-cho 7-chome, 15-3 banchi, Suzuki, Kinya, Mr. If you are going to an address for the first time, on your own, you have no choice but to first find the right ward, next the right *cho*, then the right *cho* number, then the right *banchi,* and finally the right lot number.

If your destination is near a major building or well-known landmark and you are going by taxi, whose driver is intimately familiar with the area, and you know the Japanese name of the site and can tell it to the driver, he can find the popular place easily enough. He also is usually able to get you to within a few dozen or few hundred yards of an address that is nearby.

Unfortunately, there is a steady turnover among taxi drivers, and it is not at all unusual to get one who just started, does not know the city at all, and has to depend upon his passengers, a detailed map, or stopping and asking directions.

Using Navigational Aids

The wisest thing to do, regardless of where you are going, is to have your destination written out in Japanese on a card or slip of paper (by your hotel clerk, bellboy, maid, etc.) so you can show it to a taxi driver, a policeman, or—as a last resort—passersby. And this holds true even if you are going to such famous landmarks as the Takashimaya Department Store, because you may not be able to pronounce **Takashimaya** (Tah-kah-she-mah-yah) well enough for a taxi driver to understand it.

If you are going to an out-of-the-way restaurant, shop, or private residence, or to an "unknown" place right in the heart of town, it is essential to know exactly where the place is in relation to something that *is* known, and to have a hand-drawn map showing this relationship, with the address and nearby locations (intersections, etc.) identified in Japanese on the map.

This often means that someone who speaks Japanese has to telephone the location and get specific instructions on how to get there from an individual on the spot, making sure the caller gets enough information to draw an area map if you are going by taxi or intending to find the place on your own.

Many Japanese places of business provide name cards that include maps of their location (something that I pioneered for foreign visitors in Tokyo in 1962). All Japanese, especially hotel staff, have had extensive experience at drawing maps for themselves as well as for others.

In reality, a regular pathfinder—born and raised in Tokyo and blessed with ESP—must go through one or more of the steps above each time he goes to a new place, if he wants to avoid wasting a lot of time and possibly money on an expensive cab trip. So do these steps methodically, as if a lot depended upon it.

Neighborhood policemen, stationed in Japan's famous **koban** (koe-bahn) "police boxes" at intersections and main streets, spend more time helping people find addresses than at any other task. Some of the officers speak a little English. If they do not, they will customarily call in someone who does when the need arises. Each of the *koban* is equipped with maps of their immediate areas that are detailed enough to show individual houses and buildings.

Some neighborhoods have large area maps in front of their local train stations or at key intersections. But to use the maps you must be able to read Japanese. If you are in a situation in which you have to ask someone other than a policeman to help you find an address, your best choices are restaurant delivery boys, postmen, or operators of fresh-fish shops or beauty parlors in the area.

How Not to Lose Your Hotel or Inn

Tokyo is the most difficult of all of Japan's cities in which to navigate from one place to another, and the further the distance between your starting point and your destination, the more complex the problem. In addition to the city having thousands of nameless streets, there is no overall pattern to most of the streets. In probably as much as 70 percent of the Tokyo, the streets, lanes, and alleys are like random trails that just grew haphazardly over time.

Because of the lack of street names and signs that visitors can read, and the irregularity of streets patterns, you have a situation in which newcomers are often unable to get more than two or three hundred yards from their hotel without becoming lost. All that is sometimes necessary for someone to lose his way is to turn three or four corners, get where he cannot see the hotel, and become disoriented because nothing is familiar.

My daughter Demetra, in Tokyo for the first time to go to a Japanese-language school, came out of the "wrong" exit of her local subway station one day. It took her nearly two hours to find her apartment, which was five minutes from the station. After more than forty years' experience, I know Tokyo better than most lifelong residents, yet finding a new address, particularly a private home, still can be a major, time-consuming frustration for me as well.

Generally speaking, pedestrians have the right of way on Japan's narrow, sidewalkless streets, but on large thoroughfares where there are sidewalks and stoplights, vehicular traffic comes first. If you are used to traffic moving on the right side of the street, you must be extra careful about stepping off of sidewalks without looking *right* instead of left. This really takes presence of mind and some getting used to.

At some busy intersections that have stoplights, public address systems automatically broadcast a special musical signal to let blind people know when to walk. At other crossings, the blind person must push a button to activate this recording. At some crossings, the WALK light for pedestrians does not go on until a button is pushed.

Some Useful Phrases in Japanese

I am lost. Can you help me?
Mayoimashita. Tetsudatte kudasai masen ka?
Mah-yoe-e-mahssh-tah. Tate-sue-dot-tay kuu-dah-sie mah-sin kah?

I am looking for my hotel
Watakushi no hoteru wo sagashite imasu
Wah-tock-she no hoe-tay-rue oh sah-gah-ssh-tay e-mahss

About how many minutes (is it from here)?
Nan pun gurai desu ka?   Nahn poon guu-rie dess kah?

Where is the subway station?
Chikatetsu wa doko desu ka?
Chee-kah-tat-sue wah doe-koe dess kah?

I am looking for this address
Kono jusho wo sagashite imasu
Koe-no juu-show ow sah-gah-sssh-tay e-mahss

Is it far from here?
Koko kara toi desu ka?   Koe-koe kah-rah toy dess kah?

Please draw a map for me
Maapu wo kaite kudasai   Mah-puu oh kie-tay kuu-dah-sie

I want to go to the American Embassy
Amerika Taishikan ni ikitai desu
Ah-may-ree-kah Tie-she-kahn nee e-kee-tie dess

Does this street go to the Mitsukoshi Department Store?
Kono michi wa Mitsukoshi Depaato e ikimasu ka?
Koe-no me-che wah Me-t'sue-koe-she Day-pahh-toe eh e-kee-mahss
kah?

Which way is the Ginza?
Ginza wa dochira desu ka?
Geen-zah wah doe-chee-rah dess kah?

Excuse me. Does this street have a name?
Sumimasen. Kono michi wa namae ga arimasu ka?
Sue-me-mah-sin. Koe-no me-chee wah nah-my gah ah-ree-mahss
kah?

Is the Imperial Hotel on this street?
Teikoku Hoteru wa kono michi ni arimasu ka?
Tay-e-koe-kuu Hoe-tay-rue wah koe-no me-chee nee ah-ree-mahss
kah?

I want to go to Yoyogi Park
Yoyogi koen ni ikitai desu
Yoe-yoe-ghee koe-inn nee ee-kee-tie dess

Which subway line should I take?
Dore no chikatetsu ni noru to ii desu ka?
Doe-ray no chee-kah-tate-sue nee no-rue toe ee dess kah?

CHAPTER 13

Reading
Important Signs

A Sign for Every Occasion

It has always seemed to me that Japan has more public signs than any other country. There seems to be a sign for everything and every occasion, reflecting the Japanese compulsion to communicate and educate. A problem arises for foreign visitors, however, because the signs are generally in unreadable **kanji** (kahn-jee) or **hiragana** (he-rah-gah-nah) Japanese.

Kanji are the ideograms or "characters" that make up the main Japanese writing system, which was borrowed from the Chinese some fourteen hundred years ago. *Hiragana* is a simplified phonetic system for writing Japanese that was developed in Japan several hundred years after the introduction of the Chinese characters. There is a second Japanese-created phonetic system of writing called **katakana** (kah-tah-kah-nah) that is used to write foreign words "in Japanese"—that is, break them up into syllables corresponding to the syllabic sounds of Japanese. Still another way of writing Japanese is the Latin alphabet letters used to write English and the Romance languages. This form of writing is called **Roma Ji** (Roe-mah Jee), or "Roman Letters."

Some 60 to 70 percent of all Japanese signs are written in **kanji.** Most of the rest are written in both *kanji* and *hiragana* (because children learn to read *hiragana* before they learn the Chinese ideograms), or just in *hiragana*. Some, particularly those used with transportation systems (train and subway stations and stops) and in international hotels, are generally written in Roman letters as well.

The only version of these signs the average foreign visitor can "read" are designations and names written in Latin alphabet letters, and these are meaningful only if the individual understands the meaning of the word or what it relates to. Seeing a sign that clearly says ABUNAI! doesn't do the visitor any good unless he knows it means DANGER! If he is on a subway and pulls into a station with platform and wall signs reading HIBIYA, and the signs are where station-name signs usually are, he can be pretty sure that is the name of the station and not an advertisement for a bra.

You Can't Get There without Them

Being able to recognize and read key signs outside of airports and hotels is especially important because, as we have learned, most streets are not named and addresses have nothing to do with the streets they may be on or near. And, of course, if you cannot read directional signs in banks, department stores, subway and train stations, and in dozens of other situations, you are severely handicapped and limited in what you can do on your own.

Shinjuku (Sheen-juu-kuu) Station, one of the most important commuter stations in Tokyo, is a good case in point. The station is so large and so complicated that even foreign residents who have lived in Tokyo for years still have trouble finding their way in the station if they cannot read key *kanji* signs. Just moving about in Japan, whether it is a short shopping trip down the street, looking for a district or area name, trying to find an exit, or looking for a toilet or office in a building, brings you face-to-face with dozens to hundreds of signs—some of which you need to read to know where you are.

I have selected a few key signs for reproduction here that will help you get started with some of the basics:

Understanding Key Signs

自動ドア AUTOMATIC DOORS—**JIDO DOA**

乗り場 BOARDING AREA (Platform)—**NORIBA**

バス乗場 BUS BOARDING AREA—**BASU NORIBA**

バス停留所 BUS STOP—**BASU TEIRYUJO**

会計 CASHIER—**KAIKEI**

お勘定場 CASHIER (in department store)—**O-KANJO BA**

中央口 CENTRAL GATE (exit-entrance)—**CHUO GUCHI**

閉まる CLOSE (button to close elevator door)—**SHIMARU**

準備中 CLOSED (not open for business at that time)—**JUNBI CHU**

締切り CLOSED TICKET WINDOW—**SHIMEKIRI**

本日休業 CLOSED TODAY—**HONJITSU KYUGYO**

食堂 DINING-HALL-TYPE RESTAURANT—**SHOKUDO**

降り口 DOWN STAIRWAY—**ORI GUCHI**

東口 EAST GATE (exit-entrance)—**HIGASHI GUCHI**

エレベーター ELEVATOR (directional sign)—**EREBETA**

非常呼出し EMERGENCY BUTTON (in elevator)—**HIJO YOBIDASHI**

非常口   EMERGENCY EXIT—**HIJO GUCHI**

入口   ENTRANCE—**IRIGUCHI**

エスカレーター   ESCALATOR (directional sign)—**ESUKARETA**

出口   EXIT—**DEGUCHI**

急行   EXPRESS (TRAIN)—**KYUKO**

屋内電話   HOUSE PHONE (in hotel)—**OKUNAI DENWA**

案内所   INFORMATION DESK—**ANNAI JO**

使用中   IN USE (sign on toilet cubicle door handle)—**SHIYO-CHU**

立入禁止   KEEP OUT—**TACHIRI KINSHI**

左側通行   KEEP TO THE LEFT—**HIDARIGAWA TSUKO**

右側通行   KEEP TO THE RIGHT—**MIGIGAWA TSUKO**

男
男子用   MEN (toilet signs)—**OTOKO DANSHI-YO**

横断禁止   NO CROSSING—**ODAN KINSHI**

撮影禁止   NO PHOTOGRAPHS—**SATSUEI KINSHI**

禁煙   NO SMOKING—**KIN'EN**

北口   NORTH GATE (exit-entrance)—**KITA GUCHI**

開く   OPEN (button to open elevator door)—**HIRAKU**

営業中　OPEN FOR BUSINESS—**EIGYO CHU**

24時間営業　OPEN 24 HOURS—**NIJU YOJIKAN EIGYO**

故障　OUT OF ORDER—**KOSHO**

回送　OUT OF SERVICE (on empty trains returning to the yard)—**KAISO**

ご自由にどうぞ　PLEASE TAKE ONE (FREE)—**GO-JIYU NI DOZO**

郵便局　POST OFFICE—**YUBIN KYOKU**

化粧室　POWDER ROOM—**KESHO SHITSU**

公衆電話　PUBLIC TELEPHONE—**KOSHU DENWA**

引く　PULL (on door)—**HIKU**

押す　PUSH (on door)—**OSU**

受付　RECEPTION DESK—**UKE TSUKE**

特急　SPECIAL EXPRESS (TRAIN)—**TOKKYU**

階段　STAIRS (directional sign)—**KAIDAN**

駅　STATION—**EKI**

止まれ　STOP—**TOMARE**

地下鉄　SUBWAY—**CHIKATETSU**

回送／廻送　TAXI SIGN WHEN NOT IN SERVICE—**KAISO**

空車　TAXI SIGN WHEN VACANT—**KUSHA**

タクシー乗り場   TAXI STAND—**TAKUSHII NORIBA**

改札口   TICKET GATE—**KAISATSU GUCHI**

発売中   TICKET MACHINE IN SERVICE—**HATSUBAI CHU**

発売中止   TICKET MACHINE OUT OF SERVICE—**HATSUBAI CHUSHI**

切符売り場   TICKET SALES (at subway and train stations)—**KIPPU URIBA**

トイレ／便所   TOILET/**TOIRE**—**BENJO**

登り（上り）口   UP STAIRWAY—**NOBORI GUCHI**

空   VACANT (seen on toilet cubicle handles)—**AKI**

区   WARD—**KU**

お手洗い   WASHROOM—**OTEARAI**

西口   WEST GATE (exit-entrance)—**NISHI GUCHI**

女   WOMEN (toilet signs)—**ONNA**

女の人   ONNA NO HITO
女子用   JOSHI-YO
婦人用   FUJIN-YO

円   YEN—**EN**

CHAPTER 14

Dining
In and Out

Is it Safe to Eat and Drink?

Sanitary conditions in Japan are among the highest in the world—if not *the* highest. The Japanese were endowed with an extraordinary respect for cleanliness very early in their history through the teachings of Shintoism, their native religion. Shintoism taught that cleanliness was literally next to godliness, and this was not just a slogan. Keeping both themselves and their homes clean became an integral part of the Japanese religious beliefs and practices.

The Japanese invented the hot bath long before it was known or used anywhere else in Asia, and daily bathing became a deeply ingrained ritual. In fact, their habit of bathing regularly, generally together, was shocking to the first European seamen and traders to visit the islands, who considered such behavior unhealthy. But many of the foreign visitors converted to daily bathing once they experienced its special pleasures. European missionaries who followed the traders into Japan, however, looked upon bathing, especially mixed-sex bathing, as a major sin against God. At first they tried to forbid the practice of bathing, but failing at that they limited their members and converts to bathing every other week. Finally, after developing some understanding and tolerance of the Japanese way, the missionaries allowed weekly bathing.

The natural hot springs that abound in Japan have been used for both sanitation and medicinal purposes since ancient times. Hundreds of them have been developed into major resort areas, where millions of people enjoy them annually.

This traditional concern with cleanliness was naturally carried over into the homes and kitchens of the Japanese. Housecleaning was a special skill that every woman, except those in the upper classes with servants, learned from childhood, and was a daily regime. The Japanese custom of removing their shoes before entering a home or inn grew out of their respect for cleanliness, and they still find it shocking that Westerners continue to treat their homes as dirt huts or caves, wearing outside shoes inside and on carpets that are sometimes even white.

When the presence and dangers of bacteria were discovered in the West, particularly in respect to food and drinks, this knowledge quickly spread to Japan, where it was incorporated into its food preparation and water treatment systems. All water used in Japan for household and drinking purposes, except in rural areas where wells are still in use, is purified by the most modern methods.

The infamous "tourist trot," or whatever the bug is called in other countries, is virtually unknown in Japan. From the late forties to date, during which time I have eaten in every conceivable style and quality of Japanese restaurant, I have never suffered one experience of *La Turista,* and have been aware of only one genuine case (the manager of the Chamber of Commerce of Scottsdale, Arizona, who accompanied a group I took to Japan in the sixties!).

Summing up, the food and water in Japan are certainly as safe as they are in the United States or any European country. You may be one of the few who is unlucky, but special precautions are simply not warranted by the facts.

Becoming Handy with *O'hashi*

One of the first things you will be expected to do after your arrival in Japan is try Japanese food, which means eating with **O'hashi** (Oh-hah-she), or chopsticks. *O'hashi* are the traditional eating implements of Japan, Korea, Taiwan, Hong Kong, and, of course, China, and mastering their use is one of the most interesting challenges facing most newcomers to Japan.

While all Western-style restaurants in Japan provide diners with knives, forks, and spoons, the custom of eating Japanese (and Chinese) foods with chopsticks prevails.

Whatever the food and the situation, you can request Western-type cutlery if you don't feel inclined to tackle chopsticks—but if you do take the easy way out, you will miss one of the tangible pleasures of experiencing a foreign culture. Further, metal tableware has been shown to impart an unpleasant metallic taste to the food it touches, and to the tongue—something that chopsticks do not do.

Visitors will usually be confronted at various times with three types of chopsticks. One type is made of natural wood and is primarily used in restaurants serving Japanese food. This type is called **waribashi** (wah-ree-bah-she), or "split-wood," and is usually still joined at one end as evidence that they have never been used. The diner pulls them apart, removing any splinters by rubbing the two sticks together. The *waribashi* come in a standard size.

The second type of *O'hashi* that you will likely encounter are larger than the *waribashi* and made of heavy plastic or ivory. These are favored by Chinese restaurants. In addition to being heavier and longer than *waribashi,* these chopsticks often have slightly rounded, blunt ends. Because of their weight and size, these Chinese-style chopsticks are generally more difficult for the typical visitor to use. As a result, many foreign residents and frequent travelers ask for Japanese *waribashi* when they dine at Chinese restaurants in Japan— a request that is perfectly legitimate to make.

The third type of chopstick commonly used in Japan is made of plastic or lacquered wood, and primarily used in private homes. These chopsticks come in various small sizes and colors; those for women are often smaller and more colorful. Also, they are often personalized in that individuals have their own sets that are always "served" to them. The *waribashi* are discarded after one use, whereas the lacquered, ivory, and plastic chopsticks are, of course, reused.

Lacquered chopsticks as well as ivory sticks (which I hope you will not see, because elephants are rapidly disappearing) are more difficult to use because they are slicker and much more awkward to handle, so don't hesitate to ask for the lightweight wooden ones.

The proper way to hold chopsticks is a bit tricky for the first-time user (see the following sketch). One shortcut to developing enough skill to feed yourself in just a few minutes is to keep the bottom stick stationary, pressed into the palm of your hand by your thumb, and just move the top stick up and down. Another hint for eating rice is to try not to squeeze it, but to pry a mouth-sized bite loose and then scoop it up with the sticks held parallel and about half an inch apart. Japanese rice is usually quite sticky so it holds together, making it easier to eat with chopsticks. (Chinese rice, on the other hand, is cooked much dryer and ranges from difficult to impossible to pick up with chopsticks. The only recourse may be to use a spoon or raise your rice bowl up to your mouth and scoop it in. You can make this maneuver more acceptable by placing tidbits of vegetable, meat, or seafood on top of the rice as toppings.)

There are several dos and don'ts for using chopsticks that are not essential but are good manners that should be practiced. Among the more important: Do not stick *O'hashi* into your rice bowl or any other dish and leave them protruding. This suggests death. Do not scrape off rice that adheres to the sticks. You can nibble it off (daintily), but don't scrape the sticks together. Don't use them to push or pull dishes around. Don't pick up a bowl or dish with the hand that holds your chopsticks. Don't use them to poke around in a common dish.

When not in use, chopsticks should be laid parallel on an *O'hashi* rest provided for that purpose (they are usually ceramic or wood and are often very decorative), or leaned against your plate or tray. When you are finished eating, lay the chopsticks across your plate or bowl. A pickled dish is often served for you to eat near the end of the meal to clear your palate. It is polite to rinse your chopsticks off in your teacup before eating the pickles (it serves to remove any food particles clinging to the sticks).

Japanese wives in particular often develop considerable skill with chopsticks and become adept at using them to tear items of food that are larger than bite size. When this is difficult or impossible for you to do, it is acceptable for you to raise the piece to your mouth and bite off a chunk. In this case, however, it is wise to hold your rice bowl under the piece while it is being raised to your mouth, as a kind of "backup tray" in case it gets away from your chopsticks and falls. Frequently, diners will rest the item on the rice and simultaneously raise both the bowl and the piece of food to their mouths.

It is not considered the most genteel etiquette to bring the rice bowl right up to the mouth when eating, but except on very formal occasions, most everyone does it. It is common to see people literally scraping food from an uptilted bowl into their mouths with their chopsticks.

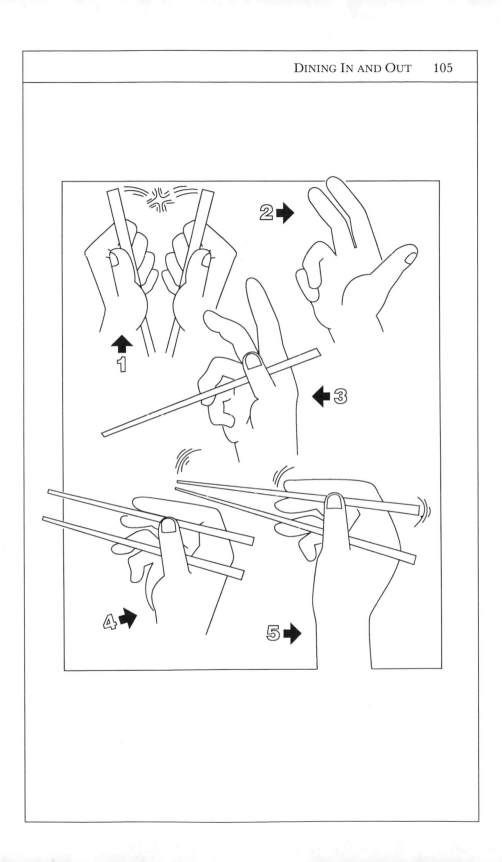

Most Japanese soups have various solid ingredients in them. To eat these ingredients without dripping soup onto the table or yourself, it is necessary to raise the soup bowl up close to your mouth. Keep the business end of your chopsticks sticking into the bowl while you are bringing it beneath your chin with both hands.

Of course, the only way you can drink soup reasonably is by raising the bowl to your mouth and sipping it. Again, it is customary to keep the business end of your chopsticks in the bowl while you are sipping.

Remember, in informal situations it is alright to use your rice bowl as a "tray" to get food items close to your mouth. This can be invaluable when you first start using *O'hashi*, because it not only helps you avoid accidents but also provides some insurance that you won't go hungry.

It is good manners to lay your chopsticks down and stop eating while you are being served additional helpings. If you help yourself from a common serving dish using your own chopsticks, it is proper etiquette for the sticks to be reversed and the opposite end used to handle the food.

Dining Japanese Style

Dining Japanese style primarily means eating traditional Japanese foods in a traditional Japanese setting, but it can also mean eating anything anywhere in the manner that the Japanese do. There are several things to keep in mind, depending on what, where, and with whom you eat.

It is not customary in many categories of Japanese restaurants— noodle shops, sushi shops, yaki-tori places, teppan-yaki houses, coffee shops—to serve water to diners automatically. If you want water you often have to ask for it. Outside of Westernized places, there is no tradition of making sure that *all* cooked foods are served piping hot, and some of the dishes we would serve hot may be served cold.

In resort inns, where meals are generally served either in the guest rooms or in large halls, often the only dish that is served hot is soup. Particularly when a large group is concerned, such things as breakfast eggs and toast—all prepared for serving at the same time—

generally arrive cold. This takes some getting used to, but once you get your expectations under control, it is not nearly as bad as it may sound.

In earlier Japan rice was normally served at the end of formal meals. Nowadays it is usually served with the rest of the meal except in exclusive *ryotei*—inn-type, Japanese-style restaurants, where traditions are still more strictly followed. The reasoning is that one should enjoy the natural taste of each of the preliminary "side dishes," in modest proportions, and then top off the meal with rice that not only fills the stomach but cleanses the palate.

If you are going to a restaurant where all seating is on the floor, a tight dress can be a problem. Also, if you have difficulty sitting for long periods of time without being able to lean up against something, remember that many such restaurants have specially designed floor seats with backrests. These legless chairs are called **zaisu** (zah-e-sue). If one is not offered to you when you first enter, it is perfectly alright to ask for it.

No kind of formal meal in Japan is complete without an alcoholic beverage, usually beer or **O'sake** (Oh-sah-kay). A traditional *sake*-drinking custom, established long ago, is to stop drinking *sake* when rice is served because the two are not regarded as compatible. This custom is still observed in formal situations such as banquets and receptions, but there are no such restrictions on beer. It is not common, however, for people to drink hard liquor with meals.

At some parties and receptions it is common for Japanese diners to leave their food untouched for up to half an hour or more while speeches and toasts flow freely. If you can anticipate such occasions, it is wise to fortify yourself with a small advance snack if at all possible.

Another thing to keep in mind when eating with Japanese friends: It is good manners to wait until the oldest or highest-ranking person starts before you begin.

There is no scarcity of delicious food in Japan, in almost any style you can imagine. In Tokyo and other large cities dozens of ethnic styles of cuisine are available. But if you plan on going off into remote areas, such as Mount Fuji, and are a finicky eater, it is wise to take along a couple of familiar snack items, which are readily available in convenience stores, supermarkets, neighborhood shops, department stores, etc.

Rice has traditionally been the main dish in all Japanese meals, and its preparation and consumption have become associated with many rules. One that you may encounter is that every grain of rice in your bowl is supposed to be eaten. If you set your bowl down with some rice left in it, it may be taken as a sign that you want more.

There are several types of restaurants in Japan that the visitor should be familiar with. These include the standard Western-style restaurant, called **restoran** (res-toe-rahn) in Japanese; the **shokudo** (show-kuu-doe), which is a cafe-type restaurant offering a mixed menu of Western and Japanese dishes; **yakitori-ya** (yah-kee-toe-ree-yah), specialty restaurants that serve barbecued chicken on spits; **O'soba-ya** (Oh-soe-bah-yah), hot- and cold-noodle-dish restaurants; **Shina ryori-ya** (She-nah rio-ree-yah), Chinese food restaurants; and **kissa ten** (kees-sah tane), or coffee shops, which serve pastries, toast, light sandwiches, coffee, soft drinks, and usually a number of ice-cream dishes.

Eating Well on a Budget

Japan appears to have more restaurants than any other country in the world (over one million, including 161,996 coffee shops that serve food and 49,825 sushi shops), and richly deserves its well-established reputation as a gourmet's Shangri La. A reputation that Japan does *not* deserve is the myth that dining out in Tokyo, Kyoto, and other large Japanese cities is like buying into a gold mine.

There are expensive restaurants in Japan, particularly in Tokyo. But these extravagantly priced places are the exception, and have their counterparts in New York, Paris, and other world-class cities where people are not shocked that dinner with drinks in an exclusive, posh eatery can run to well over a week's wages.

Most of the would-you-believe-it stories circulating about the expense of eating out in Japan concern dining in luxury-hotel restaurants and in very exclusive restaurants that cater to the very affluent and the big/ company executives on virtually unlimited expense accounts—certainly not the kind of places even the average well-to-do person would go to in his own home country unless it were a special occasion.

So where does this leave the hungry traveler? With plenty of good places to eat at prices that are not outrageous, I assure you. For many visitors, however, taking advantage of lower-priced restaurants in Japan is not that easy. It often requires a fairly substantial psychological shift that begins with a willingness to go a little out of the way and to eat foods prepared in new ways.

The economy-minded traveler must be willing to step off of the gold-lined tourist trail and eat in the restaurants that most Japanese patronize: the traditional and popular *O-soba-ya, tempura-ya, tonkatsu-ya, kamameshi-ya, Chuka ryori-ya, shokudo,* and so on. Before the traveler gnashes a gum, let me do a little translating and explaining.

There are three primary cuisines in Japan: Japanese, Western, and Chinese. Within the Japanese category there are some forty popular noodle dishes; over twenty-five equally popular rice dishes; and well over one hundred specialty dishes made up of seafoods, vegetables, meat, roots, plants, and combinations thereof.

There are three types of restaurants that serve Japanese dishes: the **O-soba-ya** (Oh-soe-bah-yah), which specializes in noodles, usually served hot in bowls in a soup stock with tidbits of meat, chicken, and/or vegetable; the *koryori-ya,* which offers an amazing variety of seafood, vegetable, and part-meat dishes; and the famous *O-sushi-ya,* which specializes in slices of raw fish and other fresh seafoods served on buns of seasoned rice.

There is a fourth type of restaurant, usually thought of as Japanese, that is something like an American cafeteria and is the Japanese equivalent of Denny's and other general-menu restaurants. This is the ubiquitous *shokudo* (show-kuu-doe), which serves a choice of the most popular Western, Japanese, and ersatz Chinese dishes.

Japan has *two* types of Chinese restaurants: the very common neighborhood type known as **Chuka ryori-ya** (Chuu-kah rio-ree-yah), or "Chinese food shop," which serves inexpensive Japanese versions of well-known Chinese dishes (primarily the noodle and rice dishes); and the relatively exclusive, far more expensive, Chinese-operated Chinese restaurants that cater to affluent Japanese and Chinese, as well as to resident and visiting foreigners.

Then there are numerous specialty restaurants, usually small and often very picturesque, mainly serving one particular kind of food at prices that go from inexpensive to very expensive.

The less expensive of these specialty shops, those that cater to typical Japanese, include **yakitori-ya** (yah-kee-toe-ree-yah), specialists in chunks of chicken and onion charcoal broiled on skewers and dipped in sauce; **tempura-ya** (tim-puu-rah-yah), seafood and vegetables dipped in a special batter and deep-fried in vegetable oil;

tonkatsu-ya (tone-kot-sue-yah), pork steaks, tenderloin or roast cuts, breaded and deep-fried; and **kamameshi-ya** (kah-mah-may-she-yah), which specialize in steamed rice in fish bouillon seasoned with soy sauce and laced with small bits of chicken, beef or pork, mushrooms, bamboo shoots, peas, etc., to taste.

Noodles, one of the most popular snack and lunch choices in Japan, are either Japanese style—with two of the most popular being *soba* (long, brownish grey, and made of buckwheat flour) and *udon* (long, white, and made of wheat flour)—or Chinese (long and yellowish).

Japanese-style noodles are usually served in soup stock and garnished with slivers of meat, seafood, and/or vegetables. They are a specialty of the *soba-ya, undon-ya,* and *shokudo.* Chinese noodles, eaten boiled or fried and usually with a vegetable/meat mixture (like chow mein), are found in both classes of Chinese restaurants and in most *shokudo.*

The next major category of both Japanese- and Chinese-style foods are the many rice dishes, served mostly in *shokudo* and *Chuka ryori-ya,* consisting of plates or bowls of rice topped with such things as pork; tempura'd shrimp; beef stew; curry-flavored stew; eggs cooked with a slice of chicken, onions, and other vegetable tidbits; etc.

How do visitors find these restaurants? They are virtually everywhere. Invariably, there are anywhere from a few to a dozen or more of each category clustered around train stations (of which there are over seventy-five in Tokyo alone). Shopping and entertainment districts also have their own collections of restaurants.

As a general rule, there are a variety of restaurants in office buildings (in basements in most, but also on upper floors in many new high-rise buildings), in department stores (also basements and upper levels), in shopping malls (particularly underground malls adjoining major stations), in and adjoining railway stations, and along shopping streets (in residential neighborhoods as well as central shopping areas)—all with prices that are not inflated because of name or location.

The variety of restaurants in these areas include specialty places that feature sushi, noodle dishes, rice dishes, and seafood dishes prepared Japanese style; there also are restaurants that have Western-style menus, with everything from spaghetti, chicken, fish, breaded pork, steak, salads, soups, and casseroles to stews. Breads and pastries in these restaurants are generally outstanding.

Hibiya Chanter

My favorite restaurant building in downtown Tokyo is the beautiful **Hibiya Chanter** (He-bee-yah Shahn-tay) at 1-2-2 Yurakucho, one block north of the Imperial Hotel Tower, adjoining the Toho Theater Building on the north and across from a Mitsui Bank building. There are more than a dozen restaurants on the second basement floor (B2F), representing as many different food styles, including sushi, noodles, seafood, spaghetti, beef dishes cooked on hot stone grills, breaded pork steak, sandwiches and pastries, and Chinese cuisine.

All of the Chanter restaurants are reasonably priced, with a variety of complete "set" meals (**teishoku**/tay-e-show-kuu) ranging from about eight hundred yen to fifteen hundred yen. Four that I patronize most often are **Vie de France Bakery,** which features excellent sandwiches and outstanding pastries; the **Menkoi** (Mane-koy), which can be translated as "love noodles"; **Tonkatsu Wako** (Wah-koe), where the specialty is breaded pork steaks and large shrimp breaded and deep-fried; and the **Kabe no Ana** (Kah-bay no Ah-nah), or "Hole in the Wall," which specializes in spaghetti dishes. If you like steak meat grilled on stone, it's the Bistro for you.

The attractive Vie de France Bakery will seat only about fifteen, so most patrons order takeout food; some of them have their lunch or snack on the plaza in front of the building. You can also get *tonkatsu* to go at *Wako.*

Other features of eating out in Japan that are very important for saving food money are the breakfast and lunch "specials" offered by thousands of restaurants that cater to office workers (and are therefore located in or near office buildings and commuter terminals). These places offer a variety of set breakfasts and lunches for prices that are approximately half and often only one-third of what the same meal would ordinarily cost. A set breakfast may consist of coffee and toast; eggs, coffee, and toast; or some other combination. Special set lunches run the gamut in both Western and Japanese dishes, depending on the restaurant, and generally include soup, salad, bread, and coffee.

"Set" evening meals, called **teishoku** (tay-e-show-kuu), are also available in a majority of the restaurants that offer special breakfast and lunch combinations in addition to their a la carte menu. These set meals are cheaper simply because of the economies of scale principle.

If you are in a restaurant and do not see (or recognize) signs or table menus listing the day's specials, you can ask the waitress or waiter whether they have them: **Special arimasu ka?** (Special ah-ree-mahss kah?) Or, **Teishoku arimasu ka?** (Tay-e-show-kuu ah-ree-mahss kah?)

"Local" restaurants are usually easy to recognize because most of them have authentic-looking plastic models of their dishes in display windows or cases outside or just inside their entrances. Prices are displayed with these replicas so the diner can decide what he wants and know its cost before sitting down. Many other nonexclusive restaurants have their menus and prices prominently displayed outside for the convenience of patrons.

Some cafeteria-style restaurants, particularly in train stations and other terminals, require that you make your selection and pay before sitting down. You receive a ticket or chit called *shokken* (shoak-ken) to hand to your waiter or waitress. Restaurants of this type have a sign at the entrance which reads: **Shokken wo omotome kudasai** (Shoak-ken oh oh-moe-toe-may kuu-dah-sie), or "Please buy a ticket." Some really inexpensive restaurants of this type use vending machines to dispense the food chits.

Besides the hundreds of thousands of independent restaurants in Japan, there are also a number of chain restaurants that serve good Western-type food at moderate prices—and seldom become known to the typical tourist or visiting businesspeople. These include the Fujiya, Morinaga, Meiji, and Benihana chains; the Aka Hyotan and Acacia Salad Shops; the Coq d'or restaurant chain; and the Tivoli (Italian) food shops.

And, of course, there are the foreign and Japanese fast-food chains: McDonald's, MOS Burgers, Kentucky Fried Chicken, Denny's, Pioneer Take Out Sandwich Shops, and others in the same category. Many shokudo-type restaurants in or adjoining commuter train stations feature what is called "Morning Service," which consists of a breakfast of eggs and/or toast and coffee at very low prices.

Coffee shops and snack restaurants, which abound in Japan, also do a thriving business during breakfast, lunch, and after hours. They mainly serve eggs, toast, coffee, sandwiches, soft drinks, pastries, and a few short-order dishes à la the *shokudo.* Coffee, tea, and soft drinks are the most expensive items (for what you get to eat or drink) on coffee shop and snack restaurant menus. But there is a valid reason for this. People use coffee shops as meeting places, for personal as well as business reasons, and commonly occupy tables or booths for up to two hours or more. During this entire period they normally order only once—one cup of coffee or tea, or a soft drink. No one hassles the patrons about ordering more or leaving, and there is often continuous music for the listening pleasure of patrons. The price for a cup of coffee covers part of this additional overhead.

The visitor who fails to buy and try Japan's delicious breads and pastries is missing a treat. Bakeries, some of them also national chains, can be found in most shopping centers and entertainment and restaurant districts, as well as in department stores and many hotels. Bread varieties include French, Russian, German, and American. The choice of pastries, mostly in one-serving pieces, numbers in the dozens, and the baked goods are as decorative as they are delicious. Some bakery chains to keep in mind: Fuji-ya, Kimura-ya, Yamazaki-ya, Coq d'or Vienna Bread, and German Bakery.

Besides this extraordinary variety and number of restaurants, convenience markets in virtually every neighborhood generally feature a variety of packaged dishes and sandwiches that are made daily. Supermarkets often have prepared food counters offering fish, chicken, and meat dishes served hot. And finally, there are sandwich and cold- or hot-drink vending machines in numerous public places.

Many hotel rooms in Japan come equipped with refrigerators. Experienced travelers, myself included, make a practice of stocking them with such items as milk, fruit, luncheon meats, rolls, honey, and peanut butter—all obtainable at nearby convenience stores and supermarkets as well as in the food departments of department stores.

Japan's National Tourist Organization (JNTO) publishes an eighteen-page booklet called *Tourist Restaurants in Japan*. The publication lists some two hundred restaurants in sixteen cities that have been rated as "Tourist Restaurants," meaning that their food is good and their prices are reasonable. The criteria for being listed in the JNTO directory are: (1) location near a main railway station or hotel frequented by tourists; (2) prices in the range of ¥250 to ¥500 for breakfast, ¥400 to ¥800 for lunch, and ¥500 to ¥1000 for dinner; and (3) clean, attractive atmosphere.

Japanese, Chinese, and Western-style restaurants, including Shakey's and McDonald's, are included in the booklet. Cities covered include (from north to south) Sapporo, Otaru, Sendai, Aizuwaka-matsu, Narita, Tokyo, Yokohama, Kanazawa, Kyoto, Osaka, Hiroshima, Fukuoka, Beppu, Kumamoto, Miyazaki, and Kagoshima.

The Tourist Restaurant membership emblem is composed of a circle with the wording TOURIST RESTAURANT over a knife and fork in its center and a dove at the bottom. The booklet is available free from JNTO offices.

The Japanization of Fast Foods

The success of American fast-food restaurants in Japan was a phenomenon that many predicted would never happen. But characteristically, the Japanese are never satisfied with leaving well enough alone. They feel compelled to improve on anything that comes their way—and to them there was nothing sacred about the franchised American hamburger, French fries, or spaghetti. Catering to the adventurous spirit of the Japanese, food merchants soon came up with chicken burgers with buns made of rice, *teriyaki* burgers garnished with *shoyu* sauce and sesame seeds, *miso* (soybean paste) burgers, *soba* dogs (hot dog buns filled with soba noodles), potato crisps sprinkled with seaweed, bread wrapped in seaweed, Japanese-style spaghetti (it is topped with seaweed instead of tomato paste and is eaten with chopsticks instead of forks), squid pizza, green tea ice cream, and more.

What is even more interesting is that these Japanese-created hybrids quickly began attracting attention abroad as "new products from Japan." While you might not appreciate soybean paste on your salad, you should certainly try some of the other innovations.

Another Japanese dish that visitors can usually relate to immediately is called **okonomi-yaki** (oh-koe-no-me-yah-kee), which consists of an omelet fried like a pancake, with various combinations of beef, pork, shrimp, and vegetables mixed in with the eggs.

A surprisingly high percentage of Japanese restaurants have their menus in English as well as Japanese, even though many only rarely if ever have foreign customers. The practice often seems to be more of a custom or fashion than a practical business decision, but it is a boon for foreign travelers who like to try restaurants off the tourist trail.

Visitors to Japan are often amazed at the number of vending machines they see and the variety of products sold in the machines. One important reason for the proliferation of these machines is because merchandisers do not have to worry about burglars or vandals. Besides the usual candy bars, sandwiches, and soft drinks, the machines also dispense fruit juices, coffee, and health drinks.

In restaurants featuring traditional Japanese dishes (*sushi,* noodles, fish, etc.) green tea is served free, as water is in other restaurants. The first *sale* of green tea apparently occurred in a Tokyo restaurant in 1988, and was so extraordinary that it became the talk of the town. It is not likely to start a trend, however.

When you order tea in coffee shops and Western-style restaurants in Japan, you get brown or black tea, which is called **kocha** (koe-chah) and is similar to Lipton's tea. If you just say *kocha* you get it plain. Variations include **remon ti** (ray-moan tee), or "lemon tea" (you get a thin slice of lemon on the side); and **miruku ti** (me-rue-kuu tee), or "milk tea" (which comes with a small serving of milk on the side).

It is common practice to sweeten *kocha,* lemon tea, and milk tea, but *never* green tea. The sight of someone putting sugar in green tea is traumatic to the Japanese and foreign afficionados of the distinctively flavored drink.

Dining Vocabulary

Menu, please
Menyu kudasai   Men-yuu kuu-dah-sie

Water, please
Mizu kudasai   Me-zuu kuu-dah-sie

Tea (brown), please
Kocha kudasai   Koe-chah kuu-dah-sie

Lemon tea, please
Remon ti kudasai   Ray-moan tee kuu-dah-sie

Milk tea, please
Miruku ti kudasai   Me-rue-kuu tee kuu-dah-sie

Coffee, please
Kohi kudasai   Koe-he kuu-dah-sie

Sugar, please
Sato kudasai   Sah-toe kuu-dah-sie

I'm hungry
Onaka suite imasu   Oh-nah-kah suu-e-tay e-mahss

Are you hungry?
Onaka suite imasu ka?   Oh-nah-kah suu-e-tay e-mahss kah?

Let's eat
Tabemasho   Tah-bay-mah-show

What time is breakfast?
Asahan wa nanji desu ka?
Ah-sah-hahn wah nahn-jee dess kah?

What time is lunch?
Hiruhan wa nanji desu ka?
He-rue-hahn wah nahn-jee dess-kah?

What time is dinner?
Yuhan wa nanji desu ka?   Yuu-hahn wah nahn-jee dess kah?

I want to eat Japanese food
Nihon ryori wo tabetai desu
Nee-hone rio-ree oh tah-bay-tie dess

I want to eat Western food
Yoshoku wo tabetai desu   Yoh-show-kuu oh tah-bay-tie dess

This is delicious
Kore wa oishii desu   Koe-ray wah oh-e-she-ee dess

My stomach is upset
Onaka no guai ga warui desu
Oh-nah-kah no gwie gah wah-rue-ee dess

I've had enough (no more, thank you)
Mo kekko desu   Moe keck-koe dess

I'm full
Ippai desu   Eep-pie dess

Is it spicy hot?
Karai desu ka?   Kah-rie dess kah?

Please cook it well done
Yoku yaite kudasai   Yoe-kuu yie-tay kuu-dah-sie

Medium well
Mejium weru   May-jee-uum way-rue

Medium
Mejium   May-jee-uum

Rare
Reah   Ray-ah

I would like some dessert
Dezato hoshii desu   Day-zah-toe hoe-she-e dess

Fruit, please
Kudamono kudasai   Kuu-dah-moe-no kuu-dah-sie

What do you recommend?
Osusume wa nan desu ka?
Oh-sue-sue-may wah nahn dess kah?

Excuse me! (call used to get attention of waiter/waitress)
Sumimasen!   Sue-me-mah-sin!

Bill, please
Okanjo kudasai   Oh-kahn-joe kuu-dah-sie

Receipt, please
Ryoshusho kudasai   Rio-shuu-show kuu-dah-sie

Thank you for a delicious meal
Gochiso sama deshita   Go-chee-sosah-mah desh-tah

Let's go out again tomorrow night
Mata ashita no ban dekakemasho
Mah-tah ah-sshtah no bahn day-kah-kay-mah-show

See you tomorrow
Ja, mata ashita   Jah, mah-tah ah-sshtah

CHAPTER 15

Nighttime Entertainment

Surviving the Pleasure Trades

Japan probably has more night life—known as **mizu shobai** (me-zoo show-by), or "water business"—than any other country, with giant entertainment districts constituting a distinct and colorful feature of every city. In Tokyo alone, over 500,000 people are employed in the entertainment trades (bars, lounges, cabarets, clubs), including some thirty thousand young women who work as cabaret hostesses. But fun in this exotic "floating world" can be very expensive, especially for the newcomer who is not familiar with the way the game is played.

Over and above the high cost of yen today, prices in first-class, prestigious places in Japan tend to be very expensive—on a par with the most elite clubs and restaurants in New York, Paris, or London. There are some aspects of exclusive hostess cabarets and certain bars, however, that can run the cost of an evening up to astronomical figures, well beyond *any* norm.

These elite (although often very small) night spots specialize in providing patrons with the company of hostesses: attractive young women who serve as conversation companions, dance partners, and foils for sexual interplay. There are two kinds of night spots that employ hostesses: so-called nightclubs, in which patrons have a choice of whether they want the company of hostesses; and "cabarets," where hostesses are automatically assigned to all customers who come in. Legally speaking, any night spot that employs hostesses is classified as a cabaret, regardless of what it calls itself—bar, nightclub, lounge, or cabaret—which causes some confusion.

Larger, name nightclubs also differ from most lounge-type cabarets in that they serve full meals and often have a live band and a dance floor.

In any event, places that offer hostesses are usually more expensive than those that don't. In a nightclub, where you "order" your hostess, she is yours for as long as you want to pay a fee, loosely based on the amount of time she spends with you. In cabarets (which often look like and are operated like what most Westerners would call a lounge), where the women are assigned by the house, you may or may not have the same woman or women very long. The practice is to rotate them among customers, to keep the customers from getting bored with or too involved with any individual hostess; give every hostess on duty a chance to earn some income; and add to the house's take, since there is a new full-hour charge every time a new hostess joins a table, even though she may stay for only twenty or thirty minutes.

The main reason for the appearance and continued existence of this system is that nearly all of the clients in this kind of "hostess lounge" are company executives living it up on entertainment expense accounts, or company owners spending company funds as they see fit. Both categories of cabaret patrons are following an age-old business practice of entertaining clients and themselves in night spots as part of their company responsibility.

Knowing that their patrons are not spending private funds, and that Japanese businessmen are conditioned to demonstrate extraordinary hospitality to their customers and guests, cabaret operators charge them all that the market will bear. They invariably know how much each manager is authorized to spend on the basis of his rank and the size of his company, and they often charge accordingly. Businessmen patrons do not pay directly; the bills are sent to their companies for payment.

The cost of an evening out in a hostess club or cabaret has no relationship to how many drinks or hors d'oeuvres have been consumed, or even how many women have kept you company. It is based on the pricing standards established by the house and how long you spend there. If you stay a long time and drink very little, the cost will be approximately the same as if you guzzled expensive liquor the whole evening.

When a foreign visitor who does not know the system wanders into one of these places on his own, without so much as an introduction from an established patron, he generally will be charged the same rate that the bar applies to its expense-account customers, and will receive a bill that is five to ten times more than what he expected. The only way to go to exclusive hostess lounges, unless you are a genuine big spender, is with a Japanese friend who, you hope, is picking up the tab.

Even more caution must be exercised when going into small bars in some of Tokyo's more notorious entertainment districts, such as Kabuki-cho in Shinjuku Ward. Some of these bars are operated by gangsters who make a practice of preying on unsuspecting Japanese visitors from out of town. Their approach is out-and-out extortion: They demand payments of several hundred dollars for a few beers, and threaten the customers with serious bodily harm if they don't pay up. They occasionally try the same thing on foreigners, who sometimes complain loudly, and the incident ends up in the newspapers.

There are, however, hundreds of thousands of bars and lounges in Japan where prices are posted and followed, and there is no danger at all—at least from operators. These include many famous bar and beer-hall chains, such as Suntory and Sapporo. There is also, in fact, a good selection of cabaret clubs that deliberately follow the Western practice of charging set prices for their drinks and women, and advertise in English-language publications to attract foreign clientele. One of these publications is the weekly *Tour Companion,* available free in hotels, airline offices, tourist information centers, service clubs, and elsewhere.

Some of the largest, most popular bar chains that cater to people not on expense accounts and have menus and set prices that are strictly adhered to are Kirin City, Lion, **Murasaki** (Muu-rah-sah-kee), **Yoronotaki** (Yoe-roe-no-tah-kee), **Kitano Kazoku** (Kee-tah-no Kah-zoe-kuu), and **Tengu** (Tane-guu)—the latter catering primarily to students.

Closing time for night spots in Japan, unless they are licensed as restaurants (which many nightclubs are), is 11:00 P.M., with a thirty-minute grace period. Many places stay open clandestinely, however, by turning out their front lights and covering any windows. They also station lookouts near buzzers at the entrance in case the police decide to spot-check.

Girls Are Not Taboo—But!

It is common knowledge that Western men find Oriental women unusually attractive, and that in any ranking of overall femininity, character, and personality, Japanese women are invariably in the top three. Japanese women are also attracted to Western men. This combination can cause problems for some visiting males if they are not aware of the etiquette involved.

The Japanese at large do not mind it when visiting foreign men enjoy themselves with Japanese women. In fact, they encourage it— but *only* with girls who are in the business of entertainment: nightclub hostesses, soapland girls, etc. Furthermore, the rules of the game ideally limit these associations to the women's place of business or to certain types of places where discreet assignations are the order of business (such as resort inns).

It goes without saying that few if any foreigners, visiting or resident, consciously follow these unwritten rules except when it serves their private purposes. And certainly there are more than enough "unprofessional" Japanese women who have no qualms about associating with foreigners any time, any place.

Probably the most common *faux pas* committed by Western men visiting Japan is taking young Japanese ladies of the evening (so to speak) to popular public places where they mix with the elite of society. At best, these men appear to be lacking in intelligence and refinement.

Japanese society has traditionally sanctioned extramarital sexual activity for both health and recreational purposes (it used to be government policy that men away from home should not be denied ample opportunity for sexual release to maintain optimum health), and the variety and volume of intimate relationships today is pursued with the same enthusiasm and dedication the Japanese apply to their successful business systems. In keeping with proper decorum, however, there is a time and a place for everything, and as long as the amorous visitor abides by accepted etiquette, anything goes.

There is a major business infrastructure in Japan that caters to and supports sexual liaisons on an astounding scale. These include not only the well-known soaplands and inns that serve as assignation places for those who desire the ultimate in discretion, but also thousands of so-called love hotels which, in American parlance, are "short-time hotels" where men and women by the hundreds of thousands go in a continuous stream.

Businessmen and others who can afford the cost who traditionally establish relationships with cabaret hostesses—among whom are some of the most gorgeous and intelligent women in the world—would never think of taking them to even casual meetings with business colleagues, but they routinely take them to fine restaurants, to luxury hotels in resort areas, and on expensive overseas trips that are ostensibly for business.

In Japan it is not what you do, it is how and where you do it—an axiom that especially applies to the pursuit of sensual pleasures.

At the same time, the newly arrived Western man should not presume that Japanese women, even cabaret hostesses, are going to fall all over him or are his for the picking. He also should not be surprised when the beautiful, provocative-acting cabaret hostess who agrees to meet him for a late-night date after closing time fails to show up at the appointed time and place.

The cabaret lothario must keep in mind that the better-looking hostesses are sought after by many men every night, and the "I'll meet you on the corner" routine is one of the standard ploys they use to fend off men they do not want to get involved with. Women who really intend to keep after-work dates with cabaret patrons usually will agree to leave the club with them at closing time—presumably to join them for a late-night snack before going home.

A male guest in a Japanese inn also should not assume that a maid is available as a pillow partner just because she helps him remove his clothing and don a *yukata* robe, and/or keeps popping in and out of his room while he is in bed or undressed.

It would be foolish to believe that the maids who do this as part of their job are completely oblivious to the masculinity of their guests, but the code of conduct followed by the average *ryokan* maid does not permit her to engage in "instant romances" with guests. She will, however, engage in stimulating banter without reserve, and will often tease a guest with artful coquetry. But this is usually as far as the game goes in the typical inn.

There are many atypical inns in Japan, however, especially on the southern island of Kyushu, that are known for maids who go beyond laying out beds as part of their regular service. This custom is a hold-over from Japan's shogunate days (which ended in 1868), when virtually every inn in the land provided female partners for male guests. This practice must have been one of the reasons the Japanese were such great travelers long before tourism became a common practice in the Western world.

With the demise of the great red-light districts in 1956, the call-girl system became more common and grew more sophisticated as time passed. Call-girl clubs and "sex banks" proliferated. Some call-girl groups distribute full-color "guide books" in the toilets of train and subway stations, in an example of direct-market merchandising that is traditionally Japanese (until the early fifties, tabloid newspapers were distributed at train stations as a means of promoting the services of prostitutes in the vicinity).

One of the Tokyo distribution points for the miniature "girl guide books" (published by the Tokyo City Press) is the men's toilet at the west end of the Akasaka Mitsuke Subway Station. Each evening the booklets are placed on a ledge in front of a long line of urinals. The booklets feature the photos of very pretty young women in varying states of undress, provocatively posed, with such headlines as "VIP Course; Whatever you want you get; I'll make your heart beat."

Outside of the *mizu shobai,* meeting and getting acquainted with Japanese women is basically no different than what it is in the United States or Europe, once you get around the language barrier. You meet them at their place of work; when shopping; in restaurants, coffee shops, or bars; on vacation trips; in schools; and so on. Of course, overcoming the communication problem is to some degree fundamental, and a newly found Japanese girlfriend is not likely to invite you to her home to meet her parents. Otherwise, the relationship can develop pretty much along standard lines as far as the two of you are concerned.

If the relationship becomes serious, however, and marriage is contemplated, most Japanese parents will oppose the union for both racial and cultural reasons. However, the more cosmopolitan the parents are, the less resistance they are likely to show, and there are a growing number who actually like the idea of their offspring opting for international marriages.

The main point for the casual visitor to keep in mind is that there are playgirls and then there are women, and it is rude and dumb to confuse the two.

How to Drink and Stay Sober

Drinking alcoholic beverages is an integral and important part of interpersonal relations in Japan. There are both social and business occasions when drinking is expected of everyone who is physically able to indulge, although many women and a few men do so only in token amounts.

The traveler in Japan very often finds himself in a situation in which he is expected to drink enthusiastically. The most common occasion is at a large Japanese-style dinner where every person may be expected to drink a toast with every other person at the party. This can present a real challenge, even when the drinking implements are the tiny, thimble-size **saka-zuki** (sah-kah-zoo-kee) from which **O'sake** (O-sah-kay) is imbibed.

If you do not drink, about the only acceptable excuse is that you have a serious disorder of the liver, kidneys, or stomach, etc., and are under strict orders from your doctor to avoid all alcohol. Older women usually are not pressured to drink, but on company trips and other social outings, young women are often unable to escape the obligation.

A very good gambit that you can use to avoid drinking more than you want is to act drunker than you really are. As soon as you show exaggerated signs of inebriation, the pressure on you to drink more usually disappears altogether.

On hundreds of occasions, I have been out drinking at night with Japanese businessmen who, after several drinks, would appear to be totally sloshed and are having a drunken brawl, singing, dancing, and falling all over themselves. However, they "sober up" in an instant, discuss some very serious business for one or two minutes, and then go back to playing drunk and enjoying themselves.

When you have had all you want or can take, turn your cup or glass upside down (in a drunken manner, if you can act), and politely but firmly resist all entreaties to reverse it. The Japanese consider it unfriendly and arrogant to refuse to get drunk with them, and if you refuse to drink without any explanation, it may spoil the whole party (and turn them against you).

Other drinking rules: It is good manners to pick up and hold your glass or cup, with both hands, when someone in your party refills it for you. It is polite to do the same when a cabaret hostess refills your glass, but such politeness is a little ostentatious. When you do pick up and hold your glass for a refill, it is also considered proper etiquette to take at least a sip before setting it down.

At parties where you are the guest, it is good form for you to pour the host a drink shortly after the party begins (he may have already poured one for you, after which it would be very impolite for you not to return the gesture). If anyone else at the party pours a drink for you, it is proper and expected that you will do the same for him. At some parties, the same *sake* cup or glass may be passed from one person to another. In this case, there should be bowls of hot water provided for rinsing the cup before passing it on to someone else.

Some Japanese are unable to drink more than one or two thimbles of *sake* or whiskey or more than a half a glass of beer without turning beet-red. If they continue drinking even the most modest amounts, they risk becoming quite ill and usually throwing up. This condition is attributed to their lacking an enzyme that metabolizes alcohol. Generally speaking, these are the only Japanese, particularly in the case of males, who drink very lightly or not at all. An exception is older Japanese men who have spent a lifetime drinking heavily five and six days a week as part of their "work responsibility," damaged their livers extensively, and had to quit to save their lives.

Many Japanese, including women, are very strong drinkers and take great pride in their ability to down large quantities of alcohol rapidly and stay upright. There are a number of sayings referring to the fact that the most important qualifications for success in business in Japan are to have an iron stomach and a hard head. However, it is not a good idea for the foreign visitor to try to outdrink anyone in Japan just to "save face"—something that happens regularly, often with serious results.

Japan's traditional drinking toast is **Kampai!** (Kahm-pie!), which means something like "Bottoms Up!" You will hear it often.

You and Miss Soapland

The *geisha* and *maiko* (apprentice *geisha*) are a lot more romantic and better known, but Japan's massage parlor hot-bath ("soapland") girls contribute a great deal more to the country's success as one of the world's best travel/vacation areas.

For the uninitiated, Japan's soaplands (formerly known as Turkish baths) are places where the patron is "prepared" in a steam or heat box (with only his head protruding), bathed, and then massaged. What makes the soapland bathhouses unusually interesting, particularly to men, is that these various ministrations are performed by attractive young women, usually dressed in short-shorts and halters, who offer various kinds of sexual services to their customers.

Soaplands have been popular in Japan for centuries. At one time they virtually replaced the formerly great red-light districts that flourished throughout country, becoming the primary houses of sensual pleasure. Today, there still are thousands of them. Some areas of Tokyo have clusters of a dozen or more in a number of entertainment districts.

Many of the soaplands are ornate, some are luxurious, and a few are gigantic. The largest one in the country at this writing is the *New Japan* in Osaka. It has eight stories above the ground and two below, and includes one floor that caters exclusively to women. Facilities and services vary to some extent in different soaplands, but most of them serve drinks to order, and some have adjoining restaurants. Room service for at least drinks is a common feature.

The typical massage bath is set up something like a hotel, with a reception desk and a lobby that may or may not have semiprivate areas (some patrons would rather not be seen entering and leaving such places). Customers may call in for specific appointments or just walk in and take their turn. Those who have patronized a place before often request a certain woman.

At the appointed time, or when the walk-in customer's turn comes, the lucky woman comes to the lobby and escorts the patron to a private bath suite. In addition to the steam cabinet and bath, the room will contain a massage table, a dressing mirror, and perhaps a chair (for the attendant to use when she doesn't have a customer).

The guest removes his shoes before stepping up on the floor of the room. The woman helps him strip, hands him a towel to wrap around his waist, and takes him to the steam box. While he is in the box, she checks the bath water, occasionally wipes the sweat from his brow, and, if he has ordered a drink, holds it up to his mouth when he wants a sip.

When the bather indicates he is "well done," the attendant lets him out of the box, takes the towel from his waist, douses him with a few buckets of warm water, and has him get into the tub and soak for a few minutes. Then he gets out and sits on a low stool while the woman scrubs him all over—or mostly all over, depending on her inclinations at this stage of the experience.

After the hard scrubbing, the soapland girl again douses the guest with more buckets of water. He may, if he chooses, get back into the tub for a few more minutes of soaking before he is dried off and directed to the massage bunk.

Most attendants will ask you to lie face down first, covering your mid-section with another towel. After thoroughly massaging your back from neck to toes (she also will get up on top of you and walk on your back if you like), she turns you over and does the front.

While soaplands are mostly patronized by men, some of them welcome female guests, and a surprisingly large number of lady visitors take advantage of them. I have had letters from Western women who said that the soaplands they visited were the highlight of their trip.

One of the special services provided by some of the massage bathhouses is washing the guest's underwear and socks. The items are returned to the rooms, heat-dried and pressed, before the guest is finished. Other special services include several "kinds" of baths, ranging from milk-and-lemon to aphrodisiac mixtures.

The soaplands naturally have a reputation that is salacious to say the least, and most of them deserve the reputation. Whether an individual attendant is available for anything beyond a straight bath and massage becomes very obvious in how she "handles" the guest during the bathing and massaging phase. In any event, the baths do not disappoint many people.

Special note: When the AIDS epidemic broke out in the mid-eighties, most of the soaplands began barring foreign guests—in particular those with tattoos, since they believed that tattooed men presented the most potential danger. This policy was later relaxed a bit, especially in the plush houses in the Tokyo vicinity that have traditionally catered to well-heeled (and presumably safer) foreign clientele.

Other Choices

Cabarets, nightclubs and soaplands make up only a small portion of Japan's nightlife. The most common and most popular night spots are ethnic restaurant/bars that serve *O'sake*, beer, and other alcoholic beverages; bars, and beer gardens, the latter being especially popular during the summer months.

Japan's "ethnic restaurant/bars" or *izaka-ya* (ee-zah-kah-yah), serve a variety of specialty dishes from *sushi* and *sashimi* and a variety of vegetables and salads to various kinds of hot stews and char-broiled fish. They are jam-packed every night except Sunday. Men and women go there not only to eat, but to drink and enjoy themselves. *Sushi* bars themselves are usually rather sedate, although practically no one eats *sushi* without drinking. But in most of the other ethnic places, the atmosphere is festive, and everyone works at having fun.

In these latter places it is common for guests to be crowded in hip to knee, with none of the distance or reserve one usually associates with the Japanese. And it is in such places that the ordinary Japanese—those who are not on company expense accounts—relax, let their hair down and enjoy each other's company. While Japanese-language ability helps one join in the joking and storytelling at these nightly gatherings, there are so many areas of communication that are universal that nonlinguists as well can have a ball.

These are the kind of places you should try to go to, not the "tourist" places. And this is where having a Japanese contact is so valuable. If you do not have a personal contact, ask your hotel bell captain to introduce you to one or more places. Almost everyone invariably knows two or three such night spots.

In the summer months, beer gardens, particularly those on rooftops, are entertaining, easy-to-find places to spend an evening. Hotel staff, taxi drivers and generally just about everyone else knows the location of two or three. Many beer gardens have live entertainment. If you have any trouble communicating, remember that in Japanese beer is **biiru** (bee-rue) and garden is **gaden** (gah-dane).

Buying Tickets

Movie and theater schedules are carried in Japan's English-language newspapers *(The Japan Times, Mainichi Daily News, Asahi Evening News, Yomiuri Daily News)* and in tourist publications. In Tokyo see *Tour Companion* or the *Tokyo Weekender*. Tickets to entertainment events and movies can be bought in advance at a chain of Play Guides found in many high-traffic locations. First-run movies are called "Road Shows" in Japan, and advance tickets are known as **mae uri ken** (my uu-ree ken).

If you want to see a live *sumo* match (highly recommended), get your tickets as early as possible, for they often sell out in advance.

Drinking Vocabulary

Beer
Biiru   (Bee-rue)

Draft (draught) beer
Nama biiru   (Nah-mah bee-rue)

Sake
O'sake   (Oh-sah-kay)

Whiskey
Uisuki   (Whiskey)

Scotch
Sukochi   (Suu-kah-chee)

Scotch and water
Mizu wari   (Mee-zuu wah-ree)

Wine
Budoshu   (Buu-doe-shuu)

Brandy
Burandi   (Buu-rahn-dee)

Champagne
Shampein   (Shahm-pain)

Drinking toast
Kampai!   (Kahm-pie!)

Some Useful Phrases in Japanese

Two bottles of Kirin beer, please
Kirin biiru ni-hon kudasai
Kee-reen bee-rue nee-hone kuu-dah-sie

Make those small bottles!
Koh bin ni shite!   Koe bean nee ssh-tay!

Another round, please
Okawari kudasai   Oh-kah-wah-ree kuu-dah-sie

I'm a little drunk
Sukoshi yotte imasu   Suu-koe-she yoat-tay ee-mahss

Let's go to some other bar
Hokano ba ni ikimasho   Hoe-kah-no bah nee ee-kee-mah-show

CHAPTER 16

Transportation Treats and Trials

From "Bullet Trains" to Ferries

Japan is noted for having one of the best public transportation systems in the world—very crowded and sometimes expensive, but clean, safe, and run with clockwork efficiency. You can go virtually anywhere in the cities or countryside, including the remotest areas, by one or more forms of public transportation, from the famed high-speed "Bullet Trains" to interisland ferries and passenger ships. (In Japanese, the Bullet Trains are known as **Shin Kan Sen** (Sheen Kahn Sin), or "New Trunk Lines."

Tokyo, Osaka, Nagoya, and Sapporo (on the northern island of Hokkaido) have subway lines. Tokyo has the most extensive subway system, made up of twelve lines, which provide residents and visitors alike with some of the best and most convenient public transportation in the world.

Each of Tokyo's twelve subway lines intersect at numerous places with other lines, giving passengers dozens of transfer points. All of the lines either bisect the central area of Tokyo or connect with lines that do. At Hibiya Station in downtown Tokyo, for example, three main lines crisscross, and three other main lines are only two to five minutes away via underground passageways.

Nagoya has five private railway lines, three National Railway (JR) lines, and three subway lines serving its central and satellite areas. Osaka is served by eight subway lines, twenty-four Japan Railway lines, and twelve other private lines, giving it a network that is as comprehensive as Tokyo's. Kyoto, on the other hand, has only one subway line, and depends primarily on an extensive bus system for its transportation needs.

Japan's subway lines are color-coded, and maps are readily available in tourist and city publications, hotels, and other key outlets.

Tokyo and its satellite villages, towns, and cities are also served by an extensive network of above-ground, high-speed trains operated by Japan Railways and a number of other private companies. This network is made up of twenty-two lines, several of which operate both local and express trains on their respective lines.

Principal transfer points within Tokyo's train system include Tokyo Station, Akihabara, Ueno, Nippori, Ikebukuro, Shinjuku, Tachikawa, Shibuya, and Shinagawa Stations. Shinjuku Station, about two miles west of the Imperial Palace grounds, is often described as the busiest train station in the world. There are also dozens of stations in Tokyo where the train and subway lines come together.

English-language route maps are readily available for all of the commuter and subway lines in Japan. Maps of Tokyo's subway system are especially well-distributed, and are available free at hotels, airline and travel agent offices, and numerous other places.

Commuter Train Tactics and Tickets

Japan's commuter trains and subways are internationally renowned for being on time, efficient, and free of graffiti—most run every two to four minutes during rush hours. Busier lines maintain this kind of schedule throughout the day and evening. They are also famous for being unbelievably crowded—sometimes up to four hundred percent beyond "normal capacity."

This **kotsu jigoku** (kote-sue jee-go-kuu), or "transportation hell" as the Japanese call it, regularly causes bodily injury, not to mention what it does to clothing, but you can avoid most if not all of the danger by learning and practicing a few countermeasures.

Japanese commuters are very good at lining up at individual coach stops along the platforms. In subway stations, especially, the places to stand are clearly marked. But once the interchange of passengers begins it is more or less every man, woman, and child for themselves. The first thing to beware of during rush hour is standing directly in front of a door when it opens to discharge passengers. You must move aside quickly to avoid being pushed aside or run down. On busier platforms there are often station employees who, like sergeants in the army, see that commuters are lined up properly in each waiting area. They also help push passengers into trains when someone has an arm, leg, or other body part sticking out, preventing the doors from closing.

When boarding an extremely crowded train, on which passengers are packed in as tightly as unoiled sardines, try to avoid being caught in the middle of the aisle, where you cannot reach an overhead bar or hand strap to hold onto. In this situation there is too much danger of your losing your footing and balance when the train starts, stops, or sways. You also are likely to be buffeted first one way then the other, each time passengers embark or disembark.

The best idea is to wedge yourself into a corner or niche formed by the seats and sides of the coach next to a door, and turn your back to the crowd. This way you will be protected on two and sometimes three sides, and by holding onto one of the vertical hand bars, you can keep yourself from swaying with the crowd. I once boarded a subway in Shibuya, got stuck in the middle, swayed to an angle of at least twenty degrees from the normal upright position, and stayed that way, held in place by the crowd, until we reached Shimbashi Station downtown some twenty minutes later.

A woman visitor who rides commuter trains during rush hours is advised to avoid wearing high heels; keep her purse in front of her, clutched to her chest; and wear clothing that is not fragile.

The main weekday rush hours are from 7:00–9:30 A.M. and again from around 4:30–7:00 P.M. On holidays and summer weekends, trains going to beach and mountain resort areas are generally packed "beyond capacity," and it is customary for vacationers to form lines several hours in advance of departure times.

Summer mountain climbers and winter skiers literally camp out by the thousands at such stations as Ueno and Shinjuku in Tokyo during the height of these two seasons, sometimes spending as much as half a day and a full night there.

If you choose to ride the commuter or vacation trains, try to do your traveling during off hours. If you plan on taking resort trains during the busiest seasons—and they can be fun with a group—get your tickets as early as possible, with reserved seats if they are available.

Trains and subway stations everywhere in Japan (except a few rural areas) have the names of the stations in Japanese spelled with Latin alphabet letters (which amounts to "English" as far as reading them is concerned), as well as in the native *kanji* (khan-jee) ideograms plus the simplified **hiragana** (he-rah-gah-nah) writing script. This is a tremendous boon for the non-Japanese reading visitor.

Furthermore, most signs, which are repeated several times in each station, include the names of the preceding and following stations, so you know in advance what the next station is going to be. These stations are at the bottom of the signs in smaller letters.

Many subway and commuter train coaches also have route-map signs above their exits, showing all of their stops and where the line intersects with other transfer lines. Some of these signs are electronic, with a light representing the train and showing its progress along the line.

Most tickets for both subways and commuter trains are dispensed by banks of vending machines. Some smaller stations in cities and more in rural areas still operate ticket windows manned by attendants. The ticket sales area is called *Kippu Uri Ba,* or "Ticket Sales Place," and is what you ask for if you are trying to locate it. On the walls above the banks of ticket machines are large route maps showing the fare to each destination on the main line you are boarding as well as on the lines to which you can transfer. Unfortunately, the station names on the maps are not always in Latin alphabet letters, so if you don't recognize the proper *kanji* ideogram, the map doesn't do you any good.

Another problem that often perplexes visitors trying to navigate via trains or subways in Japan is that they cannot identify the line they want to board, or where they want to get off, on the fare wall chart, so they cannot determine their fare. In this case, the easiest solution is to buy the cheapest ticket in the machine. When you get to your destination, go to the ticket adjustment window before you exit through the turnstiles, and hand over the ticket. The attendant will tell you how much more you owe, and will issue you a new ticket for you to give to the collector. Interestingly enough, the ticket adjustment window sign always seems to be in both Japanese and English. The Japanese words for the window are **Ryokaku Unchin Seisanjo** (Rio-kah-kuu Unn-cheen Say-e-sahn-joe).

Additional confusion can result from the fact that some lines sell tickets that are good only on that particular line or system, while others sell "through" tickets that allow you to transfer to intersecting lines; you must pass through the exit turnstiles of the first line to reach the boarding platform of the next line. In this case, of course, you do not turn in your ticket to the collector at the first turnstile. Just hold the ticket out where he can see it and go on through.

Ticket machines generally take ten-, fifty-, and one-hundred-yen coins, and automatically return change. Some newer machines will also take five-hundred-yen coins as well as one-thousand-yen bills. Many of the busier stations have change machines that accept one-thousand-yen notes, returning one-hundred-yen coins. Smaller stations may have machines that give change for one-thousand-yen bills without dispensing tickets. If there is no change machine, the ticket punchers at the turnstiles or in a facing window will give you change. Most machines dispense tickets with set fares; some machines allow you to punch in the fare you are supposed to pay.

There are two categories of tickets on subway and commuter train lines: one for adults and the other for children. The buttons to push for adult tickets are usually higher than those for children. The adult buttons are labeled 大人 **Otona** (oh-toe-nah); the children's buttons read 子供 **Kodomo** (Koe-doe-moe). Some machines have a button you can push when you want two tickets at the same price. If you put in enough money to cover both tickets, you will get them with one push. This button is labeled 二人 **Futari** (Fuu-tah-ree)—"Two (people)."

When ticket machines are out of order or not in use for some reason, they will display a Japanese-language *kanji* sign that reads 発売中止 **Hatsu Bai Chu Shi** (Hot-sue Bye Chuu She), figuratively, "Out of Service." If you can't read the sign but put your money in and nothing happens, there is a nearby button labeled

取（り）消し **Torikeshi** (Toe-ree-kay-she), or "Cancel."

Push it and you will get your money back. There is another button on the panel that you push if you want to call an attendant who works behind the bank of machines. This button is labeled 呼出し **Yobidashi** (Yoe-bee-dah-she)—"Call."

While Tokyo's combination commuter train and subway system is a marvel of efficiency and convenience, one inconvenient factor is that there are two subway systems and although their lines interconnect at several stations, they require different tickets. The various commuter train lines bisecting and crisscrossing metropolitan Tokyo are also operated by different companies and have their own tickets, ticket windows, and ticket vending machines. When two or three of these different ticket machines are lined up side-by-side, knowing which one to use can be a problem if you do not read Japanese *kanji* characters.

The subway lines are color-coded, and this code is generally (but not always) carried over to the ticket vending machines. If you know the line you want to board you can easily spot the correct color code on graphs over the vending machines. The next step is to match the line color with the correct ticket vending machine. The color bars on vending machines that do have them are not very conspicuous, so it is necessary to look closely

If you do not know the line you want to board or cannot match the proper color codes, the next bet is to ask a Japanese ticket buyer who is there at the same time by pointing to one of the ticket vending machines and saying something simple like:

Kore wa Chuo Sen desu ka?
(Koe-ray wah Chuu-oh sin dess Rah?)
Is this the Chuo Line (ticket vending machine)?

Among the main commuter train lines in Tokyo that visitors most often use are the *Chuo Sen* (used in the above example) and *Yamate Sen* (yah-mah-tay sin).

The subway lines present a bit more of a problem. Lines operated by the TRTA (Teito Rapid Transit Authority) system include: *Chiy-*

oda Sen (chee-yoe-dah sin), *Ginza Sen* (gheen-zah sin), *Hanzomon Sen* (hahn-zoe-moan sin), *Hibiya Sen* (he-be-yah sin), *Marunouchi Sen* (mah-rue-no-uu-chee sin), *Tozai Sem* (toe-zie sin), and *Yurakucho Sen* (yuu-rah-kuu-choe sin).

These operated by the TOEI group are: *Toei Asakusa Sen* (toe-eh ah-sock-sah sin), *Toei Mita Sen* (toe-eh me-tah sin), and *Toei Shinjuku Sen* (toe-eh sheen-juu-kuu sin).

Be Aware of Multiple Exits

Train and subway stations in Japan generally have several entrances and exits. It is especially important for you to go out the right exit when you are going to a place you are not familiar with. Going out the "wrong" subway station, for example, can put you as much as half a mile away from a destination that is "right in front of the station." It can also get you utterly lost even though you had specific instructions on how to find a place (since there is no relationship between streets and addresses and most streets have no names!).

Train stations in Japan may have as many as five to ten exits and entrances, with the most common ones being designated as *Kita Deguchi* (kee-tah day-guu-chee)—North Exit; *Higashi Deguchi* (he-gah-she day-guu-chee)—East Exit; *Minami Deguchi*—South Exit; *Nishi Deguchi* (nee-shee day-guu-chee)—West Exit; and *Chuo Deguchi* (chuu-oh day-guu-chee)—Central Exit.

Subway station exits, with some stations having more than a dozen, are designated by letters and numbers or a combination of letters and numbers (A-1, 1-A, A-2, B-2, etc.)

Large conspicuous signboards on train and subway platforms, unfortunately in Japanese only in most cases, specify which exit should be used for a variety of key buildings (including hotels) and named areas and districts around the station.

To avoid what can really become a serious problem, it is wise to have a Japanese print out for you in Japanese the name of the hotel, building or area you want to go to, on a slip of paper or card, so you can show it to a station attendant or fellow traveler for help.

To get directions, show the slip of paper and say:
Deguchi wa nan ban desu ka?
(Day-chuu-chee wah nahn bahn dess kah?)
What is the exit number (for the building/area on this slip)?

Getting to the Trains on Time

It is quite an experience to ride a cross-country train in Japan, particularly the famous Bullet Trains that cruise along at 127 miles per hour. There are three **Shin Kan Sen** (Sheen Kahn Sin), or "Bullet Train," lines in Japan: the **Tokaido-Sanyo** (Toe-kie-doe Sahn-yoe), the **Tohoku** (Toe-hoe-kuu), and the **Joetsu** (Joe-eh-t'sue).

The *Tokaido-Sanyo* line, which serves Yokohama, Atami, Nagoya, Kyoto, Osaka, and other cities on southern Honshu and Kyushu, begins and ends at Tokyo Central Station. The two other Bullet Train lines, which serve northern Honshu and Hokkaido, begin and end at Ueno Station, a few minutes north of Tokyo Station.

There are two kinds of trains on each line, with special names to designate the difference. On the *Tokaido-Sanyo* line, these two kinds of trains are called **Hikari** (He-kah-ree) trains, super expresses that make fewer stops; and **Kodama** (Koe-dah-mah) trains, regular express trains that stop more often.

Super express trains on the *Tohoku* line are called **Yamabiko** (Yah-mah-bee-koe); regular express trains are labeled **Aoba** (Ah-oh-bah) trains. On the *Joetsu* line, the faster trains are known as **Asahi** (Ah-sah-he), and the regular express trains are **Toki** (Toe-kee). You specify which train you want when buying your tickets, based on where you want to stop and your final destination.

Traveling by long-distance train in Japan can be complicated if you are boarding at one of the larger stations such as Tokyo Central Station, Shinjuku, and Ueno stations in Tokyo, where there are many platforms and trains coming and going. The crowds at peak hours can be overwhelming.

The difficulty for nonJapanese-speaking and reading visitors is to locate and board on the right platform, and then determine which train is theirs and where their coach is going to stop. The train number, time, coach number, and seat number (if reserved) is on the ticket, but the labels for these various things are in Japanese only. There are also overhead signs above the platforms that list all the departing and arriving trains, but if you don't know your train number, the signs are of little value.

To eliminate most of the uncertainty from the beginning, have your ticket agent or someone else write out in English the details that are on your ticket so you will know for sure the correct platform number, train number, coach number, and departure time. When you enter the station, don't hesitate to ask the turnstile ticket punchers to help you. In some stations having multiple sections, there are more than one set of platform numbers, and many entrances and exits. Have the entrance you should use clearly identified in advance.

At Tokyo Central Station, for example, if you go into the station on the west side, which is generally thought of as the main entrance, you have to go all the way through the station to the other side (with several turns) to reach the Bullet Train platforms. In this case, it is better to go in on the east or **Yaesu Guchi** (Yie-sue Guu-chee) side of the station, which is the main entrance as far as the Bullet Trains are concerned.

Both sides of the arrival and departure platforms have numbers, since trains use both, so be sure to verify that you are on the correct side of the platform.

To further minimize the chances of missing your train or getting on the wrong one, though it happens all the time, it is wise to get to the station with plenty of time to spare. Once you are in the right place, you can relax, watch the trains or passing crowds, read, or whatever. Also, when trains originate at the station, as many do at Tokyo Central, you can usually board several minutes early, find your seat at your leisure, and even order tea or other drinks and snacks from vendors on the train or the platform.

If you are buying your own ticket, keep in mind that there are several categories, depending on the train and class you are using. There are "Long Distance Tickets" *(Enkyori Kippu)*, "Express Tickets" *(Kyuko Ken)*, "Special Express Tickets" *(Tokubetsu Kyuko Ken)*, ordinary tickets, reserved seat tickets, and unreserved seat tickets. You begin with a basic fare ticket. The second ticket designates the class of seat: unreserved (no extra charge), reserved, or first class (Green Car).

In Japanese, the boarding area for trains is **noriba** (no-ree-bah). Platform is **homu** (hoe-muu), from the Japanized last half of the word "platform." The whole word, **purattohomu** (puu-raht-toe-hoe-muu), is seldom used. First-class coaches are known as "Green Cars," or **Gurin Sha** (Guu-reen Sha).

Another interesting pointer: Long-distance trains going toward Tokyo or other major cities are referred to as *nobori* (no-boe-ree), which means "going up"; in other words, "up lines." Those going away from Tokyo and other major cities are known as **kudari** (kuu-dah-ree), or "down lines."

The Japan Rail Pass

The Japanese Railway's version of the Eurailpass, the Japan Rail Pass (JRP), inaugurated in 1981, is a genuine travel bargain. Used to their fullest, the JRP allows for a 60- to 70-percent savings on all rail travel in Japan—and this includes the famous Bullet Trains. The JRP is also valid for travel on Japanese Railways (JR)-operated ferry and bus lines where such services are available. Unlike its European counterpart, the JRP offers users the option of either first class (Green Cars) or regular class.

Foreign travelers heading for Japan can buy JRP vouchers at overseas offices of the Japan Travel Bureau, Nippon Travel Agency Pacific offices, and Japan Air Lines ticket offices in the United States. After arrival in Japan, the vouchers are exchanged for passes at JR Travel Service Centers (Narita Airport, Tokyo, Ueno, Ikebukuro, Shinjuku, Shibuya, Sapporo, Sendai, Niigata, Yokohama, Nagoya, Kyoto, Osaka, Hiroshima, Shimonoseki, Kokura, Hakata, Kumamoto, and Nishi-Kagoshima). The passes are good for one, two or three weeks. (JR has a counter at Narita Airport in the central causeway building.)

Commuter Trains in Tokyo

Central Tokyo is served by three major commuter train lines, with several other lines coming into the city from outlying districts. The key to the system is the **Yamanote** (Yah-mah-no-tay) Loop Line, which begins at Tokyo Station and goes in a large loop on a northern, western, and southern course (Tokyo Bay is to the east of the central area), connecting almost all of the city's major districts, which serve in turn as terminals for lines coming from the outside (like an inner circle with spokes). *Yamanote* literally means "hilly section," and is used here in the sense of "higher town" or "uptown." (Osaka also has a loop line, called the **Kanjo Sen** [Kahn-joe Sin], which means "Loop Line.")

Tokyo's Loop Line is bisected by the **Chuo** (Chuu-oh), or "Central" Line, which begins at Tokyo Station, circles to the north around the huge Imperial Palace grounds, comes back on course and heads west for fifty miles. Major stops are Shinjuku, Ohgikubo, Tachikawa, Mitaka, and Fuchu.

Another line, the **Keihin** (Kay-heen), comes up from Yokohama, passes through central Tokyo via Tokyo Station, and goes on north to the city of Omiya, seventy-five miles away. The *Yamanote* and *Keihin* Lines run parallel to each other from Shinagawa Station on the south side of Tokyo to Nippori Station on the north side.

These three main rail lines, along with the feeder lines that connect with them at major loop terminals, make it possible to travel to all of the major business and residential concentrations of Metropolitan Tokyo in its twenty-three wards and twenty-six satellite cities. Many of the inner-city stations of these three lines also intersect with one or more of the city's eleven subway lines, adding to the extraordinary convenience of the whole network.

Those Terrific Taxis

Japan's taxi system, just like many of its other industries, is surely the most efficient and provides the highest-quality service of any other taxi system in the world. In the fifties and early sixties, when the Japanese were scrambling to rebuild their wartorn country, taxi drivers had a rather unsavory reputation for reckless driving and speeding. This reputation was not totally deserved, because it wasn't carelessness or recklessness that caused the drivers to careen through streets as if they were in some kind of derby; they simply were trying to increase their income by carrying more passengers each day. Nonetheless, accidents were rare because most of them were consummately skilled drivers.

The taxi system in today's Japan sets the standard for the world. In addition to the private taxicab companies, thousands of drivers are entrepreneurs that operate their own one-cab companies. Dress and behavior codes for drivers are very strict. Each driver must undergo training in etiquette and service. Their cars, which are seldom more than two years old, are kept immaculate. Many have white seat covers, and some drivers add a touch of ambience to their cabs with bouquets of flowers. A few have miniature television sets for the convenience of passengers.

Given the mazelike addressing system in Japan, a language that is written in a script that few foreigners can read, and other travel-related problems, the taxi system is a godsend to most foreign visitors, who would be practically immobilized without them.

Japanese cabs cruise the streets looking for fares. There are also curbside **Takushi Nori Ba** (Tock-she No-ree Bah), or "Taxi Boarding Places," on main streets in downtown areas, as well as at commuter train stations and leading hotels. When the supply of taxis runs out at hotels, doormen go into the streets and flag down cruising cabs. (At major hotels, doormen also supervise the loading and unloading of taxis, and double as interpreters for foreign passengers.)

Since driving in Japan is on the left side of the street, passengers enter and leave cabs through the door on the left side of the vehicle. In virtually all cabs in Japan these doors are opened and closed electrically by the taxi driver. The doors can be opened manually, but there are signs noting that the doors are automatic. Opening and closing the doors by hand tends to strain the automatic mechanism, and is frowned upon.

For the newcomer to Japanese taxicabs, the first thing to learn is that when you approach the left rear door (the one you are going to enter), stand back far enough, or far enough to the rear, so that the door can swing open without bumping into you.

Many taxi users in Japan prefer the privately owned cabs because their owner/drivers tend to be veterans intimately familiar with their territories (they must have a minimum of 10 years' experience to qualify for a license to operate their own company), keep their vehicles in the best possible condition, and are more solicitous of their fares. Privately owned cabs are distinguished by two large, Japanese-language characters (ideograms) either on the doors or on a sign on

top of the cab 個人 that read *Ko Jin* (Koe Jean), or "Privately Owned."

While it is against the law for a taxi driver to refuse a passenger when his cab is empty, it sometimes happens, especially late at night in entertainment districts and when it is raining. On these occasions, the drivers know they can find passengers who will pay them two or three times the meter reading (which they signal by holding up two, three or more fingers).

These less scrupulous drivers also like to pick up groups of Japanese late at night because they will likely be going to different destinations and are therefore profitable fares.

Taxi drivers are not tipped except under unusual circumstances, such as loading and unloading several pieces of luggage, or spending an inordinate amount of time asking directions at police boxes, etc., in an effort to pinpoint a hard-to-find destination for a passenger.

Determining whether a taxi is vacant is easy once you get the hang of it, especially at night. The side of the flag facing out has a red neon sign on it. The ideographic characters on this sign 空車 read **Ku Sha** (Kuu Shah), or "Empty Vehicle." When the flag is up, the red neon sign goes on, and is especially visible at night. When there is a passenger in the cab and the flag is down, the neon sign cannot be seen.

Most taxi flags in Japan also have a second sign on another "arm." This sign 回送 or 廻送 is read **Kai So** (Kie So) and means "Not in Service." It is put up when the driver is taking a break or is finished for the day and does not want to pick up any more fares.

A 20-percent surcharge is added to the regular metered taxi fare between the hours of 11:00 P.M. and 5:00 A.M. The meter also advances every 2½ minutes when the taxi is stopped or moving under ten kilometers per hour.

Going by Bus

Casual, independent bus travel in Japan is generally not recommended for visitors, primarily because of the language barrier. However, buses are certainly plentiful. Destinations are marked on the buses, and their schedules are posted at bus stops. Routes are designated by numbers, and maps in English are available for some lines.

But except at terminals, visitors often cannot recognize bus stops. Maps and signs frequently do not list the interim stops between departure points and final destinations, and only final destinations are displayed on buses. Therefore, if you are not familiar with the route, finding out which bus to board for an in-between stop becomes a problem.

Commuter buses are most often used by people who live in areas not served by trains or subways, and they take them only to the nearest train or subway station. Unless you want to go to a private residence or other place located away from train and subway terminals, buses are usually not the best way to go—not to mention that they also often get hung up in traffic, so there is no way arrival schedules can be guaranteed.

Long-distance bus travel, especially to outlying winter and summer resort areas, is a popular form of transportation, not only from the major metropolitan areas of Japan, but also from provincial capitals and other railway terminals into more remote regions. Such trips from Shinjuku in Tokyo to Mount Fuji and mountain resorts are particularly popular because of the group party aspects, and no need to transfer. Arrangements of this sort must be made well in advance through travel and resort booking agents.

If you do decide to ride the bus on your own, keep in mind that there are two payment systems. On city buses there is a set fare regardless of one's destination. Passengers board from the front of the bus and drop their fares into a fare box, which has a slot for the exact fare and another slot to be used when change is required. The no-change slot is at the back of the fare box, and has a slightly raised receptacle. The change slot is toward front of the fare box and to the left of center. The fare boxes accept one-hundred-, fifty-, and ten-yen coins. Passengers disembark from the rear of the bus.

Buses on which the fare varies with the distance (that go outside of city limits) are boarded from the rear; passengers receive a numbered ticket that is based on their destination. A large fare chart at the front of the bus tells you how much fare will be. You disembark from the front of these buses, putting your fare into the box next to the driver. Buses have buzzers for you to push when you want to get off.

Tokyo's Monorail

Tokyo's single monorail line, from **Hamamatsucho** (Hah-mah-mot-sue-choe) Station in central Tokyo to **Haneda** (Hah-nay-dah) Airport (the city's domestic airport), is a very convenient and inexpensive way to get to Haneda—if you don't have much baggage or are going out to meet someone.

The line starts on an upper-floor level of Hamamatsucho Station and terminates in an underground station beneath the entrance of the main terminal in Haneda. Trains depart every ten minutes, and the trip takes fifteen minutes—part of it over Tokyo Bay, giving passengers a panoramic view of the harbor and its ship traffic.

There are storage racks on each coach for baggage, but of course, if you have several pieces of heavy luggage, getting them on and off of the train can be a pain.

Hamamatsucho Station, where the monorail begins and ends, is the third station south of Tokyo Central Station on both the Keihin Line (which goes on to Yokohama) and the Yamanote Loop Line, which "loops" the central areas of Tokyo in a wide circle. Passengers wanting to ride the monorail may take other trains or subways that connect with either of these lines. Just make sure you get on the train or subway going in the right direction. Major connecting stations include Shibuya and Shinagawa south of Hamamatsucho, and Shimbashi and Tokyo Central on the north side.

If you are in a hurry to get to Haneda, and are near any station that connects with Hamamatsucho, the monorail plus any other public commuter line to Hamamatsucho can often get you there faster than a private car, taxi, or bus, particularly during rush hour, when getting stuck in traffic jams is the norm. Generally, no subway or train, or the monorail, is more than ten seconds off its precise schedule.

Special Disneyland Line

The most practical—and fastest—way to get to Tokyo Disneyland from central Tokyo is via the new Keiyo Line from Yurakucho (yuu-rah-kuu-choe) Station in downtown Tokyo to Maihama Station, which adjoins the Disneyland complex. The trip on this line takes only 20 minutes, versus an hour by other means and routes.

Ship and Ferry Services

Very few travelers to Japan are aware that there is ferry boat service from the ports of Tokyo and adjoining Takeshiba and Kawasaki to Hokkaido, Shikoku, Kyushu, and many of the small islands lying off the eastern coast of Japan, from Oshima in the lower reaches of Tokyo Bay to Chichijima (famed for its scuba diving).

Destinations that have ferry boat service include Kushiro and Tomakomai in Hokkaido; Katsuura on Honshu; Tokushima and Kochi on Shikoku; and Hyuga and Kokura on Kyushu. Passenger ship services are available to the islands of Oshima, Toshima, Nijima, Shikinejima, Kozujima, Miyakejima, Hachijo Jima, and Chichi Jima.

For information about reservations and other details, contact the Japan Long Distance Ferry Association, Iino Building, 9/F, 2-1-1 Uchisaiwaicho, Chiyoda-ku, Tokyo, Japan 100. Tel: 03-3501-0889. Most of the ferry ships are quite large, with passenger capacity ranging from five hundred to fifteen hundred, in addition to space for cars and trucks. Bookings, tickets, and other information are also available at Japan Travel Bureau offices and other travel services in Japan. Here are the main ferry boat operators and their ports of call.

OPERATOR	PORTS FROM/TO	ACCESS TO PORTS
Shin Nihonkai Ferry 06-345-2921 03-3553-3211	Maizuri – Otaru	JR Higashi Maizuru Station
	Tsuruga – Otaru	JR Tsuruga Station
	Niigata – Otaru	JR Niigata Station
Higashi Nihon Ferry 011-518-2718 03-5561-0211	Tomakomai – Sendai	Tagajo Station (JR Senseki Line)
	Muroran – Oarai	JR Muroran Station

Taiheiyo Ferry 052-221-6615 03-3564-4161	Nagoya – Sendai – Tomakomai	Meitetsu Bus Center (Nagoya Futo Ferry) Tomakomai Station
Blue Highway Line 03-3578-1127 06-203-4451	Orai – Tomakomai Tokyo – Tomakomai Tokyo – Nachi – Katsuura – Kochi	Tomakomai Station JR Shimbashi Station JR Kii-Katsuura Station
011-261-6321	Osaka – Shibushi	JR Shibushi Station
Kinkai Yusen 03-5400-6080 0154-24-5134	Tokyo – Kushiro	JR Kushiro Station (Tokyo Ko Ferry Futo)
Marine Express 03-3563-3911	Kawasaki – Hyuga Osaka – Miyazaki	JR Kawasaki Station Osaka Nan Ko Station
06-311-1533	Kobe – Hyuga	Motomachi Station
Ocean Tokyu Ferry 03-3567-0971	Tokyo – Tokushima – Kokura	JR Tokushima Station JR Kokura Station
Kansai Kisen 06-574-9161 03-3274-4271	Osaka/Kobe – Beppu Osaka/Kobe – Matsuyama – Beppu	JR/Subway Bentencho Station Motomachi Station JR Matsuyama Station
Diamond Ferry 078-857-9525	Oita – Matsuyama – Kobe	Hanshin Dentetsu Ashiya Station JR Oita Station
Meimon Taiyo Ferry 06-532-3651 03-3545-1741	Osaka – Shin Moji	JR Moji Station (Osaka Nan Ko)

Hankyu Ferry 078-857-1211 03-3555-3210	Izumi Otsu – Kokura Kobe – Kokura	Nankai Dentetsu Izumi Ohtsu JR/Hanshin Dentetsu Ashiya Station
Muroto Kisen 078-332-2922	Kobe – Kanno-ura – Ashizuri	Hanshin Dentetsu Ohgi Station JR Kaifu Station Tosa Shimizu Bus Terminal

Transportation Vocabulary

Airport
Hikojo   (He-koe-joe)

Boarding area
Noriba   (No-ree-bah)

Bus boarding area
Basu noriba   (Baah-sue no-ree-bah)

Bus stop
Basu teiryujo   (Baah-sue tay-e-ree-yuu-joe)

Coin lockers
Koin rokka   (Koe-inn roak-kah)

Commuter Pass
Teiki Ken   (Tay-ee-kee Ken)

Commuter Pass Sales (place)
Teiki Ken Uriba   (Tay-ee-kee Ken Uu-ree-bah)

Destination (terminus)
Yukisaki   (Yuu-kee-sah-kee)

Driver's license
Unten menjo   (Uun-tane mane-joe)

East gate (exit-entrance)
Higashi guchi   (He-gah-she guu chee)

Fare adjustment window
Ryokaku Unchin Seisanjo
(Rio-kah-kuu Unn-cheen Say-ee-sahn-joe)

Green Car (First Class)
Gurin Sha   (Guu-reen Shah)

Limited express
Tokkyu   (Toke-que)

Local trains
Futsu   (Fute-sue)

Money changer (machine)
Ryogae
(Rio-guy); or **Sen Ensatsu Ryogae** (Sin Inn-sot-sue Rio-guy)—
One-Thousand-Yen Bill Changer

North gate (exit-entrance)
Kita guchi   (Kee-tah guu-chee)

One-way (ticket)
Kata-michi   (Kah-tah-me-chee)

Ordinary express
Kyuko   (Que-koe)

Platform (train)
Homu   (Hoe-muu)

Reserved seats
Shitei seki   (She-tay-e say-kee)

Round-trip (ticket)
Ofuku   (Ohh-fuu-kuu)

South gate (exit-entrance)
Minami guchi   (Me-nah-me guu-chee)

Student's Commuter Pass
Tsu Gaku   (T'sue Gah-kuu)
   (Anyone can buy a worker's commuter pass, but to buy a student
pass, you must have an I.D. card from a recognized school.)

Ticket gate
Kaisatsu guchi   (Kie-sot-sue guu-chee)

Ticket window
Kippu Uriba   (Keep-puu Uu-ree-bah)

Track One
Ichiban Sen   (E-chee-bahn Sin)

Track Two
Niban Sen   (Nee-bahn Sin)

Track Three
Sanban Sen   (Sahn-bahn Sin)

Track Four
Yonban Sen   (Yone-bahn Sin)

Track Five
Goban Sen   (Go-bahn Sin)

Transfer
Norikaeru   (No-ree-kie-rue)

Unreserved seats
Jiyu seki   (Jee-yuu say-kee)

Waiting room
Machiai shitsu   (Mah-chee-aye sheet-sue)

West gate (exit-entrance)
Nishi guchi   (Nee-she guu-chee)

Worker's Commuter Pass
Tsu Ken   (T'sue Ken)

Useful Taxi Phrases

Please go straight
Massugu itte kudasai   Mahss-suu-guu eat-tay kuu-dah-sie

Please turn left
Hidari magatte kudasai   He-dah-ree mah-got-tay kuu-dah-sie

Please turn right
Migi magatte kudasai   Me-ghee mah-got-tay kuu-dah-sie

Please go a little further
Mo sukushi itte kudasai   Moe suu-koe-she eat-tay kuu-dah-sie

Please stop here
Koko de tomatte kudasai   Koe-koe day toe-mot-tay kuu-dah-sie

Please go to Roppongi
Roppongi ni itte kudasai
Rope-pone-ghee nee eat-tay kuu-dah-sie

Other Modes of Transportation

Bicycles, scooters, and motorcycles are popular forms of transportation in Japan, particularly in rural areas, villages, small towns, and suburbs. They are used for both recreational and business purposes, the latter including making small deliveries. Many housewives use bicycles for their daily trips to neighborhood shopping streets. In satellite towns near Tokyo and other major urban areas, bicycles are used by many people to commute to local railway stations when they are going into the city.

Generally speaking, none of these transportation modes is practical for visitors, except for recreation in resort areas, where hotels often have at least bicycles for rent. In cities, traffic congestion and unfamiliarity with the streets make it both inconvenient and dangerous. Touring by bicycle is out of the question for short-term visitors because of the distances involved. The mountainous nature of the islands is also an obstacle for all except experienced bicyclists.

Hitchhiking

The concept of hitchhiking was virtually nonexistent in Japan until it was "imported" into the country from the United States. It is still very rare among Japanese, but is becoming more common among young foreign travelers who are backpacking. Some Japanese drivers who pick up foreign hitchhikers have either been abroad or seen it in Western movies. Some do it as an expression of Japanese hospitality, while others do it to practice their English.

It helps if the foreign hitchhiker knows enough Japanese to engage in a little basic conversation—at least enough to ask for a ride. Another helpful gambit is to carry a Japanese-language *(kanji)* sign giving your destination.

The best place to get rides is roadside restaurants and service stations.

CHAPTER 17

Using Telephones

The Color of Your Phone

Japan's telephone system is one of the most modern in the world, but there are several varieties, sizes, shapes, and colors of public phones, each with different features and uses, that make it all a bit confusing to the newcomer. Japan also appears to have more public telephones than any other country, some of which can be used only for domestic calls, while international calls may be made on others.

Altogether there are five different-colored public phones: blue, green, pink, red, and yellow. All of the phones can be used to make local calls as well as in-country, long-distance direct calls. International calls can be made only from green public phones that have a gold-colored front panel. Only green phones will accept telephone cards; only yellow phones and some green phones will accept both one-hundred-yen and ten-yen coins; and the other colors (blue, pink, and red) accept only ten-yen coins.

Making Domestic Calls

Domestic calls can be made from any public telephone unless it is designated for international calls only. The basic domestic rate for local calls is ten yen for three minutes within a prescribed circumference.

Calls to any of the twenty-three wards of Tokyo and to the wards of other large cities are ten yen for the first three minutes and an additional ten yen for each additional 80 seconds or portion thereof. When using private phones, the additional charge is added automatically. When using public phones, insert additional coins as needed. A buzzer sounds just before each three-minute segment is up. If you do not insert one or more additional coins, the connection will be broken automatically.

To make a collect domestic call, dial 106 (not the area code), tell the operator you want to make a collect call, and give your name and the number to be contacted. Credit-card calls may also be made in Japan from telephone numbers registered with the telephone company for that purpose. Public telephones from which you can make credit-card calls are clearly labeled in both Japanese and English.

To call someone on one of Japan's Bullet Trains, dial 107 and tell the operator which train your party is on. The operator will connect you when your party picks up the train's phone.

Maritime radio-telephone service is also available to ships in port and to vessels sailing near the Japanese coast. Calls can be made to Japanese ocean liners anywhere in the world. Call 06-71-7131 for information.

Long-distances rates range from 30 yen to 360 yen for three minutes, depending on the distance. Night rates are cheaper. From 7:00 P.M. to 8:00 A.M. there is a 40-percent reduction on calls between 60 and 320 kilometers. From 9:00 P.M. to 6:00 A.M., a 50-percent discount is in effect on all calls over 320 kilometers in distance. On Saturdays, Sundays, and national holidays all calls over sixty kilometers in distance are reduced by 40 percent.

One of the special features of communicating by public phones in Japan is the use of telephone cards. Phone cards, good for 50 calls (Y500), 105 calls (Y1,000), 320 calls (Y3,000), or 540 calls (Y5,000), can be bought by anyone from NTT (Nihon Telephone and Telegraph) customer service windows, at retail stores displaying signs that read Telephone Card Retail Store, and from public vending machines.

Green-colored telephones are made especially for telephone cards; some of them are exclusively for cards, while others accept either cards or coins. When you use your card, a digital readout on the phone tells you how many calls you have left on the card. If you talk more than three minutes or make toll calls with your card, the additional surcharges are automatically subtracted from the calls you have remaining (the digital readout keeps you informed as the number decreases). Telephone cards can be used for international as well as domestic calls. You just need to be sure there is enough value on the card to cover the cost of an overseas call.

After you have completed a call using a telephone card, the card reappears in a return slot when you hang up, and a loud beeper sounds for several seconds, reminding you to retrieve the card.

Telephone cards may be customized with company names, logos, and advertising slogans, and are therefore immensely popular for personal use, gifts, and marketing premiums. If you are going to do quite a bit of calling on public phones, obtaining a phone card is very practical.

Sales outlets for telephone cards display a sign that depicts a phone superimposed over a card held in a hand. The Japanese writing across the top of the card in *katakana* reads **Terehon Ka-do** (Tay-ray-hone Kah-doe)—Telephone Card pronounced in Japanese.

Keep in mind that if you want to continue a local public phone conversation beyond three minutes, you must insert additional coins. If no more coins are inserted, a buzzer will sound; a few seconds later the connection is broken automatically when the time is up. If you are not sure how long you are going to talk, put in several ten-yen coins at the beginning. Any that are not used up will be returned when you hang up. You may also put in a one-hundred-yen coin, but the phone cannot return change from one-hundred yen.

For long-distance calls it is more practical, of course, to use one-hundred-yen coins or a phone card.

Making International Calls

Kokusai Denshin Denwa Co. Ltd. (KDD) provides three kinds of international telephone service: direct dial, operator assisted and home-country direct. For direct dial service, the phone you are using must be registered with KDD for International Subscriber Dialing. This includes private home phones as well as business phones. Registration is free, but not all domestic telephone numbers can be plugged into the ISD system automatically, depending on the type of exchange connection. Some require that the number be changed to be compatible with the ISD system. The access code for direct dialing internationally is 001, followed by the country code (the U.S. country code from Japan is "1"), the area code, and the phone number. To dial a number in the Los Angeles area, for example, it is 001-1-213 plus the phone number.

Operator-assisted international calls from Japan are just that, and may be station-to-station, person-to-person, collect, or credit-card calls. To book such a call from anywhere in Japan, dial 0051. For information about booking such calls, dial 0057.

To make use of KDD's home-country direct-dialing service, you dial a special country code that links you to an operator in the country you are calling. Once this operator is on the line, you can place a collect or credit-card call in the normal manner. These calls can be placed from a variety of phones, including private home phones, business phones, public phones, and special phones at major hotels and other key places.

Home-country direct-dial country codes include the following:

U.S.A. Mainland	–	0039-11
Hawaii	–	0039-111 or 0039-181
AUSTRALIA	–	0039-611
FRANCE	–	0039-331
HONG KONG	–	0039-852
UNITED KINGDOM	–	0039-441

With special home-country direct phones it is not necessary to dial a country code. These phones have individual buttons for each of the major countries, so all you have to do is push the appropriate button to get that country's operator on the line.

Telephone numbers in Japan are based on the familiar system of area code, local prefix and subscriber number. The country code for Japan is 81. Area codes for major cities include:

Tokyo	–	03
Yokohama	–	045
Nagoya	–	054
Kyoto	–	075
Osaka	–	06

Overseas phone calls, collect or with phone cards, can be dialed directly from public phones bearing a sign that reads INTERNA-

TIONAL & DOMESTIC CARD/COIN TELEPHONE, with an accompanying line drawing of the globe.

The cheapest time to make international calls from Japan is between 11:00 P.M. and 5:00 A.M. (Japan time), during which international discounts rates are automatically applied. Economy rates (lower than standard rates) are applied from 5:00 – 8:00 A.M. and from 7:00 – 11:00 P.M. The standard rate applies from 8:00 A.M. – 7:00 P.M. Monday through Saturday except on national holidays, when the discount rate is applied.

The "Japan Travel Phone"

The Japan National Tourist Organization operates two toll-free numbers for visitors seeking travel information when they are not in Tokyo or Kyoto. Tourist information numbers in these two cities operate like regular toll numbers, requiring ten-yen coins or more, depending on the length of the conversation. In Tokyo the number to call is 3503-4400; in Kyoto it is 371-5649.

In all other areas of western Japan (south and west of Kyoto), the toll-free number is 0088-22-4800; in eastern Japan (north of Tokyo), it is 0088-22-2800. These numbers can be dialed from all yellow, green, and blue public phones (but not the red ones), as well as from all private phones. When using a public phone to call these toll-free numbers, insert a ten-yen coin before dialing. It will be returned once the connection is made.

The Japan Travel-Phone service is in operation from 9:00 A.M. – 5:00 P.M. daily throughout the year.

Telephone Vocabulary

Telephone
Denwa   (Dane-wah)

Public phone
Koshu denwa   (Koe-shuu dane-wah)

House phone
Okunai denwa   (Oh-kuu-nie dane-wah)

Extension
Naisen   (Nie-sin)

Operator
Kokanshu   (Koe-khan-shuu)

Telephone directory
Denwa cho   (Dane-wah choe)

English-language telephone directory
Eigo no denwa cho   (Aye-go no dane wah choe)

Local call
Shinai denwa   (She-nie dane-wah)

Long-distance call
Cho kyori denwa   (Choe k'yoe-ree dane-wah)

Collect call
Senpo barai-no denwa   (Same-poe bah-rye-no dane-wah)

International call
Kokusai denwa   (Koke-sie dane-wah)

Busy (signal)
Hanasu-chu   (Hah-nahss-chuu)

Hello (in telephone conversation)
Moshi Moshi   (Moe-she Moe-she)

Some Useful Phrases in Japanese

You have a phone call
Denwa desu   Dane-wah dess

Where are the house phones?
Okunai denwa wa doko ni arimasu ka?
Oh-kuu-nie dane-wah wah doe-koe nee ah-ree-mahss kah?

I will call you this afternoon
Kyo gogo ni denwa wo shimasu
K'yoe go-go nee dane-wah oh she-mahss

CHAPTER 18

Driving In Japan

Rules of the Road

Many foreign residents and more and more foreign visitors are taking to Japan's roads in private or rental cars as a way of seeing the countryside and getting from city to city. This is a good idea and is highly recommended, because the island chain is extraordinarily scenic, and the more traditional Japanese lifestyle generally can be seen only in rural areas. But there are many things to know about driving in Japan.

While Japan boasts a growing number of world-class highways and freeways, its typical roadways and streets are very narrow and crowded by American and European standards. Even in the largest cities, only major streets have sidewalks. Smaller cities have fewer sidewalks still, and many towns have none at all. The average street in Tokyo, for example, was formerly a footpath. The only wheeled vehicles that ever passed through such "streets' in earlier days were hand- or horse-drawn carts.

Such streets are generally too narrow for two lanes of traffic, but most of them are two-way streets anyway. Since there are no sidewalks, pedestrians walk anywhere—and there are lots of pedestrians in all but the smaller towns and villages. Cars literally thread their way through these streets, often creeping along at walking speed, and other times moving in rapid spurts that can prove to be dangerous.

A few of Japan's large cities, notably Nagoya and Sapporo, have been partly master-planned and therefore have streets designed for automobile traffic; some sections of Kyoto and Osaka also have wide, grid-style main streets. Even in these cities, however, you are back to lanes once you get away from the downtown areas and off the main thoroughfares.

Adding to the problem of a street system that is mostly imcompatible with automobiles is the concentration of people and automobiles in urban areas. Street signs are another problem for foreign drivers in Japan, because most of the signs are in Japanese. Yet another concern is that in many cases the street signs on narrow, sidewalkless streets are relatively small and have to compete with thousands of other shop-front signs that litter both sides. Being able to spot the signs often requires the eye of an eagle and a lot of practice.

Japan uses international highway symbols on its city freeway signs, so many of them are immediately understandable to the foreign driver. The problem is that the names of locations, especially on Tokyo and Yokohama freeways, often appear only in Japanese *kanji* characters. The freeways also intersect at many locations, but there are a limited number of entrances and exits. If you can't read the *kanji* signs, you cannot determine which freeway goes where or what turnoff to take for what destination—unless you have memorized the twists and turns and recognize visible landmarks that identify where you are.

Outside of cities, virtually all highway and freeway signs are bilingual, and it is about as easy to navigate there as on American or European highways. If you do plan a driving trip that originates in Tokyo, however, you need to map your exit from the city very carefully, with precise instructions and pictorial aids that allow you to identify your route.

For a very useful English-language booklet called *Rules of the Road,* contact the Japan Automobile Federation, 3-5-8 Shiba Koen, Minato-ku, Tokyo, Japan 105.

Psychology of the Road

It is also important that you know something about the psychology of driving in Japan. A primary point is that it is not who "should" have the legal right of way in any situation regarding another vehicle or pedestrian; it is who occupies the space first that determines priority and right and wrong. In other words, if a car pulls out of a side street in front of you and you run into it because you didn't have time to stop, the accident is regarded as your fault because the other car was there first. If a car tries to pass you and gets its nose just a few inches ahead of you, then gets too close and you hit it, it's your fault—the car was "in front" of you.

The Japanese psychology of driving is based on driving defensively. It is up to you to avoid accidents no matter what the other driver does. It is especially important to keep this factor in mind when competing with trucks (particularly construction trucks) for road space. They are large, made of much stronger steel, and are much heavier. You cannot win a duel with them.

Despite these real and apparent drawbacks, seeing Japan by car is well worth the extra care and preparation that is required. As in so many other instances when functioning in a foreign environment, patience, common sense, ordinary caution, and a good sense of humor will almost always allow you to not only survive, but enjoy the experience.

Renting Cars

Rental cars are readily available in Japan from a dozen or so companies, including joint ventures with Avis and Hertz. The system works the same as in the United States and Europe. The names and phone numbers of the various companies are located in hotels, English-language phone books, yellow pages, and local tourist publications.

Driver's Licenses

If you are a visitor in Japan you may obtain an International Driver's License by presenting your passport, present license, and a five-by-four-centimeter photograph, along with the application fee. Your hotel staff can locate the nearest driver's license office for you. A better plan than this, however, is to go to your local AAA or other automobile association or club and get your IDL before leaving for Japan.

Gas Stations

Gas stations are plentiful in Japan, and usually provide a quality and quantity of service that no longer exists in most mobilized countries. When you pull into a station, several attendants swarm around your car; while one pumps gas, the others wash and wipe the vehicle. When their service is finished, one of the attendants will act as a traffic controller to get you safely back onto the usually crowded street.

One of the more interesting solutions to Japan's space problem is the elevated gas pump. Hoses come down from the rafters above, not only saving space, but also preventing potential collisions with gas-filled pumps.

Tolls

Toll roads are common in Japan. Drivers using city expressways and long-distance highways must be prepared to stop and pay at what often appears to be all-too-frequent intervals.

Photo Cops

Japan pioneered the use of remote-controlled, automated cameras as "photo cops" to catch speeders. The cameras zoom in on the license plates of offenders, and a few days later a bill comes in the mail. If you are driving a rented car the rental agency gets the ticket, and will be sure to pass it on to you.

Accidents and Road Assistance

Given the quality of streets in Japan it is amazing that the number of accidents is not much higher than it is. The reason for this is quite simple. The driver training that people must go through before they can obtain a driver's license is probably the most rigorous in the world. The driver's test also includes questions about the mechanics of automobiles that would probably flunk 80 to 90 percent of all foreign drivers.

If you are involved in an accident, it is very important that you get specific vital information from the other driver: his name, address, place of employment, telephone number, and driver's license number, plus the name of his insurance company, the number of his insurance policy, and the car registration number.

If anyone is injured, especially if it's the other party, it is equally important for you to do all you can to aid the injured, and see that an ambulance is called if needed. You also must obtain a certificate of the accident from the police as well as a certificate from the doctor rendering treatment. Without these certificates, insurance cannot be claimed.

All automobiles in Japan must have **Jibaiseki Hoken** (Jee-buy-say-kee Hoe-kaen), or "Compulsory Automobile Liability Insurance," so make sure you have the appropriate papers in the car that you rent.

Emergency telephones are placed along Japan's expressways, and there are regularly spaced pullover areas on most highways. The roadside phones are numbered so you can identify your location if you have to call for help.

The Parking Dilemma

Perhaps the biggest hindrance—and certainly one of the major cost factors—of driving in Tokyo and other large Japanese cities is the severe shortage of parking areas. Because of narrow streets and crowding, Japanese who buy cars must present a certified document providing they have off-street parking at home before they can obtain licenses for their cars.

As mentioned earlier, most city "streets" in Japan are less than two lanes wide and do not have sidewalks. An abundance of telephone poles and various kinds of other poles take up more space. Adding to the parking dilemma: in commercial areas of neighborhood streets, shopkeepers spread their wares out into a portion of the street space during store hours. Delivery trucks made small to cope with this problem buzz in and out of alleys, lanes, and streets like bees.

The percentage of city streets where curbside parking is permitted is very low—perhaps 10 or 15 percent, and this includes both business and residential areas.

Very few businesses in Japan have customer parking. The few that do are relatively new office buildings and hotels with basement parking, an occasional supermarket, and other retail outlets or restaurants where the number of cars that can be accommodated may be as little as four or five.

As a result of the parking crunch, "elevator parking towers," very slender buildings up to seven or eight stories high, are familiar sights, but not common enough to put a dent in the problem.

Renting a car in Japan therefore makes sense only for weekend trips out of the city or for touring purposes. Keep in mind that Japanese regulations require drivers and front-seat passengers to wear seat belts, and the law is strictly enforced. Penalties are charged against the driver/owner of the vehicle.

Some Useful Phrases in Japanese

Is this the road to ——— ?
Kore wa ——— e iku michi desu ka?
Koe-ray wah ——— eh ee-kuu me-chee dess kah?

What is the number of the exit for ——— ?
——— no deguchi no namba wa nan desu ka?
——— no day-guu-chee no nahm-bah wa nahn dess kah?

How many kilometers is it?
Nan kiro desu ka?
Nahn kee-roe dess kah?

Do you have an English-language map of this area?
Kono chiho no Eigo no chizu ga arimasu ka?
Koe-no chee-hoe no A-ee-go no chee-zuu gah ah-ree-mahss kah?

CHAPTER 19

Shopping Scenarios

Bargain Buying

Despite high prices in general and money fluctuations, Japan still offers many opportunities for shopping in areas other than high-tech electronics and optics, which often cost more in Japan even though they are made there. The idea is to buy things in Japan that are non-competitive in world markets—traditional items that are available only in Japan, such as woodblock prints, brocades, wind screens, lacquerware, ironware, earthenware, chinaware, and ceramics.

Another strategy is to do all or most of your shopping in the regions where the items are produced rather than in prestigious shops in luxury hotel arcades, or elite shopping districts like the Ginza in Tokyo. Just one example: buying Noritake china at a factory outlet on the outskirts of Nagoya is not only far more economical than buying it in Tokyo, but going to the factory is also an interesting experience in itself. The same can be said for the ironware of Iwate and Yamagata Prefectures, the lacquerware of Shikoku, the Hakata dolls of Kyushu, the pearls of Toba in Mie Prefecture near Nagoya, and so on.

Many visitors are inclined to do their shopping in Tokyo immediately upon their arrival, in places that are the most convenient—which often means hotel arcades. The only way this can be justified, I believe, is if your time in Japan is so short that you simply don't have time to do anything else. But there are usually other choices even under these circumstances. There are often shopping centers and discount stores within a two- or three-minute walk from your hotel. The International Arcade beneath the elevated railroad tracks immediately behind the Imperial Hotel in Tokyo is an outstanding example. The dozens of shops making up this center carry virtually all of the things visitors to Japan most often want to buy, and at prices that are 20 to 50 percent below the prices charged at hotel arcades and shops along the Ginza, which is just a few blocks farther.

Another way visitors in Japan can make sure they are getting the best possible price is to take advantage of the so-called Tax-Free Shops, which are shops authorized by the National Tax Office to sell certain items tax free to customers who are in the country on tourist visas (and will be taking the items out of the country).

Only certain categories of merchandise are eligible for tax-exempt sales. These include articles made of or decorated with precious or semiprecious stones; pearls and articles made of or decorated with pearls; articles made of precious metals, decorated with gold or platinum, or plated or covered with precious metals; articles made of tortoise shell, coral, amber, or ivory; cloisonne ware; furs; household implements made of fiber; portable TV sets; record players; and stereo equipment.

Also tax-exempt are radios; magnetic tape recorders; cameras; movie cameras and projectors, including parts and accessories; slide projectors; and watches and clocks, when the cases are decorated with precious or semi-precious stones.

The savings at tax-free shops amounts to 10 percent on such popular items as radios and tape recorders, and 15 percent on cameras, record players, movie cameras, and stereo equipment. On some items, the savings is 30 percent.

There are some fourteen-hundred tax-free shops in Japan, 170 of these are in Okinawa, with most of the remainder in Tokyo, Kyoto, Osaka. The shops are generally located in popular shopping areas, often near hotels, and have Tax-Free Shop signs conspicuously displayed at or near their entrances. Most of them advertise in English-language tourist publications that are available free from hotels, airline offices, travel agents, and tourist information centers.

To qualify for the tax exemption, visitors must have their passports on hand, and sign a tax-exempt certificate, which the shop provides and fills out at the time of purchase. The shopper gets a copy of the certificate to turn into Japanese Customs when leaving Japan.

Keep in mind that not all of the shops in hotel arcades are tax-free, and not all items in tax-free shops come under the exemption. Also keep in mind that most "tourist" shops outside of hotel arcades, including the tax-free shops, will discount if you do some good-natured haggling. In my experience over the years, they will invariably come down 10 percent, and sometimes further, especially on items that may have been out for only a year or so but have already been replaced by later models. Bargaining can be especially worthwhile if you are shopping with several friends and go for a group discount.

The Japan National Tourist Organization (JNTO) publishes a shopping directory, *Souvenirs of Japan,* available free from its offices around the world, which lists recommended shops throughout the country by merchandise category, and notes whether they are authorized tax-free shops. The directory also lists the locally produced items that are "best buys" in Sapporo, Nikko, Tokyo, Yokohama, Nagoya, Kyoto, Osaka, and Kobe.

The Japan Quality Store Association, which has members in the most popular travel destinations in Japan, produces and distributes free (also through JNTO offices) a shopper's map showing the location of member shops, with their addresses in both English and Japanese—the latter for showing to taxi drivers.

Going Native and Getting More

If your schedule permits, you often can save money and find unusual items in neighborhood stores where residents do their shopping. There are shopping districts surrounding virtually every train station in the country and "shopping streets," usually two or three blocks long, scattered throughout residential areas.

The railway terminal shopping centers range from one or more major department stores to smart boutiques and specialty stores by the score. Neighborhood shops generally include vegetable, fish, and meat markets, stores selling small kitchen and household items, and electrical appliance stores, plus a drugstore, cosmetics store, bakery, rice shop, and liquor store. There are also discount stores in most terminal shopping centers.

For snack and grocery shopping, which is a great way to save food money while in Japan, you have many choices, including the huge food sections of department stores (always in the basements), super-markets such as the Meidiya and Daiei chains, and convenience market chains (Circle K, 7-Eleven, etc.).

Using the Metric System

The metric system is the standard unit of measure in Japan. Here are metric equivalents of the American system:

One inch = 2.540 centimeters
One foot = 30.480 centimeters
One yard = 0.914 meters
One mile = 1.609 kilometers

One square inch = 6.451 square centimeters
One square foot = 0.093 square meters
One square yard = 0.836 square meters

One cubic inch = 16.387 cubic centimeters
One cubic foot = 0.028 cubic meters
One cubic yard = 0.765 cubic meters

One ounce = 28.349 grams
One pound = 0.453 kilograms

One short hundred-weight = 45.359 kilograms
One long hundred-weight = 50.802 kilograms
One short ton = 0.907 metric tons
One long ton = 1.016 metric tons

One fluid ounce = 29.573 milliliters
One fluid pint = 0.473 liters
One fluid quart = 0.946 liters
One fluid gallon = 3.785 liters

One pint = 0.550 liters
One quart = 1.101 liters
One peck = 8.809 liters
One bushel = 35.238 liters

How Big Are You in Japanese?

Clothing and shoe sizes in Japan are based on the metric system as well as a traditional Japanese numerical system. The following table shows the relationships between Japanese sizes and U.S. and European sizes:

DRESSES

Japanese size	7	9	11	13	15	
(waist)	60cm	63cm	66cm	69cm	72cm	
American size	8	10	12	14	16	18
U.K. size	32	34	36	38	40	42
French size	36	38	40	42	44	46
Italian size	38	40	42	44	46	48

WOMEN'S SHOES

Japanese size	22	$22^1/_2$	23	$23^1/_2$	24	$24^1/_2$	25
U.S. & U.K. size	$4^1/_2$	5	$5^1/_2$	6	$6^1/_2$	7	$7^1/_2$
Cont. Europe size	34	35	36	37	38	39	40

MEN'S SHOES

Japanese size	24	$24^1/_2$	25	$25^1/_2$	26	$26^1/_2$	27	$27^1/_2$
American size	$6^1/_2$	7	$7^1/_2$	8	$8^1/_2$	9	$9^1/_2$	10
U.K. size	$5^1/_2$	6	$6^1/_2$	7	$7^1/_2$	8	$8^1/_2$	9
French size	38	39	40	41	42	43	44	45

MEN'S HAT SIZES

Japanese size	53	54	55	56	57	58	59	60
American size	$6^1/_2$	$6^3/_4$	$6^7/_8$	7	$7^1/_8$	$7^1/_4$	$7^3/_8$	$7^1/_2$

LADIES' HAT SIZES

Japanese size	53	54	55	56	57	58	59	60	61
American size	21	$21^1/_4$	$21^1/_2$	22	$22^1/_2$	23	$23^1/_4$	$23^1/_5$	$24^1/_4$

SOCK SIZES

Japanese size	23	$24^1/_5$	$25^1/_2$	27	28	29	30
U.S./U.K. size	9	$9^1/_2$	10	$10^1/_2$	11	$11^1/_2$	12
Cont. Europe size	23	$24^1/_2$	$25^1/_5$	$26^3/_4$	28	$29^1/_4$	

STOCKING SIZES

Japanese size	20¼	21½	23	24¼	25⅕	27
U.S./U.K. size	8	8½	9	9½	10	10½
Cont. Europe size	20¼	21½	22¾	24	25¼	26½

JACKET SIZES

Japanese size	A4	A5	A6	A7	AB4	AB5	AB6	AB7
U.S./U.K. size	36ES	37S	38S	39R	38ES	39S	40S	41R
Italian size	44-6	46-6	48-6	50-6	44-4	46-4	48-4	50-4

SHIRT SIZES

Japanese size	36	37	38	39	40	41	42
U.S./U.K. size	14	14½	15	15⅕	16	16⅓	
Cont. Europe size	36	37	38	39	40	41	42

Shopping Vocabulary

Advertised specials
Kokoku no Shina   (Koe-koe-kuu no She-nah)

Bargain
Bagen
(Bah-gain); **Seru**   (Say-rue); **O-Uri Dashi** (Oh-Uu-ree Dah-she)

Bargain floor (in a department store)
Daisai Jo   (Die-sie Joe)

Change (money)
O'tsuri   (Oh-tsue-ree)

Country of origin
Gensan koku mei   (Gain-sahn koe-kuu may-e)

Department store cashier
O'kanjo Ba   (Oh-kahn-joe Bah)

Department store information counter
Ten-nai Go-Annai   (Tane-nie Go-on-nie)

Exchange
Torikaeru   (Toe-ree-kie-rue)

Folkcraft
Mingei-hin   (Mean-gay-e-heen)

Generic products
No burando shohin   (no buu-rahn-doe show-heen)
Also: **Mujirushi shokuhin**   (Muu-jee-rue-she show-kuu-heen)

Half price
Han Gaku   (Hahn Gah-kuu)

Instruction sheet/brochure
Setsumei sho   (Say-tsue-may-e show)

Made in Japan
Nihon sei   (Nee-hone say-e)

Newly on sale
Shin hatsu bai   (Sheen hot-sue by)

Out of stock
Genpin kagiri   (Gane-peen kah-ghee-ree)

Present, souvenir
O'miyage   (Oh-me-yah-gay)

Receipt
Ryoshusho   (Rio-shuu-show)

Sale
Seru   (Say-rue)

Sold out
Urikire   (Uu-ree-kee-ray)

Special price
Tokka   (Toak-kah)

Super special price
Cho tokka   (Choe toak-kah)

Today only
Honjitsu kagiri   (Hoan-jeet-sue kah-ghee-ree)

20-percent discount
Ni (2) waribiki   (Nee wah-ree-bee-kee)

30-percent discount
San (3) waribiki   (Sahn wah-ree-bee-kee)

Please wrap up
Tsutsunde Kudasai   (T'sue-t'soon-day Kuu-dah-sie)

Japan's Famed *Depaato*

Japan's department stores are in a class by themselves. In addition to selling dry goods, foods, and beverages, they are also venues for regular cultural activities, including art shows and handicraft exhibits. A trip to Japan could hardly be complete without a visit to one or more of the larger department stores—some of which date back more than two hundred years. Here are some of the best-known ones:

Daimaru (Die-mah-rue)   **Mitsukoshi** (Me-t'sue-koe-she)
Hankyu (Hahn-que)   **Seibu** (Say-e-buu)
Isetan (E-say-tahn)   **Sogo** (So-go)
Marui (Mah-rue-e)   **Takashimaya** (Tah-kah-she-mah-yah)
Matsuzakaya (Mah-t'sue-zah-kah-yah)

CHAPTER 20

Toilet Pointers

Finding the "Convenient Place"

Toilets in Japan have a very interesting history, and not too long ago a book by a professional toilet salesman, telling about his experiences, made the best-seller list. Probably the most memorable story about the use of Japan's pit toilets in feudal times was how a **ninja** (neen-jah) assassin was able to get the upper hand on his target by submerging himself in the pit and waiting until nature brought his victim to him.

The most recent toilet to make national news in Japan is a public privy located in the parking lot of a supermarket in northern Honshu. Designed by avant-garde architect Wasaku Kuno, it cost over $2 million to construct. The owner of the supermarket said he had the "Tokyo Tower of toilets" built to show appreciation to his customers.

There are several words for toilet in Japanese. Women generally use **gofujo** (go-fuu-joe), which means "the honorable motion place," or **O'toire** (Oh-toy-ray), which is simply the Japanese pronunciation of toilet. Both men and women frequently use the word **O'tearai** (Oh-tay-ah-rye), or "honorable hand washing," which is the equivalent of our washroom. Men (and young boys) in informal situations will often use the more colloquial **benjo** (bane-joe), which literally means "convenient place."

The traditional Japanese *benjo* deserves some comment, since you are likely to encounter one or more of them in older inns and private homes as well as in traditionally styled Japanese restaurants and mountain-climber huts.

Basically, the *benjo* consists of either (1) an aperture over a pit in the ground; (2) a ceramic flush bowl over a pit; or (3) a ceramic flush toilet that is connected to an underground sewerage system. The first type is the most primitive, and the last type is the most modern. The one common feature that all of the types share is that the user squats over the aperture or the flush bowl.

Before anyone begins putting this kind of toilet facility down, Western medical and health authorities are unanimous in saying that the natural and most desirable position for using a toilet is the squat. Of course, this is no particular help to a person who is many pounds overweight and hasn't squatted in thirty years or more. Since many Americans and Europeans are in this category, it behooves them to find out if they *can* squat before visiting a place that has only the old-fashioned *benjo* facilities.

Most public places in Japan—hotels, restaurants, better bars and clubs, and office buildings—have Western flush-type commodes and urinals. But in older private homes and buildings in rural areas, the nonflush pit-type is still common.

Japanese toilets, especially in small apartment buildings and some bars and restaurants, are very small—so small, in fact, that a large person may have difficulty getting down and up in them. One can squat in a smaller place than he can get up in, and if you find yourself in this position, the only solution is to waddle out into the hallway and stand up there. (The overall size of the Japanese has increased dramatically since 1945, but since they still see themselves as "small," the scale of things, from toilets and bus seats to doorway heights, has not yet caught up.)

At inns, guests wear felt or plastic slippers when walking around in the hallways and lobbies, but the same slippers are never worn into toilets. There are separate "toilet slippers" for that, kept just inside the toilet door. You leave your regular slippers outside (the sight of which lets others know immediately that there is someone in the toilet).

Sharing Your Toilet with Others

There still are public toilets in Japan (especially in some restaurants and night spots) that are unisex, so don't be surprised if a member of the opposite sex trots in behind you—or is already ensconced when you enter. Just act like it's old hat, and enjoy yourself. Larger night-clubs frequently have female attendants in the men's room as well as the women's. If you encounter this situation it should, of course, be taken in stride. Cleaning crews who take care of public toilets in leading hotels also are usually women who go blithely about their business while male and female users go about theirs.

Take special notice that toilets on trains, except for those on the Green Cars (first-class cars) of the famous Bullet Trains, are usually squat style. Women wearing high-heeled shoes may want to remove them before using such toilets because the motion of the train may present problems otherwise.

If you are going to be out of your hotel or inn for long periods of time, it is wise to carry toilet paper with you in your purse or pocket, because it often happens that public toilets have run out. Little pack-ets of tissue paper that are an ideal substitute are sold in many kinds of stores, from convenience markets and drug stores to places selling paper products. They are also often given away on the streets as pro-motional items.

Most larger office buildings in Japan have toilets in their base-ments and on all floors except the first or ground floor, and are open to people visiting the buildings. These can be lifesavers when you are out on the town. Larger hotels are also places to keep in mind for emergency use. Some hotels have toilets on their ground floors; oth-erwise, try the basement (especially if there is a shopping arcade there), or the second floor, where there are frequently banquet and meeting rooms requiring toilet facilities.

Some Useful Phrases in Japanese

Excuse me, where is the nearest toilet?
Sumimasen, ichiban chikai no otearai wa doko desu ka?
Sue-me-mah-sin, ee-chee-bahn chee-kie no oh-tay-ah-rye
wah doe-koe dess kah?

Is there a toilet on this floor?
Kon kai ni otearai wa arimasu ka?
Kone kie nee oh-tay-ah-rye wah ah-ree-mahss kah?

What floor is the toilet on?
Otearai wa nan kai desu ka?
Oh-tay-ah-rye wah nahn kie dess kah?

Is there a toilet in this station?
Kono eki ni otearai wa arimasu ka?
Koe-no a-kee nee oh-tay-ah-rye wah ah-ree-mahss kah?

May I use your toilet?
Otearai wo tsukatte mo ii desu ka?
Oh-tay-ah-rye oh scot-tay moe ee dess kah?

I have to go to the toilet
Otearai ni ikanakereba narimasen
Oh-tay-ah-rye nee ee-kah-nah-keh-ray-bah nah-ree-mah-sin

CHAPTER 21

Gift-Giving Etiquette

When and How to Give Gifts

Gift-giving in Japan is a major institutionalized custom that dates back to the hierarchal structure of the country's feudalistic society. Without a body of law to guarantee individual rights, staying on the good side of higher-ranking individuals and those in power could be achieved only by obeying carefully prescribed rules of conduct. Officials were catered to further with the presentation of gifts on a number of established occasions during the course of a year, as well as on special occasions when one needed a favor.

So important and so widespread did this gift-giving custom become, and so numerous and meticulous were the rules governing the custom, that each family had to have someone specialize in the details of gift-giving to do it properly and thereby avoid problems that could be more serious than not giving a gift at all.

While the sanctions against the failure to give gifts, giving the wrong gifts, or giving them improperly are no longer life-threatening, all of these details are still important in today's Japan. The reasons for so much gift-giving certainly have not changed. Companies give gifts to customers, workers give gifts to their employers, families give gifts to their doctors and to their children's teachers, newly married couples get gifts, people who travel domestically or overseas return with gifts for their families and friends, and businessmen who travel abroad give token gifts to virtually everyone who does them a good turn. Other gift-giving occasions include funerals, births, farewells, birthdays, special holidays, and visits to private homes.

Besides all the individual occasions when people give gifts, there are two major gift-giving seasons each year, when most companies as well as many people give gifts to those who have done them favors or are important to them. The first of these seasons is called **O-Chugen** (Oh-Chuu-gain), or "Mid-Year," and the second is called **O-Seibo** (Oh-Say-e-boe), or "End of the Year."

These are the two biggest sales periods in Japan, and are the equivalent of the Christmas buying season in the United States. Thousands of items especially packaged for these seasons appear in shops, and there are sales campaigns galore. Food items as well as *O'sake,* beer, wine and whiskies are favorite gifts for both seasons.

Cash is one of the most common gifts given in Japan today for birthdays, weddings, funerals, trips, and at year's end. The money is invariably in cash and usually consists of **shin satsu** (sheen sot-sue), or "new bills," since old, wrinkled bills would give a bad impression. Special envelopes called **noshi bukuro** (no-she buu-kuu-roe) which contain the cash are also important. There is one kind of envelope to be used when the cash is for a new bride and groom, another kind when it is for a family that has suffered a death, etc. The envelopes are sold in stationery stores, and if you are not sure which envelope is appropriate for the occasion, the store clerks can tell you.

The amount of money given is determined by the occasion and, of course, the financial status of the people involved. The only "safe" thing to do if you are a novice at gift-giving in Japan is to ask an older Japanese to advise you.

The kind of wrapping paper used for packaging gifts is also determined by the occasion. When you buy the paper (also at stationery stores), tell the clerk what you intend to use it for to make sure you get the proper kind.

For travelers who want to give gifts while in Japan, personal accessories (of high quality) are appropriate. Also, products made in the West, especially traditional or handcrafted items, are appreciated.

What to Give

If you are visiting someone's home, gift items that are popular and appropriate include packaged fruit, cakes, candy, cookies, and tea; gift-packaged seaweed of a name brand such as **Yamamoto Yama** (Yah-mah-moe-toe Yah-mah); roasted chestnuts; or, if you have been on a trip, the **meibutsu** (may-e-boot-sue), or "famous product," of the area you just visited, such as apples from the Tohoku region or crabs from Hokkaido.

If you are calling on a businessman at his home or office, and are in his debt for any kind of hospitality or want a favor from him, appropriate gifts include a name-brand Scotch whiskey, brandy, or wine. Cases of beer are common gifts during the year's two major gift-giving seasons. These and other heavy, bulky gifts are normally delivered by the store or a professional delivery service.

If you know a family, particularly if you have a family relationship, it is common to give the children a gift of money at New Year's, again in a special money envelope. This gift is known as **Otoshi Dama** (Oh-toe-she Dah-mah), which means something like "New Year's Gem."

Gift certificates issued by prestigious department stores and other specialty outlets are also major gift items. Telephone cards with a value of three thousand or five thousand yen also are appreciated as gifts.

When giving gifts in Japan it is best to give items in odd lots, such as three, five, or seven, to avoid any implications of bad luck.

Some Useful Phrases in Japanese

This gift is for you
Kono O'miyage wa anata ni desu
Koe-no Oh-me-yah-gay wah ah-nah-tah nee dess

Please accept this gift
Dozo, kono O'miyage wo osamete kudasai
Doe-zoe, koe-no Oh'me-yah-gay oh oh-sah-may-tay kuu-dah-sie

I'm sorry, but I cannot accept
Sumimasen ga, itadaku koto ga dekimasen
Sue-me-mah-sin gah, ee-tah-dah-kuu koe-toe gah day-kee-mah-sin

Thank you for the beautiful gift
Kirei na O'miyage ni arigato gozaimasu
Kee-ray-ee nah Oh-me-yah-gay nee ah-ree-gah-toe go-zie-mahss

Who is this for?
Kore wa dare no tame desu ka?
Koe-ray wah dah-ray no tah-may dess kah?

It's for your wife
Anata no oku-san no tame desu
Ah-nah-tah no oak-sahn no tah-may dess

Please take this to your daughter
Kore wo musume ni motte itte kudasai
Koe-ray oh muu-sue-may nee moat-tay eat-tay kuu-dah-sie

I would like to give something to your son
Nanika musuko ni agetai desu
Nah-nee-kah muu-sue-koe nee ah-gay-tie dess

What does he like?
Nani ga suki desu ka?
Nah-nee gah ski dess kah?

CHAPTER 22

In a Japanese Home

Mixed Traditions

Typical Japanese do not invite business associates or casual acquaintances, much less strangers, to their homes the way Americans and Europeans tend to do. The main reason this practice did not develop in Japan was that most homes and apartments were so small that they would not accommodate more than the family members with anywhere near the expected degree of comfort.

The size and style of Japanese houses as well as the custom of home entertaining are changing, however. Nowadays many affluent urban and rural Japanese live in homes and apartments that are larger and often basically Western style, with hardwood or carpeted floors, sofas, chairs, coffee tables, etc.

Japanese who have lived and traveled abroad and become familiar with Western customs regularly invite friends to their homes. There are also cosmopolitan Japanese living in the traditional way who delight in entertaining foreign guests as a way of sharing their culture. At present there are sixty such families in Tokyo who are registered with the city government as part of its home visit program.

JNTO's Tourist Information Center (first floor, Kotani Building, 1 Yurakucho, in downtown Tokyo) can arrange a home visit with one of these families for you. There is no charge for the visits, but taking a gift is good manners. The maximum number of visitors in a group is five; visits begin around 7:30 P.M. and usually last for around one hour. Application for home visits must be made at the TIC in person, at least one day in advance.

Home visits in Osaka can be arranged through the Osaka Tourist Information Center in the JR Shin-Osaka Station (the Bullet Train station) and the Osaka Tourist Information Office in the original JR Osaka Station.

The Tourist Information Center (tel: 305-3311) is open from 8:00 A.M.–8:00 P.M., and the Tourist Information Office (tel: 345-2189 or 345-6020) from 8:00 A.M.–7:00 P.M. Both offices will accept applications by phone. Over eighty Osaka families are registered with the Osaka Tourist Association as "host families," and each family has at least one member who speaks English.

All of the families involved in Japan's home visit programs express a deep desire to get to know foreign people on a personal basis and help spread goodwill around the world as their primary motivation for participating in the program. A number of the families say they have become lifelong friends with some of their visitors, and have visited them in their homes abroad.

If you do visit a Japanese home, whether it is totally Japanese style, partly Japanese style or fully Western style, the custom is to remove your shoes in the entrance foyer and put on slippers that will be provided for you. These slippers are to be worn only in hallways and into rooms that have wooden or carpeted floors—not *tatami* floors. If you are directed to a room with a reed-mat floor, leave the slippers in the hallway.

If you are wearing a heavy coat, it is polite to remove the coat while you are still in the entrance foyer, where you remove your shoes. There will also usually be a place for umbrellas in the foyer.

If the room is Japanese style, it will normally have a **tokonoma** (toe-koe-no-mah), or "beauty alcove," where either a flower arrangement or hanging scroll is on display. The seat nearest this alcove is the "honor seat," where guests are generally placed. A guest who is very junior to the host in age and rank should vigorously decline the "seat of honor," in deference to the host, accepting it graciously only if the host continues to insist just as vigorously.

In any event, it is polite to hold back and allow your Japanese hosts to direct you where to sit; it is very rude to sit in the place of honor without being invited to do so.

It is customary to take a gift when you are invited to someone's home, especially for the first visit, a special occasion, and other times as well if there is a long time between visits and the invitation includes a meal. Gifts that are acceptable include baskets of fruit, cakes, boxes of cookies, assortments of fresh-baked pastries, wine, brandy, whiskey, candy, special breads, or something from abroad, such as frozen steak, lobster, canned preserves, etc.

No special etiquette beyond what is mentioned above is needed for you to behave properly in a Japanese home. If you are offered some kind of refreshment or food that you are not familiar with, of course it is good manners to at least try it.

Exploring Japan's Culture

The Japan National Tourist Organization also sponsors a program called "Explore Japanese Culture," an extension of its home visit program in that it allows foreign visitors to actually participate in various cultural activities in host facilities and homes.

Among the cultural activities covered by the program are painting; ceramics; paper making; doll making; calligraphy; flower arranging; *origami; koto* and *shamisen* playing; woodblock print making; *sake* brewing; *haiku* composing; *aikido, judo* and other martial arts; carpentry; and public-bath visiting.

Cities that are participating in the program include Beppu, Fukuoka, Hiroshima, Kagoshima, Kanazawa, Kobe, Kumamoto, Kyoto, Matsue, Matsumoto, Miyasaki, Nagasaki, Nara, Okayama, Osaka, Sendai, Tokyo, and Yokohama.

Tokyo has the largest number of participating facilities, which include newspapers; stock and bond exchanges; broadcasting operations; auto-making plants; Buddhist temples; meditating, cooking, and martial arts studios; along with cultural handicrafts and arts studios.

This, of course, is the kind of personal involvement that is the basis for this book—the more things you *do,* the more you will enjoy your trip. The first step is to decide on what type or types of activity you would like to experience; next, contact the nearest office of the JNTO. It will tell you which cities offer what you want, and will provide you with the necessary information to contact the tourist office of the appropriate city for the arrangements. There is no charge, and up to five people can participate as a group.

Some Useful Phrases in Japanese

The following words and phrases are set expressions that have become institutionalized over the centuries. They are said the same way every time in the same setting.

Gomen kudasai (Go-mane kuu-dah-sie)—This phrase more or less means "Please excuse me," but is an institutionalyzed phrase used by visitors to announce their presence in the entryway, much like calling out "Hello!" It is very polite.

Ojama shimasu (Oh-jah-mah she-mahss)—This is another stock phrase that is used after you have announced yourself and been invited to enter a home. It means something like "I will bother you," and is more or less an apology.

Itadakimasu (E-tah-dah-kee-mahss)—This is the set phrase said when you are being hosted at a home or restaurant and first start to eat or drink. It is similar in meaning to "I receive it (the food or drink)," but has a more formal, gracious connotation.

Gochiso sama deshita (Go-che-so sah-mah desh-tah)—This is what you say to your host after you have finished eating or drinking at someone else's expense. It means something like "thanks to you it was delicious."

Ojama shimashita (Oh-jah-mah she-mahss-tah)—This phrase is said to your host as you are leaving. It means, "I have intruded" or "I have bothered you."

Domo arigato gozaimashita (Doe-mo ah-ree-gah-toe go-zie-mahssh-tah)—"Thank you very much." This is the final thing you say to your host as you bow in the foyer, or after you have stepped outside if there is no foyer.

I really enjoyed myself
Honto ni tanoshikatta   Hone-toe nee tah-no-she-kot-tah

Thank you very much for your hospitality
Shinsetsu-na motenashi ni taihen arigato gozaimashita
Sheen-say-t'sue-nah moe-tay-nah-she nee tie-hane
ah-ree-gah-toe go-zie-mahssh-tah

You are welcome/Don't mention it
Do itashimashite   Doe ee-tah-she-mahssh-tay

Please come again any time
Itsudemo irrashite kudasai
Eet-sue-day-moe ee-rahssh-tay kuu-dah-sie

CHAPTER 23

Mailing Things

The Postal System

If there is one area in which the West is still ahead of the Japanese, it may very likely be post offices. I have been using Japanese post offices since 1949, and have seen very few changes other than the introduction of electronic scales. Perhaps the biggest difference between a Japanese post office and most of those in the United States and elsewhere is that Japanese ones often do not have full-service windows. In some post offices virtually every function requires that you go to a different window: one for stamps for letters, one for packages, one for special delivery mail, one for airmail form letters, one for overseas letters, etc. If you have two or three items in as many categories, it may be necessary to go to as many windows. When the post office is busy, this can be a lengthy process.

Once you get beyond the style of operation, Japanese post offices offer the same services as their counterparts abroad, with a few additional ones, such as savings programs.

Postal subbranches generally do not handle overseas packages or letters requiring special services such as registration, certification, or insurance. These items must be taken to a **hon kyoku** (hone k'yoe-kuu), or "main post office." Exceptions are small stations set up especially to handle international mail; the sub-station in Tokyo's Imperial Hotel is an example.

Hours at main post offices are 9:00 A.M.–7:00 P.M. Monday through Friday, 9:00 A.M.–3:00 or 5:00 P.M. on Saturdays, and 9:00 A.M.–12:30 P.M. on Sundays and national holidays.

Street mailboxes for regular mail are red and have two slots. The one on the right side of the box is for local mail, and the one on the left is for out-of-city and foreign mail. At Tokyo Central Post Office, the boxes for foreign mail are clearly marked "Foreign Mail." Blue mailboxes are for special-delivery mail.

Size Limits

Japanese postal regulations specify acceptable envelope sizes. Post cards cannot be under nine by fourteen centimeters; have a single dimension over sixty centimeters; or have combined dimensions of more than ninety centimeters. Black or brightly colored cards are taboo.

Size specifications are divided into two categories, packages and parcels, with different specifications for parcels going to the United States, Canada, the Philippines, and the Republic of South Africa.

For general packages to all countries, the minimum size is nine by fourteen centimeters; the maximum single dimension is sixty centimeters, and the maximum combined dimensions are ninety centimeters.

For cylindrical packages to all countries, minimum length is ten centimeters; minimum combined dimensions are seventeen centimeters (length plus twice the diameter). Maximum length is ninety centimeters, and maximum combined dimensions are 104 centimeters (length plus twice the diameter).

For parcels to the United States, the maximum single dimension is $1^{1}/_{4}$ meters and overall volume is eight cubic meters. Packages to Canada and the Phillipines must have a single dimension of no more than 1.05 meters, and combined dimensions of two meters or less. For parcels to South Africa, the maximum single dimension is 1.05 meters, and the maximum combined dimensions are 1.8 meters.

For parcels to other countries there are A and B size limitations, depending on the country. A-size countries: single dimension maximum is $1^{1}/_{2}$ meters, and the maximum combined dimensions are three meters. B-size countries: the single dimension maximum is 1.05 meters, with a maximum combined dimension of two meters. The minimum for both A and B countries is nine by fourteen centimeters.

Weight limits for parcel post are ten kilograms. Parcels going to A and B countries that are oversized may be subject to a supplementary charge equal to 50 percent of the principal surface mail charge.

Postal Vocabulary

Airmail
Kokubin   (Koe-kuu-bean)

Insurance
Hoken   (Hoe-ken)

International post office
Kokusai Yubin Kyoku   (Koke-sie Yuu-bean K'yoe-kuu)

International reply coupons
Kokusai henshin kitte ken   (Koke-sie hane-sheen keet-tay ken)

Letter
Tegami   (Tay-gah-me)

Money coupons
Ko gawase   (Koe gah-wah-say)

Money envelopes
Genkin futo   (Gane-keen fuu-toe)

Post card
Ha gaki   (Hah gah-kee)

Post office
Yubin kyoku   (You-bean k'yoe-kuu)

Registered Mail
Kaki tome   (Kah-kee toe-may)

Seamail
Funabin   (Fuu-nah-bean)

Special delivery
Soku tatsu   (Soe-kuu tot-sue)

Stamp
Kitte   (Keet-tay)

Zip code
Yubin bango   (You-bean bahn-go)

Zip code directory
Yubin bango bo   (You-bean bahn-go boe)

Some Useful Phrases in Japanese

I want to mail this to France
Kore wo Furansu ni dashitai desu
Koe-ray oh Fuu-rahn-sue nee dah-she-tie dess

Please send this special delivery
Kore wa soku tatsu ni shite kudasai
Koe-ray wah soe-kuu tot-sue nee ssh-tay kuu-dah-sie

Where can I mail this package?
Kono tsutsumi wa doko de dasu koto ga dekimasu ka?
Koe-no t'sue-t'sue-me wah doe-koe day dah-sue koe-toe gah day-kee-mahss kah?

CHAPTER 24

Pronunciation Guide

How to Pronounce Key Japanese Regions, Cities, and Prefectures

One of the biggest handicaps facing first-time visitors to Japan is not being able to pronounce names of places and things that play an important role in becoming "oriented" to the country—even for the short time of a typical trip. These words include names for districts within cities, the cities themselves, and prefectures and regions of the country. Names of city districts are especially important because you often hear them and need to say them to travel on even the lowest level.

The following pronunciation guide will help alleviate this frustrating problem. The guide starts with the prefectures and their capitals, which are the principal cities in each of the prefectures. For your additional information, Japan in Japanese is **Nihon** (Nee-hone). The four main islands are **Hokkaido** (Hoke-kie-doe), **Honshu** (Hone-shuu), **Kyushu** (Que-shuu) and **Shikoku** (She-koe-kuu). Honshu is the largest of the islands, and is where Tokyo, Yokohama, Nagoya, Kyoto, Osaka, Kobe and other key cities are located.

The two regional names that you are most likely to hear are **Kanto** (Kahn-toe), which refers to the Tokyo area, and **Kansai** (Khan-sie), which refers to the Kyoto-Kobe-Osaka area. A third regional name that often is used in ordinary conversation about Japan is **Tohoku** (Toe-hoe-kuu), which refers to the large district making up the northeast portion of Honshu.

PREFECTURES	CAPITALS
Aichi (Aye-chee)	**Nagoya** (Nah-go-yah)
Akita (Ah-kee-tah)	**Akita** (Ah-kee-tah)
Aomori (Ah-oh-more-ree)	**Aomori** (Ah-oh-more-ree)
Chiba (Chee-bah)	**Chiba** (Chee-bah)
Ehime (Eh-he-may)	**Matsuyama** (Mot-sue-yah-mah)
Fukui (Fuu-kuu-ee)	**Fukui** (Fuu-kuu-ee)
Fukushima (Fuu-kuu-she-mah)	**Fukushima** (Fuu-kuu-she-mah)
Gifu (Ghee-fuu)	**Gifu** (Ghee-fuu)
Gumma (Gume-mah)	**Maebashi** (My-bah-she)
Hokkaido (Hoke-kie-doe)	**Sapporo** (Sop-poe-roe)
Hyogo (He-yoe-go)	**Kobe** (Koe-bay)
Ibaraki (E-bah-rah-kee)	**Mito** (Me-toe)
Ishikawa (E-she-kah-wah)	**Kanazawa** (Kah-nah-zah-wah)
Iwate (E-wah-tay)	**Morioka** (Moe-ree-oh-kah)
Kagawa (Kah-gah-wah)	**Takamatsu** (Tah-kah-mot-sue)
Kagoshima (Kah-go-she-mah)	**Kagoshima** (Kah-go-she-mah)
Kanagawa (Kah-nah-gah-wah)	**Yokohama** (Yoe-koe-hah-mah)
Kochi (Koe-chee)	**Kochi** (Koe-chee)
Kumamoto (Kuu-mah-moe-toe)	**Kumamoto** (Kuu-mah-moe-toe)
Kyoto (K'yoe-toe)	**Kyoto** (K'yoe-toe)
Mie (Me-eh)	**Tsu** (T'sue)
Miyagi (Me-yah-ghee)	**Sendai** (Sin-die)

Miyazaki (Me-yah-zah-kee)

Nagano (Nah-gah-no)

Nagasaki (Nah-gah-sah-kee)

Nara (Nah-rah)

Niigata (Nee-gah-tah)

Oita (Oh-ee-tah)

Okayama (Oh-kah-yah-mah)

Okinawa (Oh-kee-nah-wah)

Osaka (Oh-sah-kah)

Saga (Sah-gah)

Saitama (Sie-tah-mah)

Shiga (She-gah)

Shimane (She-mah-nay)

Shizuoka (She-zoo-oh-kah)

Tochigi (Toe-chee-ghee)

Tokushima (Toe-kuu-she-mah)

Tokyo (Toe-k'yoe)

Tottori (Tote-toe-ree)

Toyama (Toe-yah-mah)

Yamagata (Yah-mah-gah-tah)

Yamaguchi (Yah-mah-guu-chee)

Yamanashi (Yah-mah-nah-she)

Wakayama (Wah-kah-yah-mah)

Miyazaki (Me-yah-zah-kee)

Nagano (Nah-gah-no)

Nagasaki (Nah-gah-sah-kee)

Nara (Nah-rah)

Niigata (Nee-gah-tah)

Oita (Oh-ee-tah)

Okayama (Oh-kah-yah-mah)

Naha (Nah-hah)

Osaka (Oh-sah-kah)

Fukuoka (Fuu-kuu-oh-kah)

Urawa (Uu-rah-wah)

Otsu (Oh-t'sue)

Matsue (Mot-sue-eh)

Shizuoka (She-zoo-oh-kah)

Utsunomiya (Uut-sue-no-me-yah)

Tokushima (Toe-kuu-she-mah)

Tokyo (Toe-k'yoe)

Tottori (Tote-toe-ree)

Toyama (Toe-yah-mah)

Yamagata (Yah-mah-gah-tah)

Yamaguchi (Yah-mah-guu-chee)

Kofu (Koe-fuu)

Wakayama (Wah-kah-yah-mah)

Other City and Regional Names You May Need to Pronounce

Atami (Ah-tah-me)

Enoshima (Eh-no-sheem-mah)

Fuji-Yoshida (Fuu-jee-Yoe-she-dah)

Gotemba (Go-tim-bah)

Hakodate (Hah-koe-dah-tay)

Hakone (Hah-koe-nay)

Ito (Ee-toe)

Izu (Ee-zoo)

Kamakura (Kah-mah-kuu-rah)

Kawasaki (Kah-wah-sah-kee)

Karuizawa (Kah-rue-e-zah-wah)

Narita (Nah-ree-tah)

Nikko (Neek-koe)

Oshima (Oh-she-mah)

Takarazuka (Tah-kah-rah-zuu-kah)

Toba (Toe-bah)

Yokosuka (Yoe-kose-kah)

Zushi (Zuu-she)

Important Area Names in Tokyo

Akasaka (Ah-kah-sak-kah)—Major international hotel, restaurant, bar, nightclub, and geisha inn district. **Akasaka Mitsuke** (Ah-kah-sah-kah Me-t'sue-kay) at the west end of the district is a key subway terminal. Hotels here include the Akasaka Prince, New Otani Hotel, and Akasaka Tokyu Hotel.

Akihabara (Ah-kee-hah-bah-rah)—A few minutes north of the downtown area of Tokyo, this is a famous discount district that specializes in electronic and electrical products and housewares of all kinds. On weekends and holidays, the area is jammed with tens of thousands of shoppers.

Aoyama (Ah-oh-yah-mah)—Shops, offices, restaurants, and residential areas.

Asakusa (Ah-sock-sah)—Major transportation terminal, entertainment, and shopping area.

Chiyoda Ku (Chee-yoe-dah Kuu)—Tokyo's main west-side "downtown" ward. The Imperial Palace is in this ward.

Chuo Ku (Chuu-oh Kuu)—Tokyo's main east-side "downtown" ward, where the famous *Ginza* district is located.

Ginza (Geen-zah)—Tokyo's oldest and probably best-known shopping and entertainment district, which now competes with a dozen or so other districts around the city. In the central area of downtown Tokyo.

Hakozakicho (Hah-koe-zah-kee-choe)—The location of the Tokyo City Air Terminal (TCAT), which serves as the main terminal for limousine buses going to and from Narita's New Tokyo International Airport and as a check-in facility for many international airlines.

Hamamatsucho (Hah-mah-mot-sue-choe)—This is the station in south Tokyo where you board the monorail train for Haneda Airport.

Harajuku (Hah-rah-juu-kuu)—A booming young people's district on the west side of Tokyo, noted for its fashion boutiques, restaurants, and Sunday afternoon street entertainment. Meiji Shrine is located here.

Hibiya (He-bee-yah)—A popular theater and restaurant district adjoining the Imperial Palace grounds on the southeast corner. Also adjoins the *Ginza* on the east and *Shimbashi* on the south. A major subway terminal lies beneath its main thoroughfares. The Imperial Hotel is in this area.

Ikebukuro (E-kay-buu-kuu-roe)—An entertainment, shopping, and business center on the northeast side of Tokyo. Several hotels.

Minato Ku (Me-nah-toe Kuu)—Tokyo's main south-side "downtown" ward, where most embassies and many foreign residential areas are located.

Kanda (Kahn-dah)—An area noted for its bookstores and universities. It also contains a key train station.

Marunouchi (Mah-rue-no-uu-chee)—One of Tokyo's main downtown business centers, adjoining the Imperial Palace Grounds on the east side. Banks, trading companies, and Tokyo Station are in this section.

Nihonbashi (Nee-hone-bah-she)—Tokyo's original financial center (banks, security companies) and shopping center (major department stores).

Otemachi (Oh-tay-mah-chee)—A major financial business and financial center, adjoining the Marunouchi district on the north and the Imperial Palace grounds on the west. A main subway terminal.

Roppongi (Rope-pong-ghee)—One of Tokyo's most popular restaurant, bar, disco, and nightclub areas. On the Hibiya Subway Line.

Shibuya Station and area (She-buu-yah)—A major railway/subway terminal, shopping center, theater, and restaurant district. Several businessmen's hotels.

Shimbashi (Sheem-bah-she)—Hotels, entertainment, restaurants, and geisha inns. Adjoins the *Ginza* on the south.

Shinagawa (She-nah-gah-wah)—Site of several international hotels some distance south of the downtown area.

Shinjuku (Sheen-juu-kuu)—Noted entertainment and shopping district; also west-side center for international hotels and office buildings.

Toranomon (Toe-rah-no-moan)—A business and hotel district (Hotel Okura), and the location of the American Embassy.

Ueno Station and area (Way-no)—A main railway and subway terminal, also noted for its middle-class restaurants, shops, and businessmen's hotels.

Yotsuya (Yoe-t'sue-yah)—Location of Sophia University; close-in site for viewing cherry blossoms in April.

Yurakucho Station and area (Yuu-rah-kuu-choe)—Heart of what is usually considered the downtown area of Tokyo, surrounded by the *Marunouchi* business district, the *Ginza* entertainment/shopping area, and the *Hibiya* entertainment and Imperial Hotel district. The station is two short blocks from the southeast corner of the Imperial Palace grounds.

Important Places and Festivals in Kyoto

Aoi Matsuri (Ah-oh-ee Mot-sue-ree), a major festival

Daitoku Ji (Die-toe-kuu Jee), a famous temple

Fushimi Ward (Fuu-she-me)

Ginkaku Ji (Gheen-kah-kuu Jee), the Silver Pavilion

Gion Machi (Ghee-own Mah-chee), Kyoto's famed Geisha district

Gion Matsuri (Ghee-own Mot-sue-ree), a major festival

Heian Shrine (Hay-e-on)

Higashiyama Ward (He-gah-she-yah-mah)

Jidai Matsuri (Jee-die Mot-sure-ree), a major festival

Kamigyo Ward (Kah-me-g'yoe)

Katsura Rikyu (Kot-sue-rah Ree-que), the famed Katsura Imperial Villa

Kinkaku Ji (Keen-kah-kuu Jee), the famous Temple of the Golden Pavilion

Kita Ward (Kee-tah)

Kiyomizu Temple (Kee-yoe-me-zuu), one of Kyoto's most spectacular temples

Kyoto Gosho (Ke'yoe-toe Go-show), Kyoto Imperial Palace

Minami Ward (Me-nah-me)

Nakagyo Ward (Nah-kah-g'yoe)

Nanzen Ji (Nahn-zen Jee), a famous temple

Ni Jo (Nee Joe), probably Kyoto's most famous castle-palace

Nishijin (Nee-she-jeen), a famous silk-weaving area

Sakyo Ward (Sah-k'yoe)

Shimogyo Ward (She-moe-g'yoe)

Shokoku Ji (Show-koe-kuu Jee), a renowned temple

Shugakuin Rikyu (Shuu-gah-kuu-een Ree-que), Imperial Villa

Ukyo Ward (Uu-k'yoe)

Important Places in Osaka

Akenobashi (Ah-kay-no-bah-she), a place name

Dotombori (Doe-tome-boe-ree), entertainment district

Ebisubashi-suji (A-bee-sue-bah-she-sue-jee), main thoroughfare

Hankyu Department Store (Hahn-que)

Honmachi (Hone-mah-chee), a place name

Mido-suji (Me-doe-sue-jee), main thoroughfare

Minami (Me-nah-me), entertainment district

Nakanoshima (Nah-kah-no-she-mah), civic center, on a small island

Namba (Nahm-bah), shopping center, including huge underground mall

Niji-no Machi (Nee-jee-no Mah-chee), "Rainbow Town" underground shopping center

Sakuranomiya Park (Sah-kuu-rah-no-me-yah)

Shinsaibashi (Sheen-sie-bah-she), shopping area

Shinsaibashi-suji (Sheen-sie-bah-she-sue-jee), main thoroughfare

Shin Sekai (Sheen Say-kie), "New World" amusement center

Umeda (Uu-may-dah), a place name

Yotsubashi (Yoat-sue-bah-she), a place name

Other Special Words

Aka chochin (Ah-kah choe-cheen)—These are the large, red paper lanterns hung in front of bars and other eating and drinking establishments. They have long been a symbol of nightlife in Japan.

Jan Ken Pon (Jahn Kane Pone)—This is the famous "Scissors-Paper-Stone" hand game, which is probably played more often in Japan than anywhere else.

Kogen (Koe-gain)—Japan is very mountainous and has many resorts and recreational areas in the high country. The names of many of these locations are followed by *kogen,* which means "heights."

Matsuri (Mot-sue-ree)—Each year there are thousands of neighborhood, district, and regional *matsuri* all over Japan, and the word is often used without being translated. It means "festival."

Noren (No-rane)—These are the short, split, indigo-blue curtains that are hung over the entrances to Japanese-style eating and drinking places. Shops that serve *sushi,* noodles, *tempura*, and the like generally utilize *noren.* The *noren* are normally hung up when the place opens for business, and taken down when it closes. During the reign of Japan's last shogun dynasty (1603–1868), the *noren* of many businesses became nationally famous and in effect were among the world's first company logos.

Onsen (Own-sin)—This means "hot-spring spa," of which there are two thousand in Japan.

San (Sahn)—When "san" follows the name of a mountain it means "mount," as in *Fuji-san,* or Mount Fuji, *not* Mr. Fuji!

Zashiki (Zah-she-kee)—Rather freely translated, means a room or rooms in which the floor is made of **tatami** (tah-tah-me), or reed-mats; the traditional Japanese style of flooring.

PART TWO

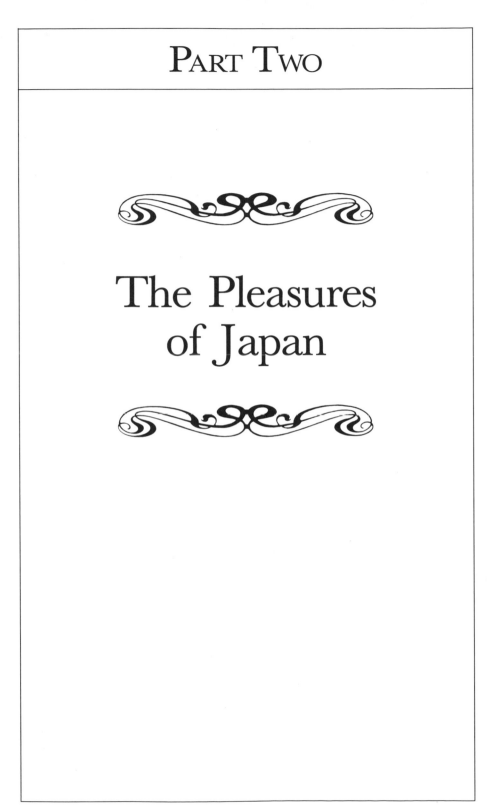

The Pleasures of Japan

Here is a random list of things you can do in Japan to add dimension, depth, and ambience to your visit.

Strolling the Back Streets

As in most countries, it is important to go behind the main-street facade of Japan to get a more comprehensive feel for the heartbeat and nuances of its culture. Once you have walked up one side and down the other of Tokyo's famed Ginza Street, for example, that's it; it is very much like the Fifth Avenue of New York or London. The really interesting part of the Ginza district is its back streets, lanes, and alleys, where shops, restaurants, bars, and other places of business are wedged together in a carnival of sights and sounds.

The same goes for any of the other dozens of centers in Tokyo, especially **Akasaka** (Ah-kah-sah-ka), **Asakusa** (Ah-sock-sah), **Roppongi** (Rope-pone-ghee), **Shibuya** (She-buu-yah), and **Shinjuku** (Sheen-juu-kuu), where visitors are most likely to go. And, of course, the same holds true for Kyoto, Osaka, etc., as well as for smaller cities and towns throughout the country. The point is that just by walking a very short distance away from the main thoroughfares, you can see, feel, and experience the other side of Japan. Wandering around Japan's back streets should be high on your list of things to do.

The Cabaret World

I have already mentioned Japan's extraordinary hostess cabarets in the book's section on entertainment. Without contacts it is not easy—and can be outrageously expensive—for a short-time visitor to experience one of the more elaborate or exclusive cabarets. But there are a number of cabarets in Japan's major cities that welcome foreign guests and advertise in English-language travel publications.

These cabarets have a menu and price system especially for foreign clientele, and while they may have departed somewhat from the pure Japanese essence of cabaret life, they nevertheless offer an exotic and exciting taste of this aspect of Japan. Probably the best way for the newcomer to experience a cabaret is to take one of the night tours offered by Japan Gray Line or the Japan Travel Bureau. Japan Gray Line has been running nighttime cabaret tours of Tokyo since the fifties. Its brochures are available in hotels, where the tours, designed for men and women, begin and end.

Samurai Dramas

Japan's version of American cowboy films are its Samurai dramas, or **chanbara** (chahn-bah-rah), movies and television shows featuring warriors who fight with swords and various **ninja** (neen-jah) equipment. Chanbara stories are set in different times during Japan's long feudal age (1192–1868), when sword-carrying **samurai** (sah-muu-rye) were both the professional warriors and the rogue cowboys of the land.

The films depict age-old themes of good sword-fighters, women as well as men, against the "bad guys." Preliminary skirmishes and derring-do culminate in the final showdown, when the "good guy"—often a rogue who has a good side—eliminates the enemy with his terrible, swift sword.

The prowess of the sword fighters is invariably exaggerated, although Japan's *samurai* as a group were probably the most skilled swordsmen who ever lived. Some of the greatest champions survived dozens of death duels, on numerous occasions engaging several enemies at the same time. Yet it is the overall psychology, setting, and lifestyles depicted in the films that are of special interest and value.

Generally speaking, the *chanbara* films are authentic depictions of life as it was in Japan during the periods concerned, and as such each one is a you-are-there sort of lesson in the economics, sociology, and politics of early Japan. The dialogue is in Japanese, and the plots are often subtle and very involved, but what you can pick up visually makes seeing at least two or three of the films worthwhile.

I recommend that you go with a Japanese companion who can explain the story line to you before the film starts, and then recap it after the showing. You also may catch one of the long-running *chanbara* serials on television. One that appears weekly is the long-running **Mito Komon** (Me-toe Koe-moan), or "Mito Advisor." Mito, a city northeast of Tokyo, was the headquarters of the most important branch of the Tokugawa Shogunate family, whose leader was the hereditary vice-shogun during the long Tokugawa Period (1603–1868). *Mito Komon* refers to what might be translated as the "Assistant Vice Shogun."

In this unending historical saga, the assistant vice shogun has retired and, with a team of trusty aides made up of three men and usually two women, all of whom are weapons experts, is on a continuous foot pilgrimage around the country. The group invariably meets up with villains in every weekly segment; at the final swordfight, the "good guys" end up revealing the identity of the vice shogun and winning the day for the local inhabitants. The show is on Channel 6 Monday nights at 8:00 P.M.

For other weekly samurai dramas, see the television guide in one of the daily English-language newspapers.

Following the Cherry Blossom Front

As spring approaches, Japan's "cherry blossom front," known in Japanese as *Sakura Zensen,* spreads up the island chain on a very reliable schedule, moving at a rate of about thirty kilometers a day. The first blossoms usually appear in southern Kyushu around 24 March. The "front" typically reaches the Tokyo area on 31 March, the southern portion of northern Honshu around 10 April, and the northern areas around 25 April. It is generally 10 May before the first blossoms open in Hokkaido, Japan's northernmost island.

If your trip to Japan coincides with the annual appearance of the nation's vaunted cherry blossoms, I strongly recommend that you spend at least one day indulging in this ancient ritual of communing with nature. It is a special experience in and of itself, and is also an occasion to experience the Japanese observing one of their oldest and most revered traditions.

Cherry tree groves abound in Japan. Some have been famous for over a thousand years. Wherever you are in Japan, virtually any adult Japanese can direct you to the nearest grove, and it is best to go on a Sunday or other holiday, when large numbers of people are out.

Popular cherry blossom viewing places in Tokyo include Ueno Park, Chidorigafuchi Park, and Shinjuku Gardens. Several areas along the Imperial Palace moat banks, particularly in the vicinity of the New Otani Hotel and Sophia University north to Ichigaya Station, also attract thousands of people during blossom season. There are dozens of blossom sites to spot around the city, including the grounds of Yasukuni Shrine in Kudan.

There are twenty-two-hundred cherry trees in Tokyo's Ueno Park, including varieties that bloom at different times and provide a variety of colors, making the park one of the favorite spots for blossom viewing. Paper lanterns are strung on overhead wires throughout the park, lighting the place at night and giving the scene an ethereal glow that goes well with hot **sake** (sah-kay) and a festive mood.

If you are in the Kyoto or Nara area and really want to make an outing out of blossom viewing, Mount Yoshino is the place. It boasts four large groves, first planted in the seventh century by a Buddhist priest named Enno Ozuna, that gradually ascend the slopes of the mountain. The main blossom-viewing festival is held there on 11 and 12 April, but the blossoms on the lower slopes begin appearing around 1 April; those highest on the mountain appear around the end of the month. Arashiyama, on the outskirts of Kyoto, also is noted for its annual blossoms.

In the northern regions, Bunsuimachi in Niigata Prefecture is nationally famous for its cherry blossoms, as is Matsume in Hokkaido.

I recommend that you reserve at least one full Sunday for the enjoyment of **Sakura no Hana Mi** (Sah-kuu-rah no Hah-nah Me), or "Cherry Blossom Viewing."

Japan's Beauty Alcoves

Japan is apparently the only nation ever to make the study and appreciation of beauty an integral part of its culture. This phenomenon was not merely an abstract concept or limited to the educated class or elite. It was a pervasive cultural characteristic that became institutionalized in the architecture, folk crafts, education and daily life of the Japanese.

This concern with beauty led to the development of specific standards for judging and appreciating beauty, and to special vocabulary to describe various aspects of beauty.

One of the most conspicuous signs of this extraordinary recognition of aesthetics as a desirable ingredient in the lives of all was the **tokonoma** (toe-koe-no-mah), or "beauty alcove" built into the living rooms of homes, *ryokan* rooms, and other places of business. There apparently has not been a single Japanese-style home built in the country in several hundred years that did not have a beauty alcove for the display of calligraphy, flowers, or paintings. Objects displayed in *tokonoma* are selected with care, and are changed to fit seasons and events.

I believe the *tokonoma* and what it represents is a concept that Westerners should adopt, and I suggest that during your stay in Japan you make a point of familiarizing yourself with this special beauty area. You could buy some scrolls that would be suitable for hanging in a special place in your own home, or adapt Western works of art for that purpose.

Roasted Chestnuts

One of the special pleasures of the late fall in Japan is the appearance of roasted chestnut vendors on the streets of entertainment and shopping districts and near major transportation terminals. Buying a bag of the delicious nuts for a quick, unplanned snack, or to take with you, is one of those little things that makes one enjoy life.

Chinzanso Garden

During the final 233-year reign of the Tukugawa Shogunate, which began in 1603 and ended in 1868, 250 of Japan's larger fief lords were required to maintain mansions in **Edo** (Eh-doe), the forerunner of Tokyo, and to spend every other year there to attend the shogun's court.

Each of the mansions was surrounded by a landscaped garden; the richer the fief, the larger and more elaborate the garden. Many of these gardens have survived to the present time and are enjoyed by great numbers of people. One of the largest and most impressive is now part of one of Tokyo's most famous resort/restaurant complexes, **Chinzanso** (Cheen-zahn-so) in Bunkyo Ward.

Several of the restaurants in the complex offer spectacular views of the area as they overlook the garden, which descends a slope into a narrow gorge. Garden barbecues are popular. To further enliven things in the fall of each year, the proprietors used to release thousands of fireflies in the huge garden, and for several nights thereafter, diners and visitors were treated to an extraordinary sight. Of course, to fully enjoy the garden, one must visit it during the day.

The *Chinzanso* is high on my list of favorite restaurants in Tokyo, and one I'm sure you will also enjoy.

Wearing Your Philosophy

A minor but fascinating facet of contemporary youth culture in Japan is the use of foreign-language words and slogans—mostly in English—on T-shirts, sweat shirts and other types of apparel. The words and phrases are not used merely for decorative purposes. They are messages, expressing the feelings and philosophies of the wearers.

Besides being interesting because of their extraordinary departure from traditional Japanese dress and values, the clothing slogans tell you a lot about today's young Japanese. While the intent is serious, the effects are often humorous when the wearer does not know the meaning of the English on his back or chest.

Reading the fronts and backs of Japanese youth during a weekend shopping or strolling trip is often enough to brighten the day, and also provides an insight into ways that Japan is changing.

Miranda Kenrick, long-time resident writer on Japan, has compiled a book of "Janglish" (Japanese-English) that includes a wonderful selection of apparel slogans. Among them: "Wokers Holic"; "Molded Fish"; "Porky Party"; "To Touch a Boy's Adventurous Brain, Dream, and Inquisity"; "It's Natural that We Should Love with This Members"; and "Have a Nice Days Today."

Other slogans spotted during a short outing: "Magic Vibrations from Sexy Tokyo," and "Hey! Take Your Hand out of Your Pocket and Come on the Courts."

Coffee-Shop Culture

Beginning in the early fifties, just a few years after the end of World War II, coffee shops became an extraordinary phenomenon in Japan. The Japanese were newly liberated from the feudalistic practices of the past and greatly influenced by the freewheeling lifestyle of Americans. They lived in tiny, crowded, unheated, and uncooled apartments and houses, and were ripe for some sort of new public facility where they could meet and socialize in comfort.

This need was fulfilled by the rapid appearance of many thousands of coffee shops ranging in size from holes in the wall to multistoried buildings, each sporting its own special kind of decor and format. Some had live entertainment, others were known for their recorded music ranging from jazz to classical, some were known for their beautiful waitresses, and others had waiters dressed in Cossack or American military uniforms. The variety was astounding.

During the day, literally hundreds of thousands of businessmen used the coffee shops as extensions of their offices, which were as small and uncomfortable as their homes. At night millions of young and middle-aged alike congregated in the shops, giving birth to a "coffee shop culture" with its own language and customs. In succeeding decades, other public places proliferated to compete with the huge number of coffee shops in Japan, but it is the coffee shops that survive and remain one of the most significant features of the Japanese landscape. I recommend that you spend half an hour or so in each of several coffee shops during your Japan visit. Ask someone to direct you to places that are out of the ordinary because of their decor, the type of clientele they cater to, or even the coffee they serve. Some shops serve only freshly ground and percolated coffee, with as many as thirty or forty blends available—something that is uncommon in other countries.

Driving Out the Devils

Another of the little winter pleasures that you can indulge in if you are in Japan on 3 February is an observation called **Setsubun** (Say-tsue-boon), which is something like Japan's Halloween. An ancient custom, it began as a religious ritual designed to exorcise ogres, devils, and other evil spirits from homes and other locations, and welcome in good luck and good fortune.

People toss parched beans (that have the power to drive devils away) around rooms and out of windows while shouting, **Oni wa soto, fuku wa uchi!** or "Out with the devils, in with good luck!" Some people don ogre masks to portray devils and allow children to chase them away while pelting them with beans.

Many shrines and other public places stage *Setsubun* ceremonies that attract large crowds, with celebrities sometimes throwing out the beans. The annual event marks another occasion when you can participate in a fun custom and see the Japanese engage in an age-old practice.

The Fire Guards

In premodern Japan virtually every building in the country, except for storage towers, was made of wood and paper. All cooking and water heating was done over open flames in small, portable pots known as **hibachi** (he-bah-chee). This was a recipe for house fires that was so much a part of life in Japan that residents of Edo (Tokyo) referred to the almost nightly occurrence of brightly flaming fires as "the blossoms of Edo," and would sometimes gather on small hills in the city to watch the glowing flames.

Because of this constant danger, residents of neighborhoods took turns walking through the streets at night, clapping two small boards together and calling out **Hi no yojin!** (He no yoe-jeen!), a warning similar to "Beware of smoldering fires!"—a reminder for everyone to make sure there were no fires smoldering in their *hibachi*.

The sound of clapping boards and the singsong call of the "fire guard" became a part of each night, serving as a signal for day's end and providing a sense of security that made it possible for people to go to sleep reassured that all was well.

Some of Japan's inns are located in residential areas where the sound of the *hi no ban* are still a part of the night. If you are lucky enough to stay at one of these inns and around 9:00 P.M. hear the clack-clack-clack followed by the *Hi no yojin!* call, you can reflect on the role this nightly custom has played in Japan in centuries past, and perhaps gain a sense of what it means to older Japanese.

Having Your Fortune Told

Fortunetelling, or *uranai,* is another age-old practice in Japan that has survived into modern times. It is one of those little bits of culture that is easily ignored but also can add spice to life.

Japan's palm readers and stick casters usually set up shop about sundown on the sidewalks of popular entertainment and restaurant districts. Their "office" consists of a stool and tiny table, lit by a small **chochin** (choe-cheen) paper lantern. Very few of them solicit customers from the streams of people flowing by. They usually sit and read, waiting patiently for the spirit to move someone to stop. If you spot one, and have a Japanese friend who can interpret for you, the experience is worth the fee.

Hot-spring Spas

One-tenth of the world's active volcanoes are in Japan, and hundreds of inactive ones dot the mountainous landscape. One of the legacies of this fiery past is the presence of thousands of natural hot mineral springs that gush out of the ground and from mountainsides throughout the country. More than two thousand of these hot springs have been developed into **onsen** (own-sin), or "hot spring spas," and have been in use for medicinal as well as sensual purposes for centuries.

Some of the best and most popular of the spas are in breathtakingly scenic areas. They are the ultimate in refined Japanese-style living, combining the sensual beauty of the traditional *ryokan* inn, the personal service of a fief lord's *honjin,* and a landscape that is the epitome of natural beauty.

If you can go only one place and do only one thing in Japan, I would not hesitate to recommend that it be an *onsen.* Here are some of the hundreds of popular ones: **Noboribetsu** (No-boe-ree-bate-sue) and **Jozankei** (Joe-zahn-kay-e) in Hokkaido; Atami, Hakone, Ito, Kinugawa, Nasu, and Shiobara in the vicinity of Tokyo; Arima near Kobe; Beppu in Kyushu; Shirahama in Wakayama Prefecture; and **Dogo** (Doe-go) in Ehime Prefecture.

Other than the two places in Hokkaido, all of the above refer to towns or cities in which there are a dozen to several dozen resort inns featuring hot springs. The Hakone area has twelve spa districts, for example; Nasu has seven; and Shiobara has eleven. The three best-known resorts in the Hakone area are Gora, Miyanoshita, and Kowakidani.

One of my favorites is the Fuji-Hakone Guest House in Sengoku-hara, Hakone, Kanagawa Prefecture, 250-06, about two hours from Tokyo. Small and intimate, it has been run by the Takahashi Family for generations.

Among the most unusual hot-spring resorts in Japan is Beppu, on the northern coast of Kyushu. There are thirty-seven hundred hot springs in Beppu, including one large section that consists of boiling ponds of water or mud that bubbles to the surface in various colors, including white, red, and blue-green. These ponds are appropriately called **jigoku** (jee-go-kuu), or "hells."

Visitors to Beppu traditionally go on an **onsen meguri** (own-sin may-guu-re), or "hot-spring spa circuit," bathing in up to a dozen or more baths. The most popular of all are the baths of the **Suginoi** (Sue-ghee-noy) Hotel—actually two baths, each of which will accommodate several hundred people. It is not necessary to stay at the hotel to enjoy its baths.

Exercising Your Nose

Appreciation of the finer things in life in Japan has traditionally included incense, not only because of its use in religious rituals, where it was used to calm the mind, expand the senses, and enhance spiritual awareness; it also was used for the sheer pleasure of it.

It is recognized everywhere that the whiff of a rose or some other agreeable scent has an immediate, positive effect on our mood and behavior, and most societies have interwoven this phenomenon into their cultures. Japan's Imperial Court and the priesthood learned the art of **kodo** (koh-doe), or incense-burning, from Chinese Buddhist priests around the sixth century, and then, as was characteristic of them in virtually everything else as well, took it much further.

Aristocrats of ancient Japan would "listen" to the fragrances of incense to inspire their poetry. From the fourteenth century on, the *samurai* warrior class used incense to create a mood of elegance and sophistication and to demonstrate their cultural learning. In the seventeenth and eighteenth centuries it spread from the court and *samurai* to the upper and middle classes, becoming a national phenomenon.

Most Japanese are now too busy to indulge themselves in the pleasures of incense, but it continues to flourish among dedicated devotees. There are several schools of *kodo,* one of them—the Oie Ryu School of Incense Appreciation—headed by a member of the Imperial Family. I suggest that you slow down long enough to "listen to the fragrances." A full incense ceremony lasts for about ninety minutes.

Each of the schools stages regular incense ceremonies that are open to the public. If you would like to do something else in Japan that could be a life gift to yourself, have someone call **Nippon Kodo** (Neep-pone Koe-doe) in Tokyo, the country's largest incense manufacturer, or the above school, and find out the local ceremony schedule.

By the Light of the Moon

You've probably seen the moon many times, but have you ever held a party to celebrate its beauty and the inspirational role it plays in human life? If not—or if you want to do it again—Japan is an ideal place: Moon viewing has been a traditional custom there for more than a thousand years. In fact, there are hundreds of celebrated moon-viewing locations around the country, some of them known and used for centuries.

Several of the distinctive facets of Japanese culture that came together long ago in the custom of moon viewing include the propensity of almost everyone to write poetry, eat specially prepared foods, drink hot rice wine, and make aestheticism an art practiced by ordinary people.

Traditionally, friends gathered in the fall at a favorable location just before the rise of a full moon; made themselves comfortable; and then proceeded to eat, drink, talk, compose poetry, and while away the evening while basking in the glow of the moon.

If you can't find or arrange this kind of party, a good substitute is a table at a rooftop beer garden. I guarantee you the muse as well as the moon will rise.

Munching Freebies

For a really unusual outing, I recommend that you visit the food department of one of Japan's large department stores. Always located in the store basement, these departments have huge displays of imported and domestic foods of every kind imaginable, plus hundreds that are new to the typical visitor.

Just strolling around and browsing among the variety of foods and ingredients, raw and prepared, is an experience. What makes it much more interesting is that on weekends and special days, anywhere from two or three dozen to five or six dozen of the counters, stands, and stalls in the department give away free food sample tidbits—everything from meatballs, roast beef, barbecued eel, and pickled fish to candies, cakes, and ice creams.

The food departments present an extraordinary picture of affluence and variety in modern-day Japan—not to mention the fact that you can make a meal out of munching here and there.

Never Say Wonderful until...

This section is not intended to be a guide to Japan's well-known attractions, but I can't resist mentioning **Nikko** (Neek-koe), about two hours north of Tokyo. A small town on the slopes of a mountain in what is now Nikko National Park, the site entered Japanese history during a period when itinerant priests searched the remotest regions of the islands for areas of exceptional beauty, and built shrines and temples there.

By the early 1600s, the site had been famous for centuries not only for its beauty but also as a religious center. After Shogun Ieyasu Tokugawa died, it was selected as the site for his mausoleum, and later the spirits of Yoritomo Minamoto and Hideyoshi Toyotomi, two of Japan's greatest heroes, also were enshrined there.

Now it is known for these mausoleums, Lake Chuzenji, the magnificent Kegon Waterfalls, and the beauty of the surrounding mountains. The scenery is especially striking in the fall, when the maple leaves turn gold and red. In an attempt to express the beauty of the area, someone years ago came up with the saying, "Never say **'kekko'** (keck-koe), or 'wonderful,' until you've seen Nikko." As a one-day or preferably a weekend trip from Tokyo, it is hard to beat.

Pachinko Parlor Psychology

Pachinko is the Japanese version of the pinball game. The "machine" stands upright and is rather narrow. Players shoot small metal balls into a maze of barriers and holes. If their ball goes into one of the holes, they win more balls—which can be exchanged for various consumer products such as cookies, cigarettes, etc. Professional players sell the goods back to the *pachinko* parlors for cash, thereby making a living at the game.

There are many thousands of *pachinko* parlors throughout Japan, some of them huge and as ornate as Las Vegas casinos. Most of the people who frequent them are not professionals. They are ordinary folk playing the game for relaxation and, some experts say, to relieve stress. Research on the subject does indicate that playing the machines helps people develop their ability to concentrate and persevere in their daily tasks.

I have not played enough *pachinko* to vouch for any kind of health benefit, but it is a very significant "slice of life" in Japan that is worth thirty minutes of your time as sociological and psychological "research." Watch the people, not the machines.

A Pickle a Day

The Japanese version of "an apple a day keeps the doctor away" could be "an *umeboshi* a day. . . ." An **umeboshi** (uu-may-boe-she) is a green plum that has been pickled in a powerful brine that includes leaves from the **shiso** (she-soe), or "beefsteak plant," to give it a bright red color and enhance its taste.

Used for centuries to help relieve stomach ailments (and hangovers) and as a general good-health supplement, *umeboshi* are served with most Japanese-style meals, particularly with the **O-bento** (Oh-bane-toe), or rice-based "box meals," that are popular as lunches and on-the-road snacks—in part to complement the bland taste of the rice.

Umeboshi take some getting used to, but they do add something to a Japanese meal that is a not-to-be-missed part of the Japanese experience. One thing's for sure, if you get up feeling blah after a night out on the town, eating a pickled plum will bring you and your taste buds back to life.

Trying Tofu Treats

If you have not yet been introduced to *tofu,* a very mild-tasting, gelatinous curd made from soybean flour, it is another culinary treat that you should experience while in Japan. *Tofu* is cholesterol-free and high in protein (higher, in fact, than meat), and can therefore be recommended for its merits as a health food.

But *tofu* goes beyond just being healthy. It is an integral part of Japan's culinary traditions. It is used in so many dishes—soup, *oden, tsukiyaki,* and so on—that it is virtually impossible to eat Japanese cuisine without coming across it.

Tofu is eaten raw, deep-fried, and boiled, and takes on some of the taste of whatever condiments, stock, or sauces it is used with. I suggest that you make a special point of developing a taste for it during your Japan sojourn, and then add it to your regular choices of foods after returning home.

Pleasure on the Floor

One of the more subtle of the sensual pleasures that is woven into Japan's traditional lifestyle is the feel and aroma of new **tatami** (tah-tah-me), the three-by-six-inch reed mats, built onto wooden frames, that are the floors of **Nihon ma** (Nee-hone mah), or "Japanese rooms." The mats have a soft, smooth, cool feel that invites touching, and a delicate, piquant aroma that is soothing and stimulating at the same time.

If you find yourself in a *Nihon ma* that is still greenish in color, meaning it is still fairly new, get down on the *tatami* and absorb some of its ambience. (As the reeds age, they turn golden.)

Tea, Please

Tea was introduced into Japan by a Chinese priest named Ganjin sometime around the year 725. At that time, Ganjin presented some herbal medicines to Japan's Emperor Shomu, among which was tea. The practice of drinking tea for its health benefits quickly grew within the Imperial Court and among the Buddhist priesthood. As the centuries passed, tea drinking spread among the masses, eventually becoming a daily ritual.

During the 1500s a famous Osaka merchant named Sen-no Rikyu elevated formalized tea drinking to an art form that was institutionalized as **Chano-yu** (Chah-no yuu), or the "Tea Ceremony."

The tea used in the tea ceremony does not have a pleasant taste, but I do recommend that you try several other kinds of tea while you are in Japan. The cheapest and most commonly served tea is a green tea that goes by one of three names: **ocha** (oh-chah), which is generic for "tea," also **ban-cha** (bahn-chah), literally "number tea," or **Nihon cha** (Nee-hone chah), which is "Japan tea." The latter two terms are frequently used to clearly distinguish the kind of tea you want. It is greenish in color and has an agreeable taste. Occupying the next level of quality and price is **sen-cha** (sane-chah), which is the variety usually served to special guests. The highest quality tea, **gyokuro** (g'yoe-kuu-roe), is served on very, very special occasions.

Stick with *ban-cha;* it is inexpensive enough that you can drink copious amounts, and is very refreshing.

A popular summertime chilled "tea" drink I recommend is called **mugi-cha** (muu-ghee-chah). It is actually made of roasted barley and is not a tea in the strict sense. Another "tea" drink that is very healthy is **kobu-cha** (koe-buu-chah), made from powdered seaweed. It tastes like salty soup, and takes some getting used to, but is full of minerals the body needs.

The Tea Ceremony

Japan's famous Tea Ceremony has nothing to do with enjoying a drink of tea. It is a way of developing character, refined manners, sensitivity, and the ability to appreciate natural beauty. The formalities of the Tea Ceremony are very mechanical, and precisely prescribed. It is following these formalities exactly and doing so in the right frame of mind that is the essence of the ceremony.

Benefits to be derived from the Tea Ceremony include learning how to control one's body in a highly stylized manner, which first requires good mind control, and then polishing one's spirit and intellect to achieve philosophical peace with the cosmos. Heavy stuff, in which tea is only the visible vehicle.

If you have a philosophical bent and an appreciation of refined manners, I highly recommend that you participate in a Tea Ceremony while in Japan. There are numerous schools and teahouses, with ceremonies regularly arranged for visitors. Also reading Kakuzo Okakura's *Book of Tea* in advance would be very beneficial.

Street of Books

Tokyo's **Kanda** (Kahn-dah) district is one of the original areas of the city. During its long heyday during the Tokugawa Shogunate, its residents were known far and wide as representing the epitome of the distinctive character and spirit of the city. Today it is known as a university town and as the location of the "Street of Books."

Dozens of bookstores line the main east-west thoroughfare and some of the side lines in the Jinbo-cho section of Kanda, attracting shoppers and browsers from all over the world. Antique bookstores abound in the area.

Unless you are seriously into books you may not want to make a special trip to Jinbo-cho, but you might combine it with a visit to Japan's best-known Shinto shrine, **Yasukuni Jinja** (Yah-sue-kuu-nee Jeen-jah), which is on a small hill a short distance away.

Shrines and Temples

Foreign visitors to Japan who are not familiar with the Buddhist and Shinto religions generally have problems separating the two and distinguishing a shrine from a temple. There are over one-hundred-thousand shrines in Japan and many thousands of temples, so the difficulty arises often.

To begin with, shrines are Shintoist and temples are Buddhist. Larger Shinto shrines are invariably marked by one or more of the famous **torii** (toe-ree-e), or "gates," that consist of two upright pillars and one or two crosspieces at the top. *Torii* have long been used as a symbol of Japan.

Worshippers do not enter Shinto shrines. They pay their respects and say their prayers outside, standing before the shrine altar. The *torii* are symbolic gates to the interior of a shrine, and mark the boundary between the outside world and the inside world of the shrine. After passing through the *torii* you are supposed to begin preparing yourself for communion with the divine spirit of the shrine.

Shintoism has no founder or sacred literature, but it does have colorful ceremonies on festive and other auspicious occasions. Shintoism is the source of the ancient Japanese idea that they were the direct descendants of godly beings who created the islands of Japan and then came down from the heavens to dwell on them. In Shinto mythology, the emperor of Japan was divine and was worshipped as a "god on earth." Shintoism teaches that all things, animate and inanimate, have spirits and are linked together in a great cosmic scheme requiring a symbiotic relationship for a harmonious world.

Over the centuries, Shintoism was primarily used in a political sense to maintain the status quo between the emperor and the common people, and to inspire nationalistic feelings among the people. It also was the origin of the Japanese belief that they had a divine mandate to spread **wa** (wah), or "harmony," to the four corners of the globe.

In a more practical sense, Shintoism was primarily concerned with the fertility and fecundity of both the land and its people. The religion was the mainspring of many of Japan's traditional festivals that were designed to please the gods of nature so that crops and children would be abundant. The thousands of stone and wooden replicas of the erect male organ that once dotted the landscape and are still used in a number of fertility festivals held around the country each year sprang from this deep concern with fertility.

In modern-day Japan, most weddings and the blessings of new buildings are Shintoist. Shinto priests wear white robes and headgear.

Among the best-known and most impressive Shinto shrines in Tokyo are the Yasukuni and the Meiji. The Yasukuni Shrine is where Japan's war dead are enshrined, and from shortly after the fall of the Tokugawa Shogunate in 1868 until the end of World War II was the national shrine of Japan. What could be called the true national shrine of Japan is the Grand Shrine of Ise, near Nagoya, where emperors are enthroned and the spirits of past emperors are enshrined. It is a large complex with dozens of buildings in an incredibly beautiful setting.

Buddhism, introduced into Japan from China, is a much more contemporary religion. It has an extensive literature and has inspired great works of art. The religion also supports the construction and use of great temples which have indoor meeting halls for worshippers. Buddhism is primarily a moral and ethical concept aimed at helping people behave properly while on earth to prepare themselves for entry into the afterworld when they die. It teaches the Japanese the concepts of heaven and hell, but was not nearly as restrictive as the social concepts of Christianity or as primitive as the theological dogmas of Christianity. It was a tolerant, nonaggressive religion that allowed the Japanese to carry on their daily lives without significant interference.

Thousands of famous Buddhist temples still exist in Japan today, some of them dating back more than a thousand years. Noted temples in Tokyo include the Zojo, the Sengaku, and the Asakusa Kannon. Dozens of temples in Kyoto have been nationally famous for centuries. Among them: Chion-in, Kyomizu, Nansen, Higashi Hongan, Ryoan, and Daitoku. The Japanese word for temple is *ji* (jee), which is always attached to the end of the temple name when it is written in Latin alphabet letters—for example, Nansenji, Ryoanji.

Buddhist priests wear black robes. One of their most common functions is to conduct rites for the dead.

You should certainly visit two or three representative shrines and temples while you are in Japan. Many temples offer overnight accommodations to visitors and serve distinctive vegetarian meals. Zen temples also offer lessons in the Zen sect of Buddhism and in meditation. Narita, where the New Tokyo International Airport is located, has been reknowned for nearly a thousand years for its many temples. A little while spent in a Zen temple is not a bad way to end a trip to Japan.

Rice Cracker Heaven

Another traditional Japanese food that you should try while in Japan are the country's famous **senbei** (sin-baye), or rice crackers. These ethnic crackers come in various shapes and sizes, from flat to round like a joint of your finger. While baking they are coated with **shoyu** (show-yuu), a soy-based flavoring. Some are then wrapped in sheaths of dried **nori** (no-ree), or seaweed.

Perhaps oddly tasting at first, most people, especially children, quickly develop a liking for *senbei*. They make very good snacks and are popular as gifts. Vendors sell them aboard long-distance trains, and they are available in food markets as well as specialty *senbei* shops. Try them. They go particularly well with green tea *(bancha)*.

A New Taste Treat

Yet another taste treat that I recommend, and one that most visitors love immediately, is **shabu shabu** (shah-buu shah-buu), which some describe as a Japanese fondue. It is a hotpot dish in which thinly sliced beef, various vegetables, and tofu are fast-boiled in a lightly flavored, clear broth, and dipped in a light sauce before eating.

Cooking is done at the table, with the diner acting as his own chef. The meat, which is eaten first, gets cooked so quickly most people simply hold it with chopsticks in the bubbling stock for a few seconds. The vegetables and tofu stay in longer, cooking and soaking up the flavor of the stock.

Once you have had your fill of solid ingredients, the stock is poured into bowls to be eaten as soup. Real aficionados pour it over bowls of rice, served last, to savor both the stock and the rice to the very end. In my experience, four out of five first-time visitors to Japan say they liked *shabu shabu* best of all.

Strolling Your Cares Away

One of the favorite weekend pastimes of the Japanese is *sanpo*, or "strolling." I recommend it highly for visitors as well, and suggest that you make sure it is on your itinerary as a legitimate activity. On holidays and weekends, its seems that just about everyone in Japan turns out to stroll in favorite areas: along rivers and beaches, mountain trails, city canals, and shop-and-restaurant streets, as well as in parks and department stores. You should join them.

I especially recommend the most popular shop-and-restaurant areas, including huge underground malls in places like Kobe, Osaka, Nagoya, Tokyo, and Sapporo. A place in Tokyo that you should not miss is **Omote Sando** (Oh-moe-tay Sahn-doe) Boulevard in the Harajuku district of Shibuya Ward. About a mile long, this broad, tree-lined avenue gives you modern Japan in a microcosm. A mecca for the young and avant garde, its restaurants, boutiques, and specialty shops throb with energy. On Sundays, the avenue is blocked off to traffic and becomes a pedestrian haven.

Streets in the downtown areas of Shibuya and Shinjuku as well as the popular Ginza are also turned into pedestrian malls on Sundays and national holidays.

Sweet Potato Treats

Street vendors selling baked sweet potatoes have been a part of the Japanese scene for a long time. Some still use the time-honored pushcarts. Others, taking advantage of affluence and modern-day technology, use small trucks with ovens built onto the beds, and electric loudspeakers to announce their presence in neighborhoods. The long musical cry of *Yah-kee ee-mooooooh!* is still enough to send both children and adults rushing out to buy the succulent potatoes.

Vendors still using pushcarts generally set up shop around dusk in entertainment and restaurant districts, rather than cruise the neighborhoods. If you run across one, buying and eating a steaming hot sweet potato is another of those little, easy-to-do things that will add another gem to your travel treasury.

Welcoming New Year's

New Year's is worthy of note because it is such an extraordinary annual event in Japan. In addition to being the most significant national holiday, with many people taking off five to seven days, it incorporates a number of cultural traditions that have long been a vital part of Japanese life.

The two parts of the New Year's celebration that I want to bring to your attention are visits to Shinto shrines and the ringing of bells at Buddhist temples. Many people choose to make their first shrine-visit of the year just after midnight. Huge crowds gather in the vicinity of shrines as midnight approaches, and then arrive at the shrines as close to the beginning of the new year as possible. Joining one of these pilgrimages—and then eating hot **oden** (oh-dane) and toasting the New Year with *O-sake* at a sidewalk food cart on the way home—is a rewarding thing to do.

Chicken on a Stick

Small chunks of chicken, grilled over an open fire with pieces of onion and green peppers if you like is another Japanese taste treat that visitors invariably take to without any trial period. The **yaki tori** (yah-kee toe-ree) tidbits are coated with a soy-based sauce or lightly salted to add a succulent flavor, and this is what gives them the Japanese touch.

While good *yaki tori* is delicious, it is not so much the food but the ethnic character of the shops serving it that makes it worth recommending to visitors. There are two styles of *yaki tori* shops. One style of shop is enclosed in the normal manner, generally with a counter and row of stools instead of tables and chairs. The shop interior is built and decorated in traditional Japanese style, with sliding front doors, **noren** (no-rane) curtains hanging across the front, and a large red **chochin** (choe-cheen) lantern serving as a lighted sign.

The second "style" consists of open-air stands or shops, some of them tucked into railroad and freeway underpasses in central areas where there is much foot traffic. These very casual, outdoor barbecue-type places cater to a dedicated core of *yaki tori* eaters who are not concerned about the trappings and appreciate the basics. I began patronizing one such shop between the Imperial Hotel and the Ginza in the early fifties, and it is still flourishing.

The picturesque *yaki tori* shops—both styles—serve beer and *O-sake* along with *yaki tori,* and are convivial places where one goes to eat, get a little tipsy, commune with friends, and have a good time. I recommend them for the food as well as the atmosphere.

Letting It All Ring Out

The Buddhist practice of tolling temple bells just before the end of the old year is something to see and experience. Temples all over the country begin the tolling as a countdown to midnight, when the new year starts. Bells toll a total of 108 times to banish the 108 illusions that cause conflict and pain to humanity, so the whole nation can start the new year afresh.

Many thousands of people congregate at famous temples around the country to witness the tolling of the bells, and, following the stroke of midnight, to say a prayer for health and happiness during the new year. In some of the temples, the bells are huge, with the clappers consisting of great logs suspended on ropes from the ceiling.

Among the temples that attract the largest number of people on New Year's Eve and the following three days are Daishi Temple in Kawasaki (between Tokyo and Yokohama) and Shinsho Temple in Narita, about an hour northeast of Tokyo. Visitors to each of these temples number well over three million every year. Other popular places in Tokyo include the Eiji Temple in Ueno and the Zojo Temple in Shiba.

Participating in this sanctified custom is one of the special joys of the winter season. If you can make your way New Year's Eve to Kawasaki or Narita or any of the other great temples following this annual practice, you will find that it beats standing in New York's Times Square and counting down to the New Year.

Some of these New Year's celebrations feature throngs of *sake*-warmed young men, dressed only in white loin cloths despite the cold weather, taking turns ringing the bells. If you are not in the vicinity of one of the bell-ringing temples, you can watch the celebration on one of the television networks.

If you cannot make it to a bell-ringing temple and are in Tokyo, the next-best thing is to go to Harajuku at about 11:00 P.M. (via the Chiyoda Subway Line, exiting at Meiji Jingu Mae Station), and there join the huge throng of people for the final mile-long walk to Meiji Shrine, which annually marks the ending of the old year and the beginning of the new.

Afterward, hot food and drinks are very much in order.

Getting It All Back!

There is one way you can get all the money you spent in Japan back, and then some—if the gods are with you. You can play the lottery! All of Japan's forty-seven prefectures and a number of other institutions, including the post office, sponsor **takarakuji** (tah-kah-rah-kuu-jee), or lotteries, throughout the year. The three largest are the "Dream Jumbo" in the spring, the "Summer Jumbo," and the **Nenmatsu** (Nane-mot-sue), or "End-of-the Year" lottery.

All of the national lotteries are administered by the Dai-Ichi Kangyo Bank (largest bank in the world), with the profits going to the prefectures and cities to build roads, bridges and other public works.

Tickets cost from three hundred yen to one thousand yen. Winners of Jumbo tickets (which cost three hundred yen) can receive as much as Y60 million. Tickets for local lotteries cost from one hundred yen to three hundred yen, and may yield such noncash prizes as trips, travel coupons and cars.

There are some thirty million winners annually in the national drawings, with prizes ranging from only ¥300 to about ¥10 million. Those hoping to win big usually buy several tickets in numbered sequence to improve their chances. Winnings, no matter how large, are totally tax free. After a drawing, winners have one year to collect their prizes. Any prize over ten thousand yen must be collected from the Dai-Ichi Kangyo Bank. Anything from ten thousand yen and below can be collected from any ticket vendor.

Tickets can be purchased from lottery booths or windows in any Dai-Ichi Kangyo Bank, at department stores and tobacco shops, from sidewalk "lottery ladies," and other locations throughout the country. Two of the most popular places in Tokyo are the Dream Center next to Hibiya Park downtown, and, the most popular of all, the Chance Center in the Nishi Ginza Department Store, which has sold more winning tickets than any other outlet.

Players in the three major annual lotteries pick up reservation cards several weeks before tickets go on sale. You can buy up to thirty tickets with each reservation card you fill out and send in, and there is no limit to the number of cards you can send in. The reservation cards help the Lottery Association predict how many tickets they will need to print up for each drawing.

Winning numbers are announced at bank lottery windows and street booths and in major daily newspapers the day after the drawing. If you have to leave Japan before the drawing, you can leave your tickets or ticket numbers with a trusted friend.

Doing Things in the Cold

Some Western countries have groups or clubs whose members dip themselves in ice-filled water in mid-winter. Not surprisingly, the Japanese took this form of ascetism much further, making it an institutional practice among large numbers of people, from Buddhist monks to sumo wrestlers and singers of traditional music forms.

It has long been believed in Japan that practicing a religious ritual—or certain skills, such as singing loudly in extreme cold—not only demonstrated devotion but also contributed intrinsically to the development of mind over matter, and thereby to the learning process. This custom is known as **kan geiko** (kahn gay-e-koe), or "cold practice," which normally takes place in the coldest time of the winter.

I'm not suggesting that you take up any *kan geiko*, but observing the ritualistic way the custom is performed by large numbers of Japanese provides valuable insight into the character and personality of the people. You can witness such practices (while warmly dressed) at the Kodokan Judo Hall in Tokyo's Suidobashi district each January, and at *sumo* stables (where *sumo* wrestlers live and train) in the Ryogoku district each January and February.

The Kabuki Za

The center of *kabuki*, Japan's famed classical theater that is now recognized as one of the world's greatest theatrical arts, the **Kabuki Za** (Kah-buu-kee Zah) is another place to put on your itinerary—even though you may not be a dedicated fan of the classical arts.

Kabuki originated shortly after the beginning of the Tokugawa Shogunate in 1603 as comic and licentious dances performed by women, and the word meant "unorthodox" or "eccentric." After running afoul of the shogunate authorities, the art was taken over by men and during the next century was perfected into the classically styled art we see today. In this process, the original meaning of the word *kabuki* was changed to song (*ka*), dance (*bu*), and skill or technique (*ki*).

I recommend an afternoon or evening at the *Kabuki Za* as a "multi-cultural" experience, regardless of your feelings about *kabuki* as entertainment. The whole experience is another window to Japan—another opportunity to learn more about the Japanese etiquette, philosophy and morals. "Earphone guides" are available for those who want English-language commentary on the stories as they unfold.

Recognizing that foreign visitors may not want to sit through four or five hours of kabuki drama, the theater sells special "limited" tickets for fourth-floor mezzanine seats (but earphone guides are not available on the fourth floor). For reservations, call 541-3131. Tickets must be booked at least one day in advance.

The *Kabuki Za* is located on Harumi Street in East Ginza, in central Tokyo. It is within walking distance of the Ginza hotels, and is in front of the **Nishi** (Nee-she) Ginza Subway Station on the Hibiya Line.

A Special Trip from Tokyo

For a special fall adventure from Tokyo, which can be accomplished in half a day or stretched out to a full day if you like, I recommend an ascent of Mount Takao. Only forty-seven minutes from Shinjuku Station in Tokyo via the Keio Line, Takao is actually within metropolitan Tokyo.

After disembarking at the end of the line (Takao-San Guchi), exit from the station and go to the right along a lane that leads past noodle and fish restaurants to a cable-car station. From the end of the cable-car line it is only a short walk to a Shingon sect temple complex. From there it is an easy walk on to the summit of the mountain, where you will find restaurants and viewpoints, including some that, on clear days, provide spectacular views of Mount Fuji. From the summit, there are several marked walks leading back to the cable-car station.

The short, easy trip not only gets you out of Tokyo for a respite from the crowds and concrete canyons, but it also is a good reminder of what life used to be like in the city during its early years—western residents living in Edo (Tokyo) during the Tokugawa Period wrote of horseback riding among the pine-forested hills and streams that have long since been paved over.

The Water Ritual

The purification or lustration effects of water are well-known in the West and are reflected in the religious practices of baptism and sprinkling holy water on babies and objects. On an individual basis, we all know how good a bath or shower feels when we are grimy as well as when we just feel unclean, but these are minor rituals in the overall scheme of things.

The use of water as a purifying element was taken much further in Japanese culture, and **misogi** (me-so-ghee), or the "purification" process, was extended to cover social as well as physical and spiritual contamination. In the Japanese context, *misogi* also refers to publicly acknowledging guilt and shame (when one is guilty of something), thereby gaining redemption. In other words, confess your sins, ask for forgiveness, and your soul slate is clean.

I am not suggesting that you join Zen priests and other ascetics beneath bone-chilling waterfalls or plunge into one of the Imperial Palace moats. But an understanding of how *misogi* works in Japanese society, and possibly adopting it to some degree, can psychologically be a very healthy thing to do.

The Flower-Friday Syndrome

In the seventies, when Japan's frenetic rush to economic wealth and its workaholic image began to come under serious criticism both at home and abroad, companies gradually began converting to a five-day workweek. To encourage people to go out and enjoy themselves on Friday evenings (since more and more of them had Saturdays off), someone came up with the brilliant idea of labeling Fridays **Hana Kin** (Hah-nah Keen), or "Flower Fridays," the inference being that people should go out on the town Friday nights to drink, eat, and generally make merry—something that was indeed still very rare for the average Japanese. A more festive translation of *Hana Kin* was "Golden Friday", since "golden" was associated with a week of back-to-back national holidays in the spring.

The message hit home. *Hana Kin* was a huge social and economic success as millions of Japanese began spending their hard-gotten gains on the good life. But as prosperity continued despite the shorter working hours (of at least part of the population), the Japanese began to discover other ways to enjoy their weekends away from work, including quickie trips to Korea, Hong Kong, Taiwan, and Guam. This resulted in growing numbers of people switching from "Flower Fridays" to "Flower Thursdays" (**Hana Moku**/Hah-nah Moe-kuu), doing their bar- and restaurant-hopping on Thursdays and then taking off Friday evenings for long weekends to out-of-town destinations.

Now it is difficult to tell Mondays, Tuesdays, and Wednesdays from *Hana Moku* or *Hana Kin*. The great restaurant/entertainment districts of Japan's cities are filled to virtual capacity every night except Sundays. But the crowds are part of the attraction, and I urge you to spend several of your evenings in the busiest districts, absorbing the atmosphere and enjoying the ambience of what has to be the most varied and colorful concentration of high-tech industrialization, economic affluence, and hedonism the world has ever seen.

In Tokyo I recommend the following districts (out of a total of several hundred), listed in alphabetical order for convenience:

AKASAKA (Ah-kah-sah-kah)

This is an area in mid-town, near government center, within walking distance of the Akasaka Prince Hotel, Akasaka Tokyo Hotel, Ana Hotel, Capitol Tokyo Hotel, New Otani Hotel, and Hotel Okura. The area is about three blocks wide and half a mile long, and includes hundreds of restaurants, bars, clubs, discos, and geisha inns (the latter being primarily preempted by political bigwigs and lobbyists, whose offices are on the adjoining government hill).

As for public transportation to the area, the Marunouchi and Ginza subway lines converge at Akasaka Intersection. The Chiyoda Subway Line cuts through the district, and the Hanzomon Line is only a block away from Akasaka Intersection.

ASAKUSA (Ah-sock-sah)

On the northeast side of Tokyo, Asakusa is one of the oldest and best-known entertainment districts in the city, dating back to the early days of the Tokugawa Shogunate, when it became the site of the shogunate capital's largest red-light district—the **Yoshiwara** (Yoe-she-wah-rah).

Now a dense concentration of bars, clubs, geisha inns, massage parlors (where the *Yoshiwara* used to be), restaurants, specialty shops, temples, and shrines, Asakusa has retained much of its traditional atmosphere and is where many Tokyo residents go when they want to experience the "real" Japan. The heart of the area is the great Kannon Temple.

Asakusa is at the northeast end of the Ginza Subway Line (the other end of the line is Shibuya Station), about twenty minutes from downtown Tokyo.

HARAJUKU (Hah-rah-juu-kuu)

For the most part, the Harajuku district is just one street, the very broad (for Tokyo), tree-lined **Omote Sando** (Oh-moe-tay Sahn-doe) Boulevard, which begins at Harajuku Station (where the Yamanote train line and the Chiyoda subway line connect) and the east entrance to the large Meiji Shrine grounds. It runs eastward for about one mile to **Aoyama Dori** (Ah-oh-yah-mah Doe-ree), or Aoyama Avenue, which connects the Akasaka area with Shibuya (see below).

Harajuku's primary attractions are restaurants and smart boutiques along with such specialty shops as the Oriental Bazaar (which mainly attracts foreign residents and tourists and predates the emergence of the area as a popular entertainment district). There are few bars in the area and a number of "love hotels" on the back side, but overall it is a place for the young and for families.

Omote Sando, to me at least, is now far superior as a place to stroll in the evenings and on holidays than the Ginza in downtown Tokyo, which has been famous since before the 1890s. On Sunday afternoons the street is blocked off to vehicular traffic and becomes a long parkway. The promenade extends beyond the station area and the entrance to Meiji Shrine into what was Japan's Olympic Village in 1964—now a sports and recreation center.

ROPPONGI (Rope-pone-ghee)

On a low hill about three kilometers from downtown Tokyo and one kilometer southwest of the Akasaka area, Roppongi emerged in the 1970s as a new entertainment and restaurant district that was geared to the young crowd. It has flourished ever since, and by the 1980s was equally popular with middle-aged revelers as well.

The area is small as such districts go, centering around Roppongi Intersection and extending two to six or seven blocks in all directions. Its attractions include some of the most popular discos in the city, and numerous specialty restaurants.

SHIBUYA (She-buu-yah)

One of the many large commuter terminals in Tokyo, where the Ginza Subway Line connects with the Yamanote (Look) train line and several feeder lines, Shibuya is a shopping, restaurant, and night-life mecca that covers about a square mile. In addition to several department stores (the train/subway station is in the Tokyu Department Store building) and a dozen theaters, the area is a good example of what modern urban Japan is all about.

My favorite area in Shibuya is called the **Shibuya Senta Gai** (She-buu-yah Sin-tah Guy), or "Shibuya Center Shop-Street," which is a maze of lanes that begins just across the street on the west side of Shibuya Station. There is a large, inverted V-shaped sign over the entrance to the section that gives the name in Japanese characters, and is visible from the front of the station. (The front of the station has a plaza with a bronze statue of Japan's most famous dog, **Hachiko** [Hah-chee-koe]. For several years the dog came to the station every evening to meet its master coming home from work. After its owner died, the dog continued to come to the station and wait for several hours each evening, until it also died eight years later.)

The Shibuya Senta Gai consists of a maze of streets and lanes that stretch up one of Tokyo's many small hills (rises might be more appropriate than "hills") for a distance of about a quarter of a mile. It is a jungle of neon signs, shops, restaurants, theaters, and department stores, as well as a haven for those who go for Japanese- and Western-style fast foods, ethnic foods, stylish boutiques of every kind and description, and masses of young people. It is, again, modern Japan in microcosm.

SHINJUKU (Sheen-juu-kuu)

About four miles west of downtown Tokyo and two miles beyond the Imperial Palace grounds, Shinjuku emerged in the early eighties as Tokyo's newest and largest commercial/business areas landmarked by high-rise office buildings and plush international hotels, including the Hilton, Hyatt-Regency, Keio Plaza, and Sheraton.

The primary entertainment district in Shinjuku is a large area about four blocks north of Shinjuku Station that is called **Kabuki-cho** (Kah-buu-kee-choe). It is the gaudiest and most flamboyant of all of Tokyo's large, popular entertainment districts, and is noted for the prevalence of Japan's notorious **yakuza** (yah-kuu-zah), or organized crime gangs, among its landlords and business operators.

Despite this underside element, however, *kabuki-cho* is unsafe only in the sense that some of its bars and other night spots are rip-off joints that systematically overcharge naive rural folk and foreign visitors. Otherwise, the area is about as safe as a Sunday School classroom.

Here, as in Shibuya, you find an almost unbelievable concentration of restaurants, bars, clubs, coffee shops, theaters, massage parlors, love hotels, boutiques, and specialty shops—the difference being a less-refined, less-sophisticated quality that adds a raw, crass element to the scene. You might say it is picturesque in a cleaned-up New York way.

Famous Gardens in Tokyo

Despite its modern facade, Tokyo still boasts some of the most beautiful and famous of Japan's landscaped gardens. Here are five that are easy to get to and offer a quick course in why Japanese gardens have become world famous.

IMPERIAL PALACE EAST GARDEN

Over 210,000 square meters in size, this noted garden contains several buildings, including a famed teahouse. It is open from 9:00 A.M.–4:00 P.M. daily except Mondays, Fridays, New Year's Eve, and New Year's Day. No admission charge. Enter the Imperial grounds through the Otemon Gate.

HAMA RIKYU GARDEN

Built during the Edo period and owned by successive Tokugawa shoguns, this garden is part of the Imperial Detached Palace which adjoins Tokyo Bay, and is only a ten-minute walk from Shimbashi Station in downtown Tokyo. It is open from 9:00 A.M.–4:30 P.M. daily except Mondays, the year-end, and New Year's.

KOISHIKAWA KORAKUEN GARDEN

A Chinese-style garden with a lake in its center, this famous beauty spot was built in the 1600s. It is a seven-minute walk from Korakuen Station on the Marunouchi Subway Line. Open from 9:00 A.M.–4:30 P.M. daily except Mondays, the year-end, and New Year's.

SHINJUKU GARDEN

Also designed in the 1600s, this garden is the site of an annual chrysanthemum show (1–15 November) that is attended by hundreds of notables, including members of the Imperial Family. The site contains a Western as well as a Japanese-style garden. Open from 9:00 A.M.–4:00 P.M. daily except Mondays, the year-end, and New Year's. The entrance is a short block from the Gyoen-mae Station on the Marunouchi Subway Line.

RIKUGIEN GARDEN

Built in the seventeenth century and once owned by the Iwasaki family, founders of the great Mitsui empire, the Rikugien is especially noted because it duplicates several of Japan's most famous scenic views, first extolled in a history book written in the ninth century. It took seven years to build. Open from 9:00 A.M.–4:30 P.M. daily except Mondays, the year-end, and New Year's. Five-minute walk from the JR Komagome Station.

The Symbol of Japan

Mount Fuji has long been the sentinel as well as the symbol of Japan. Towering some 3,776 meters into the sky and dominating every other geographic feature in the country, it is the centerpiece of the Fuji Hakone Izu National Park as well as of Japan. Visible from much of central Honshu, Mount Fuji is surrounded by lesser mountains, lakes, and forests and is one of the largest recreational areas in the nation.

Whether or not you are into mountain climbing, I recommend that Mount Fuji be put on your itinerary. Just seeing it close up from the many cities, towns, and villages around its base and waist is worth the visit, and in the process you will see a lot more of Japan. Of course, you get a lot more out of it if you climb at least partway up the magnificent mountain.

You can ride in comfort to Station Five (there are twelve stations to the top of the mountain) and then climb just high enough to see the world stretched out beneath you. There are several climbing routes, but the two that offer bus service to Station Five are Fujinomiya on the south side of the mountain and Fuji-Yoshida on the north side. Station 5 is 2$^4/_{10}$ meters high. The climbing season is from 1 July to 31 August.

The easiest access from Tokyo is by train from Shinjuku Station to Fuji-Yoshida—about an hour's trip. The bus ride from Fuji-Yoshida to Station Five takes about forty-five minutes. The view of the towering peak from Fuji-Yoshida is worth the trip.

Fukiya International Villa

One of seven villages in Okayama Prefecture that have been designated as **Furusato** (Fuu-rue-sah-toe), or "Home Villages," Fukiya is a living museum of Japan's past. A visit here is like stepping back in time. The traditional homes and storefronts, with their burnt-red and mustard-colored walls of **bengara** (bane-gah-rah), or charred sidings, and their calico and red tiles, specially designed to complement the seasons, evoke both the appearance and the atmosphere of bygone days.

Among the many specific attractions in Fukiya are the Fukiya Historical Museum, the Nishie Residence, the Bengara Factory Museum, Enmei Temple, Yama Jinja Mountain Shrine, Fukiya Primary School, the Hirokane Residence, and the Fukiya International Villa, where visitors stay.

Situated on a tree-covered hill overlooking the village, the International Villa was designed by noted architect Kazuhiro Ishii, and modeled after the traditional **shoyu gura** (show-yuu guu-rah), or soy sauce storehouse that once stood on the site. Guest-room facilities at the villa are Western style but in traditional Japanese decor.

Operated by the Okayama prefectural government as a historical property, the villa is available for regular guests as well as for business retreats and company parties. A large community center adjoins. Nightly rates are well below those of regular inns and hotels. To make reservations, contact the International Exchange Section of the Okayama Prefectural Government, 2-4-6 Uchisange, Okayama 700, Japan; Tel: 0862-24-2111, ext. 2805; Fax 862-23-3615.

Fukiya is about ninety-five minutes from Okayama City—sixty minutes by train to Takahashi on the JR Hakubi Line, and thirty-five minutes by car from Takahashi. If you want to both see and experience traditional Japan, and be very comfortable at the same time, the Fukiya International Villa is highly recommended.

Going Back to Edo

Japan's traditional culture reached its zenith during the Tokugawa or Edo Period, which began in 1603 and lasted until 1868. I suggest that you combine a visit to Kanazawa with a brief stopover at **Edo Mura** (Eh-doe Muu-rah) or "Edo Village," which is the recreation of how people lived during that period. Among the structures in the village is the mansion of the chief retainer of the great Maeda clan, the home of a low-level *samurai* warrior, a merchant's house, and a farmer's home.

Also of special interest is the home of a **ninja** (neen-jah), one of the professional secret agents and assassins of Japan's feudal era.

Residents of the village demonstrate traditional Japanese crafts, and displays of ninja skills are staged daily.

Lords, Ladies, and Castles

Japan, like Europe, had its castle age, and castles played a seminal role in the social and economic life of the country for many centuries. Each of the 270 clans that existed during the long Tokugawa Era had its own castle where the clan lord and his entourage lived. The larger and richer the fief, the larger and more impressive the clan castle was apt to be.

Japan's castles were built around a high tower known as a **tenshu-kaku** (tane-shuu-kah-kuu) or *donjon*. Numerous defensive features and mechanisms, including secret passageways, were built into the castles to help defend them against enemy attack. All were surrounded by **hori** (hoe-ree), or moats, which served as additional barriers against enemy forces.

Most of Japan's castles were destroyed during the revolution that toppled the Tokugawa Shogunate government in the 1860s; others fell to Allied bombers during World War II. Among those that survived or have been reconstructed, the following are outstanding:

HIKONE CASTLE

Completed in 1622 by Lord Naotsugu Ii, this castle stands on a tree- and flower-covered hill overlooking Lake Biwa, near Kyoto.

HIMEJI CASTLE

Often described as the most impressive castle in Japan, Himeji Jo was first built as a fort in the fourteenth century, converted to a castle in 1581 by the famous Hideyoshi Toyotomi (a vagabond peasant who rose to supreme power), then greatly enlarged by Lord Terumasa Ikeda, one of Hideyoshi's generals, in 1608. Called **Hakuro Jo** (Hah-kuu-roe Joe), or "Egret Castle," because when seen from a distance its white-plastered walls suggest the silhouette of the bird, the castle is located in the center of Himeji on a hill, a short walk from Himeji Station. It faces the offshore Ejima Islands. This is where many of the scenes in the movie extravaganza *Shogun* were filmed.

NAGOYA CASTLE

Built in 1612 for Ieyasu Tokugawa, founder of the Tokugawa Shogunate, this was the most modern and sophisticated castle of its time. It was home for Ieyasu's descendants for almost three hundred years. One of its most famous features was a pair of golden dolphins mounted on the roof of its main turret. It is now a museum open to the public.

MARUOKA CASTLE

Better known as **Kasumiga Jo** (Kah-suu-me-gah Joe), or "Misty Castle," this impressive edifice was built in 1576 by Lord Katsutoyo Shibata, one of Nobunaga Oda's generals. It was originally surrounded by a moat that was ninety meters wide. Today it is surrounded by pine and cherry trees. Maruoka is on the Hokuriku Train Line in Fukui Prefecture.

MATSUMOTO CASTLE

Now in the center of Matsumoto City (Nagano Prefecture), this great castle was completed in 1594 by Kazumasa Ishikawa, one of the most famous castle builders in Japan's history. Its *donjon* is six stories high. The primary color of the castle is black, resulting in it being known as the "Crow Castle."

Japan's Grand Canyon

Given its mountainous terrain and high rainfall and snowfall, Japan has numerous picturesque gorges, one of which is big enough to qualify as a canyon. Cut by a river flowing down from the Northern Japan Alps on the Sea of Japan side of Honshu, **Kurobe** (Kuu-roe-bay) Canyon is the deepest and steepest gorge in Japan. Weaving its way between two high mountain ranges, the canyon is two thousand meters deep at some points. The waters of the canyon river are fed by numerous tributaries and by dozens of hot springs gushing out from its banks.

A favorite place to view Kurobe Canyon is Unazuki Hotsprings.

From there you can ride a small train that follows the canyon, crossing it several times, for some 20²/₁₀ kilometers down to the town of Keyakidaira (Kay-yah-kee-die-rah). Best season is from June through October.

Ukai: Fishing with Birds

Ukai is a "spectator" event that I recommend because its ethnic atmosphere makes the overall experience culturally rich. Using cormorants, a large pelican-like bird, to catch **ayu** (ah-yuu), a sweet, freshwater trout, has been carried on in Japan for at least two thousand years. For centuries the emperors and shoguns had their own private *ukai* preserves and teams of cormorant masters.

The art continues today on a greatly reduced scale, providing *ayu* to specialty restaurants in the areas where it is practiced, and at the same time serving as a spectator event for visitors. The large birds, on neck leashes, are controlled by fishing masters, who use exactly the same techniques and wear the same gear that was developed by their predecessors prior to the year 712, when it was first mentioned in a history book.

Cormorant fishing is done at night. Bonfires on the boats attract the fish, and make it possible for viewers, in accompanying boats, to see the action. Each fishing master handles twelve cormorants at a time, controlling them with the neck leashes. The best-known *ayu* fishing grounds are along the Nagara and Kiso Rivers near Gifu City in Aichi Prefecture; Inuyama, a short distance from Gifu; Arashyama and Uji, near Kyoto; and Hakata in northern Kyushu.

Taking in Gifu

Twenty-six train minutes from Nagoya, Gifu, on the Nagara River and near the foot of Mount Kinka, is another off-the-track prefectural city that is worth a visit as a contrast to the major metropolises. The city retains much of its charm from an earlier age, and is in a particularly scenic area at the foot of the Southern Japan Alps.

Gifu is perhaps best known to the tourist industry as one of the most famous **ayu** (ah-yuu) fishing areas in the country. The season starts on 11 May and lasts until 15 October each year. The best months are June and August.

Another reason for adding Gifu to this list is its famous **Gujo Odori** (Guu-joe Oh-doe-ree), or "Gujo Dance," performed nightly in the streets of Gujo Hachiman Town each year during **O'Bon** (Oh-bone) period from July through August, with 13–16 August being the main days of the festival. The *Gujo* dance festival is particularly notable because the dances are performed with a vigor that distinguishes them from other dance festivals, and are therefore much more exciting to watch and perform.

The dance festival was originated in 1630 by clan lord Endo Tajima as a way of developing harmony among the four classes of people—*samurai* warriors, farmers, artisans and merchants.

Water Women of Japan

For centuries women in some coastal areas of Japan have followed the profession of **ama** (ah-mah), literally "ocean women," earning a living for their families by diving for abalone, wreath shells, seaweed, and, more recently, pearl oysters. Women have traditionally done the diving because they can withstand the chilly ocean water better than men.

Women begin diving at the age of fourteen or fifteen, gradually developing an extraordinary lung capacity that allows them to reach depths of thirty meters and stay under water for several minutes. When the *ama* surface they let their breath out in a distinctive whistle that has long been associated with the trade.

Among the places in Japan where *ama* are still an economic mainstay is the village of Shima in Mie Prefecture, the island of Hekura off of western Honshu (and part of Ishikawa Prefecture), Shirahama on Boso Peninsula southeast of Tokyo, and also the nearby Onjuku village, and Waga village on Shima Peninsula near Toba and Nagoya.

Seven-Five-Three

Being able to see large numbers of children is one of the special joys and rewards of visiting any country. The children are not only beautiful and charming, but their innocence and promise help to renew faith in mankind. The best time to see large numbers of Japanese children, combined with a colorful pageantry and overall holiday spirit, is during the so-called **Shichi Go San** (She-chee Go Sahn), or "Seven-Five-Three" Festival held in the first week of November each year.

The festival originated centuries ago to mark important milestones in the lives of children in Japan's highly formalized society. At the age of three, the hair of children was first styled in a special ceremony. At the age of five, boys first donned the traditional **hakama** (hah-kah-mah), or pleated trousers, and at seven girls began wearing **obi** (oh-bee), the wide sash that holds the *kimono* and *yukata* in place. On all of these occasions, children were taken to the local shrine as part of the ceremony. It was also the custom in old Japan to take children to shrines when they were about seven as formal recognition that they had become responsible members of society.

During the early years of Japan's last shogunate, which began in 1603 and ended in 1868, Edo merchants began promoting the idea of dressing children up in their best finery for their visits to local shrines. The custom gradually spread throughout the country.

Nowadays, the festival is held either on 3 November (Culture Day) or the Sunday before or after 15 November; most parents take their children to large, well-known shrines instead of small, neighborhood shrines. Thus, once a year, Japan's several hundred thousand children aged three, five, and seven are dressed to the hilt in their *kimono* and *hakama* and paraded for the world to see. Specifically, the celebration applies to girls who are seven, boys who are five, and boys and girls who are three years old.

In Tokyo the three most popular *Shichi Go San* shrines are the Meiji Shrine near Harajuku Station, Yasukuni Shrine in Kudan, and the Myojin Shrine in Kanda. Others include the Fukagawa Hachiman, Hie, and Hikawa Shrines.

A Sight to See

You have surely heard of Japanese-style wrestling and perhaps seen a bit of it on television. In any case, it is one of the most extraordinary and spectacular events one can witness—something that is totally unique to Japan, and the kind of thing that helps make a visit to Japan memorable.

Sumo features wrestlers who have undergone special training and dieting to turn them into behemoths weighing up to four hundred pounds. Originated as a Shintoist ceremony during Japan's mythical age, *sumo* had become a national sport by the year 600, patronized by emperors and later shoguns. It continues today as an exotic heritage from ancient Japan.

The sport is controlled by the Japan Sumo Wrestling Association, which sponsors six fifteen-day tournaments each year—three in Tokyo (in January, May and September), and one each in Osaka (March), Nagoya (July), and Fukuoka (November)—which means there are tournaments going on for three months out of the year. Wrestlers belong to **beya** (bay-yah), or "stables," that are usually owned and presided over by ex-champions in a feudalistic setting and fashion that also goes back for ages.

Wrestlers are divided into two levels: a lower level that includes beginning wrestlers as young as the mid-teens and might be called the "minor leagues," and an upper level that corresponds to the major leagues in baseball terms. There are several grades or ranks within each of these levels. All bouts are elimination matches, with class and rank based on the number of wins—not on size or weight.

Before each tournament wrestlers are equally divided into east and west "camps." The half with the best win-loss record during the previous tournament is placed in the east camp; the other half is assigned to the west camp. Since ranking is based on the number of wins and not size, the youngest and smallest "big league" wrestler may therefore go up against a veteran grand champion who is twice his size. Each *sumo* fights a different opponent each day during the fifteen-day tournaments. The winner of each tournament is the one who had the most wins.

There are three ranks of winners or champions in sumo: **yokozuna** (yoe-koe-zuu-nah), or grand champions; **o-zeki** (oh-zay-kee), or champions; and **sekiwake** (say-kee-wah-kay), or junior champions. The referee is a **gyoji** (g'yoe-jee). The sumo wear only a large loincloth called a **mawashi** (mah-wah-she).

Bouts take place in a raised ring in the center of a huge, colorful arena. The circular ring is called **dohyo** (doe-h'yoe). The bouts themselves are usually over within seconds and seldom go beyond two or three minutes, but what makes the experience worthwhile is the pomp, pageantry, and ritualistic nature of the games. The ultimate for many sumo fans is to go to one of the stables and watch wrestlers train. Both are worth the effort and time.

In the case of a tournament, however, the idea is to make a day-long party out of it. The bouts end at approximately 6:00 P.M. following which people go out to dinner, often to nearby restaurants that feature the special **chanko nabe** (chahn-koe nah-bay) foods eaten by the *sumo*.

An afternoon of *sumo* followed by a Japanese-style meal with good friends is worth two or three days of sightseeing.

The Great Fish Market

Not many people would think of putting a visit to a fish market on their list of things to do while in Japan, but Tokyo's Tsukiji Fish Market is in fact a visitor attraction. Some people go as early as 2:00 A.M. to see the spectacle of shiploads of fish being unloaded, sorted, sectioned, and sold in daily auctions. Others go also as early as 4:00 A.M. to patronize the *sashimi* and *O-sushi* restaurants which surround the market.

Japan Gray Line offers early-morning tours to the market. One of the main reasons they get a surprising number of takers is because people arriving from the United States and other distant eastern points often wake up between 2:00 and 3:00 A.M. on their first couple of days in Tokyo.

Training in Spirit

One might wonder where the Japanese get the spirit that allows them to change from their usually calm and passive ways to dedicated workers and deadly fighters without missing a beat. For many Japanese, part of the answer lies in the training they receive in the martial arts, particularly **kendo** (ken-doe), or "the way of the sword."

During Japan's feudal age (1192–1868), all members of the *samurai* class (about ten percent of the population) underwent years of *kendo* training to steel their spirit and master sword fighting. After the last shogunate fell in 1868, anyone could attend a *kendo* school, and eventually the art was introduced into the regular school system. In *kendo* matches, combatants use "swords" made of bamboo slats bound together, and wear heavy protective clothing.

Today *kendo* clubs abound in Japan, and the art is a key part of the training of police. Some young businessmen also take the training to help them develop strong, aggressive spirits. The ancient art, stylized and ritualistic, is an exciting drama to watch, as well as being educational. Visitors are welcomed at training gyms, and exhibitions and tournaments are frequent. A call to the All-Japan Kendo Federation will give you locations and times.

Feasting in Chinatown

Yokohama's Chinatown is world famous for its seventy restaurants, bars, cabarets and shops selling imported Chinese herbs, foodstuffs, and souvenirs. Besides being a wonderful place to indulge yourself in a wide range of Chinese food, it is also place to see. The area is within a short walk of the city's equally noted Motomachi shopping district (and not far from where one of the first foreign communities in Japan was located—behind a great barrier wall).

A good starting point for both Chinatown and Motomachi, as well as the port of Yokohama just three blocks to the east, is the Yokohama Holiday Inn. The inn adjoins the southeast corner of the Chinese district and is a five-minute walk from Motomachi.

Beauty Spots

Japan is blessed with some of the most beautiful landscapes on earth, which is perhaps one of the reasons the Japanese were among the few people anywhere to incorporate the appreciation of beauty into their culture very early in their history. Seeking out and communing with natural beauty was an integral part of Shintoism, Japan's native religion.

This feeling for beauty resulted in the naming and ranking of especially beautiful areas around the country. Since ancient times, the three most scenic spots in Japan have been listed as **Ama-no Hashi-date** (Ah-mah-no Hah-she-dah-tay), or "The Bridge of Heaven," on the Sea of Japan coast west of Kyoto; Matsushima (Pine Islands) Bay near Sendai on northeastern Honshu; and Miyajima (Shrine Island) on the Inland Sea.

If your sightseeing itinerary in Japan brings you within reach of any of these extraordinary places, I suggest you make a point of adding them to your list. My favorite among the three is Matsushima. There are literally thousands of other places in Japan that are noted for their extraordinary beauty. If you get outside of the large cities, you will surely see several of them.

Kyoto's Geisha Town

One of the most historic spots in Kyoto is the **Gion Machi** (Ghee-own Mah-chee) district, Japan's most famous geisha quarters since the early 1600s. On the east bank of the Kamo River, near several of Kyoto's major hotels, the site is also the location of the country's oldest theater, the *Minami Za*, which also dates from the early 1600s. A second theater in the district, the **Kaburenjo** (Kah-buu-rane-joe), sponsors the annual spring Cherry Dance Festival. Kabuki performances are still staged at the *Minami Za*.

The district is noted for its Kyoto-style bars and restaurants, for the refined Kyoto dialect of its residents, and for its traditional architecture. It is definitely a place to put on your list to balance out the temples and palaces of this former imperial capital. Phone 794-1868 for information.

Letting It All Hang Out

You have probably heard of **karaoke** (kah-rah-oh-kay), which means "empty orchestra" and refers to patrons singing to recorded orchestra music in bars that provide the equipment and the stage for this kind of self-entertainment.

Karaoke originated in the seventies after Japan's electronic firms began selling home microphone systems that could be plugged into stereo sets. This innovation allowed people to add a very professional touch to their traditional custom of practicing singing at home to sing well at parties and other public functions, such as weddings.

Bars and clubs soon picked up on the idea and began offering their patrons the opportunity to perform in public. It went over big. *Karaoke* bars proliferated, even spreading to Los Angeles, New York, and other expatriate communities of Japanese overseas.

Singing in bars gave the Japanese an opportunity to show off their talent, but even more important it became a way for businessmen to relieve some of the stress that comes with their highly formalized etiquette system and the extraordinary pressures of their work.

I recommend that you spend an hour or so in a *karaoke ba* (bar) not only to see the Japanese at play but to take your turn at the mike. It takes a lot of courage, but the rewards are real and worthwhile. You have to do it to fully understand and appreciate it.

Bathing in the Woods

It is well known that a walk in the woods will make anyone feel better under almost any circumstances. But leave it to the Japanese to develop **shinrin yoku** (sheen-reen yoe-kuu), or "woods bathing," into an institutionalized form of preventive and remedial health care.

Of course, you do not have to be in Japan to "bathe" yourself in the refreshing and rejuvenating atmosphere of a wooded area, but doing so is still another way to benefit from your trip. The term *shinrin yoku* has the connotation of submerging yourself in the essence of a forest, and letting its sounds, aromas and sights soak in to relieve fatigue and stress.

This concept is part of the overall traditional Japanese philosophy of merging themselves and their homes, shrines, and temples *with* nature and trying to become a part of it—something that has suffered ingloriously in modern times, but still exists in the rural areas of the country. Just having words for the concept encourages its practice, and maybe this will lead you to deliberately making it a part of your life.

Enjoying Children

Putting the children of a country on your travel schedule may seem rather odd, but I learned long ago that visitors to Japan often got more out of a one- or two-hour visit to a Japanese kindergarten or grade school than days spent traipsing around looking at old buildings (which, if you don't possess a deep sense of their history, are little more than "bones" of the long dead).

Use your free time to go out of your way to visit at least one school. Arrange it in advance with the principal. Be prepared to make a little speech to the kids. They will love it and so will you (although they will probably not understand more than "hello" and "goodbye").

Let-Your-Hair-Down Parties

If you are fortunate enough to be invited to a **Bu Rei Ko** (Buu Ray Koe) party, don't be afraid to go. *Bu Rei Ko* means "Party without Etiquette," and in this case refers to a gathering in which social class and rank are put aside and everyone participates as an equal—something that is exceptionally rare in Japan. A *Bu Rei Ko* party is specifically a drinking party. (Japanese men generally let their hair down—and their true feelings out—only when in informal drinking situations.)

Sumida River Cruise

Another offbeat thing to do in Tokyo is take a forty-minute cruise on the Sumida River, which cuts through the famous entertainment-restaurant district of Asakusa in northeast Tokyo and empties into Tokyo Bay. The trip is run by the Tokyo Cruise Ship Company, and can start in Asakusa or at Hinode Pier near Hamamatsucho Station on the south side of central Tokyo. The ship goes by the famed Hamarikyu Garden, which is part of the former Imperial Detached Palace. For details call the cruise ship company at 841-9178.

An Easy Shrine to See

Yasukuni Jinja (Yah-suu-kuu-nee Jeen-jah), Japan's best-known shrine, is in the middle of Tokyo in a setting that is far less spectacular than what is characteristic of most of the country's other noted shrines. It was founded in the name of Emperor Meiji in 1896 to commemorate members of Japan's military forces who died in war. After Shintoism was declared the state religion during the early years of the Meiji Era, the shrine was administered by the Imperial Army and Navy. Since the end of World War II in 1945, it has been run by a religious corporation, in accordance with Article 20 of the Japanese Constitution, which prohibits the state from getting involved in religious activities.

On a small hill within walking distance of the northwestern side of the Imperial Palace Grounds, *Yasukuni* is accessible from any of the city's tourist and business hotels in five to thirty minutes. The nearest subway stop is Kudanshita Station on the Tozai Line.

The Great Sapporo Snow Festival

One of the biggest annual winter events in Japan, the Sapporo Snow Festival attracts over two million people each year, including thousands from abroad. The festival began in 1950 when high school students created six snow statues in Sapporo's Odori Park. Now there are three sites: Odori Park, Makomanai, and Susukino. The sculptures number in the hundreds, and many are huge, measuring several stories high and covering as much as a square block.

Sculptures include mythical as well as modern depictions, from castles to the United States's Statue of Liberty. In a typical year, over six-thousand five-ton truckloads of snow are brought in from the suburbs for construction of the sculptures.

Part of the attraction of the snow festival is international competition among teams from countries all over the world. Competing sculptures are all located in International Square. Another feature is a Snow Queen Contest, with the winner automatically becoming

Miss Sapporo and serving until March of the following year. Other events include a Festival Night Gathering, concerts, and a fashion show. All of the events receive national television coverage.

Many visitors who take in the Snow Festival also take advantage of the opportunity to ski at one of the several resorts in the vicinity. There are also other attractions—the Susukino entertainment district (one of the sites for snow sculptures) has over four-thousand bars, cabarets, nightclubs, and restaurants.

The Snow Festival is held on the first weekend in February, but the sculptures are completed well in advance and can be enjoyed over a period of several days. If you decide to put the festival on your itinerary, make your hotel and flight reservations several months in advance. (You will appreciate the layout of Sapporo. Its streets are constructed like a chessboard, making it much easier to find your way around.)

Fun in the Snow

With its high volcanic mountain ranges and their abundant natural hot springs, Japan has some of the world's most spectacular combination ski resort/hot-spring spas. In central Japan (the nine prefectures making up central Honshu, the main island) there are 150 ski grounds, some of them internationally known.

Here are some that are especially noted: **Akakura Onsen** (Ah-kah-kuu-rah Own-sin), **Shiga Kogen** (She-gah Koe-gane), **Zao** (Zah-oh), **Naeba** (Nie-bah), **Togari** (Toe-gah-ree), **Nozawa Onsen** (No-zah-wah Own-sin), and **Myoko Kogen** (M'yoe-koe Koe-gane).

Shiga Heights, approximately five hours from Tokyo by train and bus, is the largest ski resort in Japan, with twenty-two slopes. Both Japan Air Lines and All Nippon Airways offer several packaged ski tours to Hokkaido during the season, including a number that coincide with the famed Sapporo Snow Festival in early February.

Joining a packaged ski outing is one of the best ways to experience this aspect of Japan (the hot-spring spas being as important as the snow in the overall pleasures), and is highly recommended.

The Island That Pearls Built

Mikimoto Pearl Island is on the established tourist trail, but is nevertheless worthy of mention because it is such an unusual attraction. Consisting of a tiny island in Toba Bay in Mie Prefecture about three and a half hours southwest of Tokyo, this is where the famous Kokichi Mikimoto learned how to culture pearls, ultimately creating one of Japan's most important industries.

While Mikimoto achieved his goal of producing genuine pearls in 1893, Pearl Island was not opened to the public until 1951, and since has been turned into a showplace that attracts people, including royal celebrities, from all over the world. Connected to the shore by an elevated causeway, the island's attractions include a pearl museum, the Kokichi Mikimoto Memorial Hall, and a Mikimoto Pearl Shop.

Visitors may watch demonstrations by women pearl divers and the extraction and sorting of pearls. The shop, of course, is a great place to indulge yourself.

In addition to Pearl Island, Toba is the gateway to the famed Imperial Ise Jingu Shrines at Ise in Ise Shima National Park, one of the grandest beauty spots on the globe. This is the place where the spirits of Japan's past emperors are enshrined and where each new emperor goes to pay respects to his forebears. If you especially appreciate natural beauty combined with history, a visit to the ancient Ise Jingu Shrines is very rewarding.

Peace Memorials

If you are planning on visiting either Hiroshima or Nagasaki, the two cities that were atom-bombed in 1945 by the U.S. Air Force during World War II in a bid to end the war with Japan, there is a **Heiwa Kinen Shikiten** (Hay-e-wah Kee-nane She-kee-tane), or Peace Memorial Ceremony, in Hiroshima on 8 August, and a **Genbaku Kinenbi** (Gane-bah-kuu Kee-nane-bee), or "Atom-bomb Anniversary" (peace memorial ceremony), in Nagasaki on 9 August. Both are worth seeing because of their historical significance.

Selecting a Hot-Spring Spa

Out of Japan's two-thousand hot-spring spas (each of which has from a few to a hundred or more "hot-spring inns" within each spa area), here are a number that have been preselected on the basis of their authentic *onsen* atmosphere, their convenience, reasonable prices, and experience in accommodating foreign visitors. All of them have one or more staff members who speak English well enough to communicate.

In the Vicinity of Tokyo:

Sugiyoshi Ryokan (Sue-ghee-yoe-she Rio-khan) in Moto-Hakone, about two hours via the "Romance Car" from Shinjuku Station. Tel: 0460-3-6327.

Fuji Hakone Guest House (Fuu-jee Hah-koe-nay) in Sengoku-bara, via the same route. Tel: 0460-4-6577.

Nanzentei (Nahn-zen-tay) in Yugawara, 1½ hours from Tokyo on the Tokaido Line. Tel: 0465-62-5188.

Marin Hills (Mah-reen) in Ito, two hours from Tokyo via the Tokaido and Ito Lines. Tel: 0557-45-4537.

Surigahama-so (Sue-ree-gah-hah-mah-soe) in Shimoda, two hours and fifty minutes from Tokyo on the Tokaido and Ito Lines. Tel: 05582-2-0238.

Village Nunoba (Nuu-no-bah) in Nunoba (Echigo Yuzawa Spas), eighty minutes from Ueno Station (Tokyo) via JR Joetsu "Bullet Train" *Asahi* (Ah-sah-he). Tel: 0257-84-2409.

In central Honshu alone there are over three-hundred hot-spring spas, with a combined total of several thousand hot-spring inns. Several of the most famous ones are in the spectacularly beautiful Lake Hakone area a little over an hour from Tokyo by train. A minimum of one weekend (Friday night to Sunday) should be allotted for the special experience of staying in a traditionally styled **ryokan** (rio-khan) inn.

Public Hot-Spring Baths in Tokyo

For the adventurous, there are three public (**sento**/sin-toe) hot-spring baths in Tokyo that give you both the feel and taste of traditional Japan. Unfortunately, they are all unisex...but still worthwhile.

Asakusa Kannon Onsen (Ah-sock-sah Kahn-noan Own-sin), 2-7-10 Asakusa, Taito-ku. Adjacent to the famous Asakusa Kannon Temple, a ten-minute walk from Asakusa Station on the Ginza Subway Line. Open from 6:30 A.M. to 6:00 P.M. except first and third Thursdays. Tel: 844-4141.

Azabu Juban Onsen (Ah-sah-buu Juu-bahn Own-sin), 1-5-22 Azabu Juban, Minato-ku. A ten-minute walk southeast from the Roppongi Subway Station on the Hibiya Line. Open from 3:00–11:00 P.M. daily except Tuesdays (or Wednesday if Tuesday falls on a national holiday). Tel: 404-2610. A popular place for weekend parties by some foreign residents of the city.

Shibaura Yokujo (She-bah-uu-rah Yoe-kuu-joe), 3-13-6 Shibaura, Minato-ku. Five-minute walk southeast of Tamachi Station on the Yamanote and Keihin train lines. Open 4:00–11:00 P.M. daily except Tuesdays. Tel: 451-7948.

Public Hot-Spring Baths
Near Kyoto and Osaka

Takayama-So (Tah-kah-yah-mah-soe) in Arima, forty-five minutes to one hour from Kyoto or Osaka, depending on which train line. Tel: 078-904-0744.

The Lantern Festival

Long one of Japan's most important annual observances, **Obon** (Oh-bone), which is often translated as "The Festival of the Dead," or "The Lantern Festival," was originally a religious ritual designed to relieve the suffering of the dead and ensure their happiness in the afterlife, as well as to ensure that the living would not be punished for ignoring their ancestors.

The first record of the *Obon* ritual was at a temple in Nara, then the Imperial capital of Japan, in the year 657. During the Tokugawa Shogunate/Edo period (1603–1868), 13–16 July was set aside each year for people to visit the graves of their ancestors, make offerings to them and invite their souls back to their homes for brief visits (in the evenings, lighted lanterns were carried from the graves to nearby homes to show the spirits the way home).

Following the downfall of the Tokugawa Shogunate, the annual ritual gradually became more of a fun festival and a vacation period, when people visited their ancestral homes to see their families and enjoy themselves. Traditional folk dances, performed at temple grounds and in the streets, became a major focal point of the festival period in most cities and communities around the country.

Some people still visit family gravesites and follow other ritual practices in mid-July, but most *Obon* observances are now in mid-August, usually from the 13th to the 16th, when the majority of the people take a week's vacation.

Virtually every city and town in the country has one or more **Obon Odori** (Oh-bone Oh-doe-ree), or "Obon Dances," during this period. They are colorful and exciting events that are well worth a few hours of your time if you are in Japan during this period. Some of the biggest dances that involve whole towns are staged in Kiso in Nagano Prefecture, in Tokushima on Shikoku Island, on Shiraishi Island in the Inland Sea, and on Sado Island off the coast of northwest Honshu. These events are generally televised nationally.

Those Naked Festivals

January, Japan's coldest month, is the month of naked festivals. Actually, the participants in these festivals—always men—are not completely naked. They wear white **fundoshi** (foon-doe-she), which is a long strip of cloth worn wrapped around the waist and between the legs in the fashion of a wide G-string.

"Naked" festivals are held during the coldest part of the year because withstanding the cold temperature is regarded as both demonstrating and developing dedication, strength, stamina, will, and spirit. It seems to me that most such events today have very little if any pious content and are more of a lark, with the participants protected from feeling most of the cold by filling themselves with "anti-freeze" *sake* in advance.

Action consists of hundreds of young men snake-dancing through the streets, with some of them supporting a portable shrine on their shoulders, giving the godly spirits a joyous ride (to make the gods feel better and win their favor).

The three biggest "half-naked" events in January are in Yanaizu Town in Fukushima Prefecture on 7 January (**Yanaizu-no Hadaka Mairi**/Yah-nie-zoo-no Hah-dah-kah My-ree, or "Yanaizu Naked Coming"); Osaka's **Doyadoya** (Doe-yah-doe-yah) on 14 January; and the **Konomiya Hadaka Matsuri** (Koe-no-me-yah Hah-dah-kah Mot-sue-ree), or the "Kono Temple Naked Festival," in Aichi at the end of January.

The town of Warabi (Wah-rah-bee) in Chiba Prefecture near Tokyo also has an annual "Naked Festival" on 25 February. Several of the festivals are televised nationally, but, as always, it is much better to see them in the flesh than on film to fully appreciate the essence of the celebration.

National Theater

Japan's **Kokuritsu Gekijo** (Koe-kuu-reet-sue Gay-kee-joe), or "National Theater," a short distance from the Diet Building in Tokyo's "government center" and overlooking the Imperial Palace grounds, is one of the most impressive architectural sights in the country. A combination of traditional Japanese motifs and modern construction technology, it is an outstanding setting as a venue for present-day entertainment.

In addition to regular kabuki performances, the theater is used for a variety of other kinds of traditional entertainment, including dance and musical programs. I recommend that you combine a visit to this impressive theater with attendance at one of its special events. Just being able to mingle with the Japanese audience makes the experience worthwhile. Check the local newspapers, or call 265-7411 for current programs.

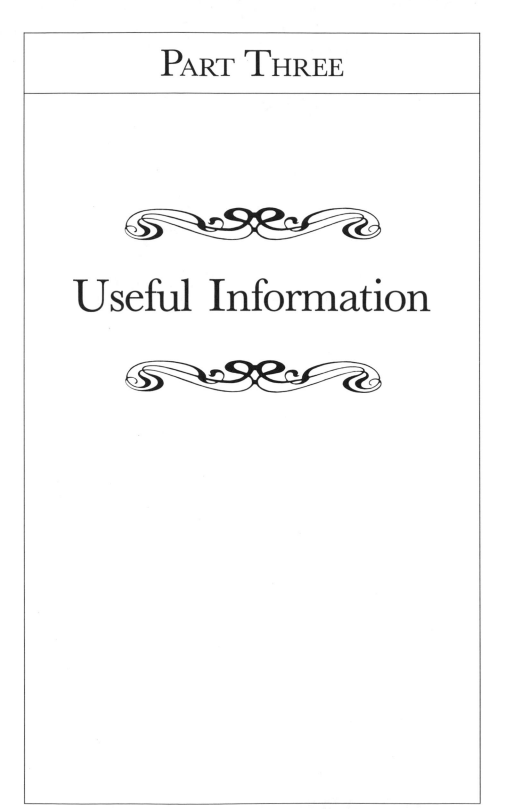

PART THREE

Useful Information

Plugging in

Electrical current in Japan is 100 volts throughout, but the cycle rating differs in the northern and southwestern parts of the country. In eastern and northern Japan, which includes Yokohama, Tokyo, and all points north, the current is 50 cycles. In southern and southwestern Japan, including the Nagoya, Kyoto, Osaka, and Kobe areas, the current is 60 cycles.

Appliances such as hair dryers, shavers, and the like made for the U.S. market will work but at reduced efficiency in the areas where the current is 50 cycles. Voltage regulators are readily available in electrical supply shops, and some hotels have them on hand for guests.

Sizes, Weights, and Distances

Japanese apparel sizes are based on the metric scale, in which 1 inch equals 2.54 centimeters, and 1 centimeter equals 0.39 inches. Women who wear a Size 8 shoe in the American scale need a Size 26 in Japanese.

For men, a shirt with a fifteen-inch neck becomes Size 38 in Japanese. A Japanese girl who measures an impressive 76-50-81 in the metric system is a modest 30-20-32 in inches.

Weights in Japan are measured in grams. One pound equals 0.4436 kilograms, and 1 kilogram equals 2.2 pounds. Therefore, a 180-pound man weighs a little more than 81 kilograms.

Distances are measured in kilometers. One kilometer equals 0.62 miles. One mile equals 1.60 kilometers. It is 318 miles or 514 kilometers from Tokyo to Kyoto.

The Temperature Scale

0 degrees Fahrenheit = -18 degrees Celsius

23°F = -5°C   68°F = 20°C

32°F = 0°C   77°F = 25°C

41°F = 5°C   86°F = 30°C

50°F = 10°C   95°F = 35°C

59°F = 15°C   105°F = 40°C

Train Time between Tokyo and Other Cities

Aomori — 5 (hours)   Kyoto — 3

Atami — 2   Nagasaki — $9^3/_4$

Beppu — $8^1/_2$ Nagoya — 2

Fuji-Yoshida (Mt. Fuji) — $1^1/_2$ Nara — $3^3/_4$

Gifu — 3   Niigata — $1^1/_2$

Hakone — $1^1/_2$ Nikko — $1^3/_4$

Hakata (Fukuoka) — 7   Okayama — $4^1/_4$

Hiroshima — 5   Osaka — $3^1/_4$

Kobe — $3^1/_2$ Sendai — 4

Kagoshima — 12   Takamatsu — 5

Kamakura — 1   Toba — $3^1/_2$

Kanazawa — $5^1/_2$ Yokohama — 30 minutes on
                                        limited express;
Kobe — $3^1/_2$ 40 minutes on
                                        local train
Kumamoto — $7^1/_2$

                                        Zushi — 1 hour, 5 minutes

TRAVEL AND CULTURE BOOKS

"World at Its Best" Travel Series
 Britain, France, Germany, Hawaii,
 Holland, Hong Kong, Italy, Spain,
 Switzerland, London, New York, Paris,
 Washington, D.C., San Francisco

Passport's Travel Guides and References
 IHT Guides to Business Travel in Asia &
 Europe
 Only in New York
 Mystery Reader's Walking Guides:
 London, England, New York, Chicago
 Chicago's Best-Kept Secrets
 London's Best-Kept Secrets
 New York's Best-Kept Secrets
 The Japan Encyclopedia
 Japan Today!
 Japan at Night
 Japan Made Easy
 Discovering Cultural Japan
 Living in Mexico
 The Hispanic Way
 Guide to Ethnic Chicago
 Guide to Ethnic London
 Guide to Ethnic New York
 Guide to Ethnic Montreal
 Passport's Trip Planner & Travel Diary
 Chinese Etiquette and Ethics in Business
 Korean Etiquette and Ethics in Business
 Japanese Etiquette and Ethics in Business
 How to Do Business with the Japanese
 Japanese Cultural Encounters
 The Japanese

Passport's Regional Guides of France
 Auvergne, Provence, Loire Valley,
 Dordogne & Lot, Languedoc, Brittany, South
 West France, Normandy & North West
 France, Paris, Rhône Valley & Savoy,
 France for the Gourmet Traveler

Passport's Regional Guides of Indonesia
 New Guinea, Java, Borneo, Bali, East of
 Bali, Sumatra, Spice Islands,
 Sulawesi, Exploring the Islands of
 Indonesia

Up-Close Guides
 Paris, London, Manhattan, Amsterdam,
 Rome

Passport's "Ticket To..." Series
 Italy, Germany, France, Spain

**Passport's Guides: Asia, Africa, Latin
 America, Europe, Middle East**
 Japan, Korea, Malaysia, Singapore, Bali,
 Burma, Australia, New Zealand, Egypt,
 Kenya, Philippines, Portugal, Moscow,
 St. Petersburg, The Georgian Republic,
 Mexico, Vietnam, Iran, Berlin, Turkey

Passport's China Guides
 All China, Beijing, Fujian, Guilin,
 Hangzhou & Zhejiang, Hong Kong,
 Macau, Nanjing & Jiangsu, Shanghai,
 The Silk Road, Taiwan, Tibet, Xi'an,
 The Yangzi River, Yunnan

Passport's India Guides
 All India; Bombay & Goa; Dehli, Agra
 & Jaipur; Burma; Pakistan;
 Kathmandu Valley; Bhutan; Museums
 of India; Hill Stations of India

Passport's Thai Guides
 Bangkok, Phuket, Chiang Mai, Koh Sumi

On Your Own Series
 Brazil, Israel

"Everything Under the Sun" Series
 Spain, Barcelona, Toledo, Seville,
 Marbella, Cordoba, Granada, Madrid,
 Salamanca, Palma de Majorca

Passport's Travel Paks
 Britain, France, Italy, Germany, Spain

Exploring Rural Europe Series
 England & Wales, France, Greece,
 Ireland, Italy, Spain, Austria,
 Germany, Scotland, Ireland by Bicycle

Regional Guides of Italy
 Florence & Tuscany, Naples & Campania,
 Umbria, the Marches & San Marino

Passport Maps
 Europe, Britain, France, Italy, Holland,
 Belgium & Luxembourg, Scandinavia,
 Spain & Portugal, Switzerland, Austria
 & the Alps

Passport's Trip Planners & Guides
 California, France, Greece, Italy

PASSPORT BOOKS
a division of *NTC Publishing Group*
Lincolnwood, Illinois USA